P9-BYE-864

THE
MAXWELL
DAILY
READER

365 Days of Insight *to* Develop
the Leader Within You
and Influence Those Around You

JOHN C.
MAXWELL

HarperCollins
Leadership

An Imprint of HarperCollins

© 2007 by John C. Maxwell

All rights reserved. No portion of this book may be reproduced, stored in a retrieval system, or transmitted in any form or by any means—electronic, mechanical, photocopy, recording, scanning, or other—except for brief quotations in critical reviews or articles, without the prior written permission of the publisher.

Published by HarperCollins Leadership, an imprint of HarperCollins Focus, LLC.

Published in association with Yates & Yates, www.yates2.com

ISBN 978-1-4041-7478-8 (custom)
ISBN 978-1-4002-0339-0 (trade paper)
ISBN 978-1-4002-8001-8 (SE)
ISBN 978-1-4002-8052-0 (IE)

The Library of Congress has catalogued the hardcover edition as follows:

Maxwell, John C., 1947–
    The Maxwell daily reader : 365 days of insight to develop the leader within you and influence those around you / John C. Maxwell.
        p. cm.
    Includes bibliographical references.
    ISBN 978-1-4002-8016-2
    1. Leadership. I. Title.
    HD57.7.M394263 2008
    658.4'092—dc22

                                                                2008032087

Printed in China
15 16 17 18 19 TIMS 7 6 5 4 3

CONTENTS

INTRODUCTION

What is the key to being successful? What separates people who achieve much from those who merely get by? It's what they do every day. The secret to your success can be found in your daily agenda.

People who achieve their potential do so because they invest in themselves every day. They take the time to add value to themselves. Because they do, they are also able to add value to others.

The Maxwell Daily Reader has been designed to help you make that investment in yourself every day of the year. Each entry contains an excerpt from one of my books to encourage you, teach you, challenge you, or prompt you to grow. And each ends with a thought that captures the essence of the day's reading and helps you to apply it as you approach your day.

You cannot grow unless you are willing to change. And you will not change unless you change something you do every day. My prayer is that this book will help you with that process in the coming year.

—*John C. Maxwell*

JANUARY

JANUARY 1

TAKE CARE OF THE LITTLE THINGS

When I teach at a conference or go to a book signing, people sometimes confide in me that they desire to write books too. "How do I get started?" they ask.

"How much writing do you do now?" I ask in return.

Some tell me about articles and other pieces they are writing, and I simply encourage them; but most of the time they sheepishly respond, "Well, I haven't really written anything yet."

"Then you need to start writing," I explain. "You've got to start small and work up to it."

Leadership is the same. You've got to start small and work up to it. A person who has never led before needs to try to influence one other person. Someone who has some influence should try to build a team. Just start with what's necessary.

St. Francis of Assisi said, "Start doing what is necessary; then do what is possible; and suddenly you are doing the impossible." All good leadership begins where you are. It was Napoleon who said, "The only conquests which are permanent and leave no regrets are our conquests over ourselves." The small responsibilities you have before you now comprise the first great leadership conquest you must make. Don't try to conquer the world until you've taken care of things in your own backyard.

—*The 360° Leader*

WHAT ONE SMALL, SPECIFIC
LEADERSHIP STEP CAN YOU TAKE TODAY?

THE INSTRUMENT OF LEADERSHIP

John W. Gardner observed, "If I had to name a single all-purpose instrument of leadership, it would be communication." Perhaps you are familiar with my books on leadership; then you know that I believe everything rises and falls on leadership. What I haven't mentioned before is that leadership rises and falls on communication.

If you lead your team, give yourself these standards to live by as you communicate to your people:

1. *Be consistent.* Nothing frustrates team members more than leaders who can't make up their minds. One of the things that won the team over to Gordon Bethune when he was at Continental was the consistency of his communication. His employees always knew they could depend on him and what he said.

2. *Be clear.* Your team cannot execute if the members don't know what you want. Don't try to dazzle anyone with your intelligence; impress people with your straightforwardness.

3. *Be courteous.* Everyone deserves to be shown respect, no matter what the position or what kind of history you might have with him. By being courteous to your people, you set the tone for the entire organization.

Never forget that because you are the leader, your communication sets the tone for the interaction among your people. Teams always reflect their leaders. And never forget that good communication is never one-way. It should not be top-down or dictatorial. The best leaders listen, invite, and then encourage participation.

—*The 17 Indisputable Laws of Teamwork*

BE AWARE TODAY THAT YOUR COMMUNICATION
IS SETTING THE TONE WITH THE PEOPLE YOU LEAD.

DISCERNMENT

Discernment can be described as the ability to find the root of the matter, and it relies on intuition as well as rational thought. Discernment is an indispensable quality for any leader who desires to maximize effectiveness. It helps to do several important things:

1. *Discover the Root Issues.* Leaders of large organizations must cope with tremendous chaos and complexity every day. They are never able to gather enough information to get a complete picture. As a result, they have to rely on discernment to see a partial picture, fill in the missing pieces intuitively, and find the real heart of a matter.

2. *Enhance Your Problem Solving.* If you can see the root issue of a problem, you can solve it. The closer a leader is to his area of gifting, the stronger his intuition and ability to see root causes. If you want to tap into your discernment potential, work in your areas of strength.

3. *Evaluate Your Options for Maximum Impact.* Management consultant Robert Heller has this advice: "Never ignore a gut feeling, but never believe that it's enough." Discernment isn't relying on intuition alone, nor is it relying only on intellect. Discernment enables you to use both your gut and your head to find the best option.

4. *Multiply Your Opportunities.* People who lack discernment are seldom in the right place at the right time. Although great leaders often appear to be lucky to some observers, I believe leaders create their own "luck" as the result of discernment, that willingness to use their experience and follow their instincts.

—*The 21 Indispensable Qualities of a Leader*

USE DISCERNMENT TODAY TO POSITION YOURSELF
AND YOUR TEAM SO THAT THEY CAN SUCCEED.

YOU ARE YOUR LENS

Who you are determines the way you see everything. You cannot separate your identity from your perspective. All that you are and every experience you've had color how you see things. It is your lens. Here's what I mean:

A traveler nearing a great city asked an old man seated by the road, "What are the people like in this city?"

"What were they like where you came from?" the man asked.

"Horrible," the traveler reported. "Mean, untrustworthy, detestable in all respects."

"Ah," said the old man, "you will find them the same in the city ahead."

Scarcely had the first traveler gone on his way when another stopped to inquire about the people in the city before him. Again the old man asked about the people in the place the traveler has just left.

"They were fine people: honest, industrious, and generous to a fault," declared the second traveler. "I was sorry to leave."

The old man responded, "That's exactly how you'll find the people here."

The way people see others is a reflection of themselves: If I am a trusting person, I will see others as trustworthy. If I am a critical person, I will see others as critical. If I am a caring person, I will see others as compassionate.

If you change yourself and become the kind of person you desire to be, you will begin to view others in a whole new light. And that will change the way you interact in all of your relationships.

—*Winning with People*

BE AWARE OF YOUR "LENS" TODAY AS
YOU INTERACT WITH OTHERS.

PUT PEOPLE IN THEIR (RIGHT) PLACE

Moving someone from a job they hate to the right job can be life changing. One executive I interviewed said he moved a person on his staff to four different places in the organization, trying to find the right fit. Because he'd placed her wrong so many times, he was almost ready to give up on her. But he knew she had great potential, and she was right for the organization. Finally, after he found the right job for her, she was a star!

Because this executive knows how important it is to have every person working in the right job, he asks his staff once a year, "If you could be doing anything, what would it be?" From their answers, he gets clues about any people who may have been miscast in their roles.

Trying to get the right person in the right job can take a lot of time and energy. Let's face it. Isn't it easier for a leader to just put people where it is most convenient and get on with the work? Once again, this is an area where leaders' desire for action works against them. Fight against your natural tendency to make a decision and move on. Don't be afraid to move people around if they're not shining the way you think they could.

—*The 360° Leader*

LOOK FOR CLUES THAT SOMEONE ON
YOUR TEAM COULD BE BETTER PLACED.

CHARACTER IS EVERYTHING

What makes people want to follow a leader? Why do people reluctantly comply with one leader while passionately following another to the ends of the earth? What separates leadership theorists from successful leaders who lead effectively in the real world? The answer lies in the character qualities of the individual person.

My friend, do you know whether you have what it takes to become a great leader, the kind who attracts people and makes things happen? I mean, if you took the time to really look at yourself deep down, would you find the qualities needed to live out your boldest dreams, the ones so big that you've never shared them with anybody? That's a question each of us must have the courage to honestly ask—and answer—if we want to achieve our real potential.

—The 21 Indispensable Qualities of a Leader

CULTIVATE THE CHARACTER QUALITIES NECESSARY
TO BE A SUCCESSFUL, PASSIONATE LEADER.

THE LAW OF INFLUENCE

The true measure of leadership is influence—nothing more, nothing less. True leadership cannot be awarded, appointed, or assigned. It comes only from influence, and that cannot be mandated. It must be earned.

The proof of leadership is found in the followers. So why do some people emerge as leaders while others can't influence no matter how hard they try? I believe that several factors come into play:

1. Character—who they are
2. Relationships—who they know
3. Knowledge—what they know
4. Intuition—what they feel
5. Experience—where they've been
6. Past Success—what they've done
7. Ability—what they can do

I love the leadership proverb that says, "He who thinks he leads, but has no followers, is only taking a walk." If you can't influence people, then they will not follow you. And if people won't follow, you are not a leader.

—*The 21 Irrefutable Laws of Leadership*

ARE PEOPLE FOLLOWING YOU, OR
ARE YOU ONLY TAKING A WALK?

JANUARY 8

POINT OUT PEOPLE'S STRENGTHS

People often make a mistake in their personal development when they focus too much on their weaknesses. As a result, they spend all their time trying to shore up those weaknesses instead of maximizing the strengths they possess. Similarly, it's a mistake to focus on the weaknesses of others. The self-proclaimed "experts" who spend their time telling others what's wrong with them never win with people. Most people simply avoid them.

Instead, we need to focus on finding people's strengths and pointing them out. Most people have strengths that they rarely get to use. Those strengths may be job skills, knowledge, general abilities, personality characteristics, or other attributes. I once read an interesting fact based on research, saying that every person can do at least one thing better than ten thousand other people. Think about that! You possess an ability that can't be matched by anyone in your town or neighborhood . . . or in your college or university . . . or in your company or maybe even in your industry.

Have you discovered that ability? If so, you are probably well on your way to pursuing your life's purpose. If you haven't, wouldn't you love it if someone came alongside you and pointed it out? How would you feel about that person? I bet you'd be pretty grateful.

Why not try to become that kind of person in someone else's life? When you do, you just might be helping others to discover the thing God created them to do.

—*25 Ways to Win with People*

POINT OUT A GREAT STRENGTH OF
SOMEONE IN YOUR LIFE TODAY.

THE POWER OF FOCUSING

What does it take to have the focus required to be a truly effective leader? The keys are priorities and concentration. A leader who knows his priorities but lacks concentration knows what to do but never gets it done. If he has concentration but no priorities, he has excellence without progress. But when he harnesses both, he has the potential to achieve great things.

I frequently meet people in leadership positions who seem to major in minor things. So the important question is, How should you focus your time and energy?

Effective leaders who reach their potential spend more time focusing on what they do well than on what they do wrong. To be successful, focus on your strengths and develop them. That's where you should pour your time, energy, and resources.

Growth equals change. If you want to get better, you have to keep changing and improving. That means stepping out into new areas. If you dedicate time to new things related to areas of strength, then you'll grow as a leader. Don't forget: in leadership, if you're through growing, you're through.

Nobody can entirely avoid working in areas of weakness. The key is to minimize it as much as possible, and leaders can do it by delegating. For example, I delegate detail work to others. A team of people handles all the logistics of my conferences. That way when I'm there, I stick to the things I do best, such as the actual speaking.

—*The 21 Indispensable Qualities of a Leader*

SET YOUR PRIORITIES AND FOCUS
ON YOUR STRENGTHS TODAY.

CHARTING THE COURSE

Nearly anyone can steer the ship, but it takes a leader to chart the course. Before leaders take their people on a journey, they become navigators and go through a process in order to give the trip the best chance of being a success:

Navigators Draw on Past Experience: Most natural leaders are activists. They tend to look forward—not backward—make decisions, and move on. But for leaders to become good navigators, they need to take time to reflect and learn from their experiences.

Navigators Examine the Conditions Before Making Commitments: Good navigators count the cost *before* making commitments for themselves and others. They examine not only measurable factors such as finances, resources, and talent, but also intangibles such as timing, morale, momentum, culture, and so on.

Navigators Listen to What Others Have to Say: No matter how good a leader you are, you yourself will not have all the answers. That's why top-notch navigators gather information from many sources.

Navigators Make Sure Their Conclusions Represent Both Faith and Fact: Being able to navigate for others requires a leader to possess a positive attitude. You've got to have faith that you can take your people all the way. On the other hand, you also have to be able to see the facts realistically. If you don't go in with your eyes wide open, you're going to get blindsided.

—*The 21 Irrefutable Laws of Leadership*

HAVE YOU TAKEN THE TIME TO CHART THE
COURSE FOR THE PEOPLE YOU'RE LEADING?

JANUARY 11

THE LAW OF PRIORITIES

When we are busy, we naturally believe that we are achieving. But busyness does not equal productivity. Activity is not necessarily accomplishment. Prioritizing requires leaders to continually think ahead, to know what's important, to know what's next, to see how everything relates to the overall vision.

- *What Is Required?* What must I do that nobody can or should do for me?
- *What Gives the Greatest Return?* Work in your areas of greatest strength. Is there something you're doing that can be done 80 percent as well by someone else? If so, delegate it.
- *What Brings the Greatest Reward?* Life is too short not to do some things you love. What energizes you and keeps you passionate?

—*The 21 Irrefutable Laws of Leadership*

TODAY GIVE YOUR TIME ONLY TO THINGS THAT PASS
THE REQUIREMENT, RETURN, REWARD TEST.

PEOPLE NEED TO KNOW THEY HELPED

Whenever someone tells me how valuable the people on my team are to them, I encourage him to tell the individuals who were so helpful. Why? Because people need to know that they helped someone.

"Good leaders make people feel that they're at the very heart of things, not at the periphery," says author and leadership expert Warren Bennis. "Everyone feels that he or she makes a difference to the success of the organization. When that happens people feel centered and that gives their work meaning." Walter Shipley of Citibank says, "We have 68,000 employees. With a company this size, I'm not 'running the business.' . . . My job is to create the environment that enables people to leverage each other beyond their own individual capabilities. . . . I get credit for providing the leadership that got us there. But our people did it." Shipley understands what successful leaders know: people need to know that they made an important contribution to reaching the goal.

It's not a sign of weakness to let others know you value them. It's a sign of security and strength. When you're honest about your need for help, specific with others about the value they add, and inclusive of others as you build a team to do something bigger than you are, everybody wins.

—*25 Ways to Win with People*

TELL THE MEMBERS OF YOUR TEAM
WHY THEY ARE VALUABLE TO YOU.

CONTROL WHAT'S IN YOU

Former UCLA basketball coach John Wooden, one of the greatest coaches who ever lived, said, "Do not let what you cannot do interfere with what you can do." Wooden was known for stressing excellence to his players and encouraging them to work toward their potential. He never made winning a championship his goal. He focused on the journey, not the destination. Yet his work ethic and focus on the things within his control earned his UCLA teams four undefeated seasons, an eighty-eight-game winning streak, and an incredible ten national championships. No one had ever done that before him, and no one has done it since.

As you move forward on the success journey, you need to remember that what happens *in* you is more important than what happens *to* you. You can control your attitudes as you travel on the journey, but you have no control over the actions of others. You can choose what to put on your calendar, but you can't control today's circumstances. Unfortunately, the majority of the fear and stress that people experience in life is from things they can do nothing about. Don't let that happen to you.

—Your Road Map for Success

FOCUS ON THE THINGS YOU CAN
DO SOMETHING ABOUT TODAY.

LEADERS SEE WITHIN
THE LARGER CONTEXT

Most people evaluate events in their lives according to how they will be personally affected. Leaders think within a broader context. They start by asking themselves, *How will this impact my people?* But then they also look at how something will impact those above and beside them. They try to see everything in terms of the entire organization and beyond.

Effective leaders know the answers to the following questions:

* How do I fit in my area or department?
* How do all the departments fit into the organization?
* Where does our organization fit in the market?
* How is our market related to other industries and the economy?

And as industries in our economy become more global, many good leaders are thinking even more broadly!

You don't have to become a global economist to lead effectively from the middle of your organization. The point is that 360-Degree Leaders see their area as part of the larger process and understand how the pieces of the larger puzzle fit together. If you desire to be a better leader, then broaden your thinking and work at seeing things from a larger perspective.

—The 360° Leader

WHAT POSITIVE IMPROVEMENTS CAN YOU MAKE TODAY
BASED ON YOUR UNDERSTANDING OF HOW YOU FIT WITHIN
YOUR AREA, ORGANIZATION, MARKET, AND INDUSTRY?

BE IMPRESSED, NOT IMPRESSIVE

Too often we think that if we can impress others, we will gain influence with them. We want to become others' heroes—to be larger than life. That creates a problem because we're real live human beings. People can see us for who we really are. If we make it our goal to impress them, we puff up our pride and end up being pretentious—and that turns people off.

If you want to influence others, don't try to impress them. Pride is really nothing more than a form of selfishness, and pretense is only a way to keep people at arm's length so that they can't see who you really are. Instead of impressing others, let them impress you.

It's really a matter of attitude. The people with charisma, those who attract others to themselves, are individuals who focus on others, not themselves. They ask questions of others. They listen. They don't try to be the center of attention. And they never try to pretend they're perfect.

—*The 360° Leader*

SPEND TODAY LISTENING TO OTHERS
AND LETTING THEM IMPRESS YOU.

MANAGE YOUR ATTITUDE DAILY

One of the most significant discoveries of my life was realizing that we often place too much emphasis on making decisions and too little on managing the decisions we've already made. This discovery was so significant to me that I wrote a book about it called *Today Matters*. The thesis of the book is that successful people make right decisions early and manage those decisions daily. You can make a decision to have a good attitude, but if you don't make plans to *manage* that decision every day, then you are likely to end up right back where you started. But here's the good news: *maintaining* the right attitude is easier than *regaining* the right attitude.

How do you do that? A Chinese proverb I came across gives insight: "Assume a cheerfulness you do not feel, and shortly you feel the cheerfulness you assumed." Or as editor and publisher Elbert Hubbard says, "Be pleasant until 10 a.m. and the rest of the day will take care of itself." When you get up in the morning, you need to remind yourself of the decision you've made to have a positive attitude. You need to manage your thinking and direct your actions so that they are consistent with your decision.

If you take responsibility for your attitude—recognizing that it can change how you live, managing it every day, and cultivating and developing positive thoughts and habits—then you can make your attitude your greatest asset. It can become the difference maker in your life, opening doors and helping you overcome great obstacles.

—The Difference Maker

MAKE THE DECISION TO HAVE A GOOD ATTITUDE TODAY,
THEN MANAGE THAT DECISION THE REST OF THE DAY.

THE LAW OF CONNECTION

The stronger the relationship you form with followers, the greater the connection you forge—and the more likely those followers will be to want to help you. Whether you're speaking in front of a large audience or chatting in the hallway with an individual, the guidelines are the same.

1. *Connect with Yourself:* You must know who you are and have confidence in yourself if you desire to connect with others.

2. *Communicate with Openness and Sincerity:* Legendary NFL coach Bill Walsh said, "Nothing is more effective than sincere, accurate praise, and nothing is more lame than a cookie-cutter compliment."

3. *Know Your Audience:* Learn people's names, find out about their histories, ask about their dreams. Speak to what *they* care about.

4. *Live Your Message:* Practice what you preach. That's where credibility comes from.

5. *Go to Where They Are:* I dislike any kind of barrier to communication. I adapt to others; I don't expect them to adapt to me.

6. *Focus on Them, Not Yourself:* The number one problem of inexperienced speakers and ineffective leaders is that they focus on themselves.

7. *Believe in Them:* It's one thing to communicate to people because you believe you have something of value to say. It's another to communicate with people because you believe they have value.

8. *Offer Direction and Hope:* French general Napoleon Bonaparte said, "Leaders are dealers in hope."

—The 21 Irrefutable Laws of Leadership

INTENTIONALLY CONNECT WITH
THE PEOPLE YOU LEAD TODAY.

TAKE TIME TO UNDERSTAND PEOPLE

How are you doing when it comes to being relational? Do you spend a lot of time and energy building solid relationships with your teammates, or are you so focused on results that you tend to overlook (or overrun) others as you work to achieve team goals? If the latter is true of you, think about the wise words of George Kienzle and Edward Dare in *Climbing the Executive Ladder*: "Few things will pay you bigger dividends than the time and trouble you take to understand people. Almost nothing will add more to your stature as an executive and a person. Nothing will give you greater satisfaction or bring you more happiness." Becoming a highly relational person brings individual and team success.

—The 17 Essential Qualities of a Team Player

BUILD SOLID RELATIONSHIPS WITH YOUR
PEOPLE AND THE RESULTS WILL FOLLOW.

THE 30-SECOND RULE

When most people meet others, they search for ways to make themselves look good. The key to the 30-Second Rule is reversing this practice. When you make contact with people, instead of focusing on yourself, search for ways to make *them* look good.

Every day before I meet with people, I pause to think about something encouraging I can tell them. What I say can be one of many things: I might thank them for something they've done for me or for a friend. I might tell others about one of their accomplishments. I might praise them for a personal quality they exhibit. Or I might simply compliment their appearance. The practice isn't complicated, but it does take some time, effort, and discipline. The reward for practicing it is huge, because it really makes a positive impact on people.

—25 Ways to Win with People

TAKE THIRTY SECONDS WITH EACH PERSON YOU
MEET TODAY TO ADD VALUE TO THEM.

DEVELOP RELATIONSHIPS
BEFORE STARTING OUT

Leaders often make the common mistake of trying to lead others before developing relationships with them. As you prepare to develop other people, take time to get to know each other. Ask them to share their story with you—their journey so far. Find out what makes them tick, their strengths and weaknesses, their temperaments. And spend some time with them outside the environment where you typically see them. If you work together, then play sports together. If you know each other from church, meet with them at their workplace. If you go to school together, then spend some time together at home. You can even use this principle with your family. For example, if you spend time with your children outside your everyday environment, you'll learn a lot more about them. It will develop your relationship in ways it hasn't before, and it will help you grow.

—Your Road Map for Success

GET OUT OF YOUR NORMAL ENVIRONMENT
TODAY WITH SOMEONE YOU LEAD.

THE VALUE OF TIME

Time is valuable. Psychiatrist and author M. Scott Peck said, "Until you value yourself, you won't value your time. Until you value your time, you will not do anything with it."

In *What to Do Between Birth and Death*, Charles Spezzano says that people don't pay for things with money; they pay for them with time. If you say to yourself, *In five years, I'll have put enough away to buy that vacation house*, then what you are really saying is that the house will cost you five years—one-twelfth of your adult life. "The phrase *spending your time* is not a metaphor," said Spezzano. "It's how life works."

Instead of thinking about what you do and what you buy in terms of money, think about them in terms of time. Think about it. What is worth spending your life on? Seeing your work in that light just may change the way you manage your time.

—The 360° Leader

ARE THE TASKS ON TODAY'S AGENDA WORTHY OF YOUR LIFE?

ENLARGING OTHERS

Team members always love and admire a player who is able to help them go to another level, someone who enlarges them and empowers them to be successful.

Players who enlarge their teammates have several things in common:

1. *Enlargers Value Their Teammates:* Your teammates can tell whether you believe in them. People's performances usually reflect the expectations of those they respect.

2. *Enlargers Value What Their Teammates Value:* Players who enlarge others listen to discover what their teammates talk about and watch to see what they spend their money on. That kind of knowledge, along with a desire to relate to their fellow players, creates a strong connection.

3. *Enlargers Add Value to Their Teammates:* Adding value is really the essence of enlarging others. It's finding ways to help others improve their abilities and attitudes. An enlarger looks for the gifts, talents, and uniqueness in other people, and then helps them to increase those abilities.

4. *Enlargers Make Themselves More Valuable:* Enlargers work to make themselves better, not only because it benefits them personally, but also because it helps them to help others. If you want to increase the ability of a teammate, make yourself better.

How do your teammates see you? Are you an enlarger? Do you make them better than they are alone through your inspiration and contribution? Do you know what your teammates value? Do you capitalize on those things by adding value to them in those areas?

—*The 17 Essential Qualities of a Team Player*

TAKE SOME SPECIFIC STEPS TO
ENLARGE YOUR TEAMMATES TODAY.

OVERCOMING BARRIERS TO EMPOWERMENT

Leading well is not about enriching yourself—it's about empowering others. Only empowered people can reach their potential. When a leader can't or won't empower others, he creates barriers within the organization that followers cannot overcome.

When leaders fail to empower others, it is usually due to three main reasons:

1. Desire for Job Security
2. Resistance to Change
3. Lack of Self-Worth

The truth is that empowerment is powerful—not only for the person being developed, but also for the mentor. Enlarging others makes you larger. It is an impact you can experience as a leader as long as you are willing to believe in people and give your power away.

—*The 21 Irrefutable Laws of Leadership*

ARE YOU WILLING TO GIVE YOUR
POWER AWAY TO ENLARGE OTHERS?

LEADERS CANNOT RISE ABOVE THE LIMITATIONS OF THEIR CHARACTER

Have you ever seen highly talented people suddenly fall apart when they achieved a certain level of success? Steven Berglas, a psychologist at Harvard Medical School and author of *The Success Syndrome*, says that people who achieve great heights but lack the bedrock character to sustain them through the stress are headed for disaster. He believes they are destined for one or more of the four A's: *arrogance*, painful feelings of *aloneness*, destructive *adventure-seeking*, or *adultery*. Each is a terrible price to pay for weak character.

If you've found yourself being sucked in by one of the four A's that Berglas identifies, do what you must to step away from some of the stress of your success, and seek professional help. Don't think that the valley you're in will pass with time, more money, or increased prestige. Unaddressed cracks in character only get deeper and more destructive with time.

If you're not struggling in any of these four areas, you should still examine the condition of your character. Ask yourself whether your words and actions match—all the time. When you say you'll finish an assignment, do you always follow through? If you tell your children that you'll make it to their recital or ball game, are you there for it?

As you lead others, recognize that your character is your most important asset. G. Alan Bernard, president of Mid Park, Inc., stated, "The respect that leadership must have requires that one's ethics be without question. A leader not only stays above the line between right and wrong, he stays well clear of the 'gray areas.'"

—*The 21 Indispensable Qualities of a Leader*

EXAMINE THE CONDITION OF YOUR CHARACTER,
AND MAKE SURE YOUR WORDS AND ACTIONS MATCH UP.

VISION

One of the great dreamers of the twentieth century was Walt Disney. Back when Walt's two daughters were young, he used to take them to an amusement park in the Los Angeles area on Saturday mornings. Walt was especially captivated by the carousel. As he approached it, he saw a blur of bright images racing around to the tune of energetic calliope music. But when he got closer and the carousel stopped, he could see that his eye had been fooled. He observed shabby horses with cracked and chipped paint. And he noticed that only the horses on the outside row moved up and down. The others stood lifeless, bolted to the floor. The cartoonist's disappointment inspired him with a grand vision: Disneyland and Walt Disney World.

Vision is everything for a leader. It is utterly indispensable. Why? Because vision leads the leader. It paints the target. It sparks and fuels the fire within, and draws him forward. It is also the fire lighter for others who follow that leader. Show me a leader without vision, and I'll show you someone who isn't going anywhere. At best, he is traveling in circles.

If you lack vision, look inside yourself. Draw on your natural gifts and desires. Look to your calling if you have one. And if you still don't sense a vision of your own, then consider hooking up with a leader whose vision resonates with you. Become his partner. That's what Walt Disney's brother, Roy, did. He was a good businessman and leader who could make things happen, but Walt was the one who provided the vision. Together, they made an incredible team.

—The 21 Indispensable Qualities of a Leader

FIND YOUR VISION, AND LET IT
GUIDE YOU IN ALL THAT YOU DO.

EVERYONE INFLUENCES SOMEONE

Sociologists tell us that even the most introverted individual will influence ten thousand other people during his or her lifetime! This amazing statistic was shared with me by my associate Tim Elmore. Tim and I concluded that each one of us is both influencing and being influenced by others. That means that all of us are leading in some areas, while in other areas we are being led. No one is excluded from being a leader or a follower. Realizing your potential as a leader is your responsibility. In any given situation with any given group, there is a prominent influencer.

The prominent leader of any group is quite easily discovered. Just observe the people as they gather. If an issue is to be decided, who is the person whose opinion seems most valuable? Who is the one others watch the most when the issue is being discussed? Who is the one with whom people quickly agree? Most importantly, who is the one the others follow? Answers to these questions will help you discern who the real leader is in a particular group.

—*Developing the Leader Within You*

WHO IS THE REAL LEADER IN YOUR WORKPLACE,
AND HOW WILL THAT IMPACT THE WAY YOU LEAD?

JANUARY 27

THE HEART OF LEADERSHIP

Where is your heart when it comes to serving others? Do you desire to become a leader for the perks and benefits? Or are you motivated by a desire to help others?

If you really want to become the kind of leader that people want to follow, you will have to settle the issue of servanthood. If your attitude is to be served rather than to serve, you may be headed for trouble. If this is an issue in your life, then heed this advice:

- Stop lording over people, and start listening to them.
- Stop role-playing for advancement, and start risking for others' benefit.
- Stop seeking your own way, and start serving others.

It is true that those who would be great must be like the least and the servant of all.

Albert Schweitzer wisely stated, "I don't know what your destiny will be, but one thing I know: The ones among you who will be really happy are those who have sought and found how to serve." If you want to lead on the highest level, be willing to serve on the lowest.

—*The 21 Indispensable Qualities of a Leader*

EXAMINE YOUR MOTIVATION FOR LEADING OTHERS TODAY.

ACT YOURSELF INTO CHANGING

The quality of your life and the duration of your success depend on your attitude, and you are the only person in this world with the power to make it better. Dr. William Glasser maintained, "If you want to change attitudes, start with a change in behavior. In other words, begin to act the part, as well as you can, of the person you would rather be, the person you most want to become. Gradually, the old, fearful person will fade away."

Change requires action. Most people wait until they feel like it to change their attitudes. But that only causes them to keep waiting because they have the whole process backward. If you wait until you *feel like it* to try to change your attitude, you will never change. You have to *act* yourself into changing.

> An act of your will
> Will lead you to action;
> And your positive action
> Will lead to a positive attitude!

According to Henry Ford, "Whether you think you can or think you can't—you are right." The mind, more than anything else, determines how far you can go on the success journey.

—Your Road Map for Success

ACT YOUR WAY INTO FEELING POSITIVE
TODAY AS YOU FACE ADVERSITY.

LET PEOPLE KNOW YOU NEED THEM

The day that I realized I could no longer do everything myself was a major step in my development as a person and a leader. I've always had vision, plenty of ideas, and vast amounts of energy. But when the vision gets bigger than you, you really only have two choices: give up on the vision or get help. I chose the latter.

No matter how successful you are, no matter how important or accomplished, you *do* need people. That's why you need to let them know that you cannot win without them. President Woodrow Wilson said, "We should not only use all the brains we have—but all that we can borrow." Why stop with just their brains? Enlist people's hands and hearts too! Another president, Lyndon Johnson, was right when he said, "There are no problems we cannot solve together, and very few that we can solve by ourselves."

—25 Ways to Win with People

TAKE TIME TODAY TO LET THE PEOPLE AROUND YOU
KNOW HOW MUCH YOU NEED AND APPRECIATE THEM.

STEER A COURSE

If you could go anywhere, where would you like to go? Not in terms of vacations, but in your life. Your answer to that question does a lot to determine whether or not you're successful. You see, we're all on a journey, whether we know it or not. We are traveling inevitably toward the ends of our lives. So the real question for us is whether we're going to select a destination and steer a course for it, or allow ourselves to be swept along with the tide, letting others determine where we'll end up. The choice is entirely up to us.

—Your Road Map for Success

WHAT SPECIFIC DESTINATION ARE
YOU STEERING YOUR LIFE TOWARD?

GROWING TO YOUR POTENTIAL

Novelist H. G. Wells held that wealth, notoriety, place, and power are no measures of success whatsoever. The only true measure of success is the ratio between what we might have been and what we have become. In other words, success comes as the result of growing to our potential.

It's been said that our potential is God's gift to us, and what we do with it is our gift to him. But at the same time, our potential is probably our greatest untapped resource. Henry Ford observed, "There is no man living who isn't capable of doing more than he thinks he can do."

We have nearly limitless potential, yet too few ever try to reach it. Why? The answer lies in this: We can do *anything*, but we can't do *everything*. Many people let everyone around them decide their agenda in life. As a result, they never really dedicate themselves to *their* purpose in life. They become a jack-of-all-trades, master of none—rather than a jack-of-few-trades, focused on one.

If that describes you more than you'd like, you're probably ready to take steps to make a change. There are four principles to put you on the road to growing toward your potential:

1. Concentrate on one main goal.
2. Concentrate on continual improvement.
3. Forget the past.
4. Focus on the future.

When you know your purpose in life and are growing to reach your maximum potential, you're well on your way to being a success.

—Your Road Map for Success

ARE YOU FOCUSED ON THE ONE TRADE
THAT WILL SET YOU APART?

FEBRUARY

GIVE PEOPLE THE TRIPLE–A TREATMENT

A ll people feel better and do better when you give them *attention, affirmation,* and *appreciation.* The next time you make contact with people, begin by giving them your undivided attention during the first thirty seconds. Affirm them and show your appreciation for them in some way. Then watch what happens. You will be surprised by how positively they respond. And if you have trouble remembering to keep your focus on them instead of on yourself, then perhaps the words of William King will help you. He said, "A gossip is one who talks to you about other people. A bore is one who talks to you about himself. And a brilliant conversationalist is one who talks to you about yourself."

—25 Ways to Win with People

GIVE MEMBERS OF YOUR TEAM ATTENTION,
AFFIRMATION, AND APPRECIATION TODAY.

TO TEAMWORK, ADD FRIENDSHIP

Why do I recommend that you work to develop friendships on the job?

Friendship Is the Foundation of Influence: President Abraham Lincoln said, "If you would win a man to your cause, first convince him that you are his sincere friend." Good relationships make influence possible, and friendship is the most positive relationship you can develop on the job with your coworkers.

Friendship Is the Framework for Success: I believe long-term success is unachievable without good people skills. Theodore Roosevelt said, "The most important single ingredient in the formula of success is knowing how to get along with people." Without it, most achievements are not possible, and even what we do achieve can feel hollow.

Friendship Is the Shelter Against Sudden Storms: If you're having a bad day, who can make you feel better? A friend. When you have to face your fears, who would you rather do it with? A friend. When you fall on your face, who can help pick you up? A friend. Aristotle was right when he said, "True friends are a sure refuge."

—The 360° Leader

DON'T JUST BE A TEAM MEMBER—
BE A FRIEND TO THOSE YOU WORK WITH.

FEBRUARY 3

RATCHET UP YOUR PASSION

What makes it possible for people who might seem ordinary to achieve great things? The answer is passion. Nothing can take the place of passion in a leader's life.

Take a look at four truths about passion and what it can do for you as a leader:

1. *Passion Is the First Step to Achievement:* Your desire determines your destiny. Anyone who lives beyond an ordinary life has great desire. It's true in any field: weak desire brings weak results, just as a small fire creates little heat. The stronger your fire, the greater the desire—and the greater the potential.

2. *Passion Increases Your Willpower:* There is no substitute for passion. It is fuel for the will. If you want anything badly enough, you can find the willpower to achieve it. The only way to have that kind of desire is to develop passion.

3. *Passion Changes You:* If you follow your passion—instead of others' perceptions—you can't help becoming a more dedicated, productive person. And that increases your ability to impact others. In the end, your passion will have more influence than your personality.

4. *Passion Makes the Impossible Possible:* Human beings are so made that whenever anything fires the soul, impossibilities vanish. A fire in the heart lifts everything in your life. That's why passionate leaders are so effective. A leader with great passion and few skills always outperforms a leader with great skills and no passion.

—*The 21 Indispensable Qualities of a Leader*

FIND OR REKINDLE YOUR PASSION TODAY
TO INCREASE YOUR INTENSITY FOR SUCCESS.

REMEMBER THEIR GOOD DAYS, NOT THEIR BAD ONES

We all have good days and bad days. I don't know about you, but I'd like to be remembered for my good ones. And I can only ask to be forgiven for my bad ones. Fuller Theological Seminary Professor David Augsburger observes, "Since nothing we intend is ever faultless, and nothing we achieve without some measure of finitude and fallibility we call humanness, we are saved by forgiveness." If you desire to mine the gold of good intentions in others, then forgiveness is essential. And it's rarely a one-time thing. Civil rights leader Martin Luther King Jr. was right when he said, "Forgiveness is not an occasional act; it is a permanent attitude."

And remember, it is with the attitude with which you judge others that you will also be judged. If you mine the gold of good intentions in your relationship with others, then people will more likely do the same for you.

—25 Ways to Win with People

POSSESS AN ATTITUDE OF FORGIVENESS
TODAY AS YOU WORK WITH OTHERS.

TRUST ME ON THIS

If you boil relationships down to the most important element, it's always going to be trust—not leadership, value, partnership, or anything else. If you don't have trust, your relationship is in trouble.

In his book *On Becoming a Leader*, Warren Bennis says, "Integrity is the basis of trust, which is not so much an ingredient of leadership as it is a product. It is the one quality that cannot be acquired but must be earned. It is given by coworkers and followers, and without it, the leader can't function."

That can be said not only of leaders and followers, but also of all relationships. Developing trust is like constructing a building. It takes time, and it must be done one piece at a time. As in construction, it's much quicker and easier to tear something down than it is to build it up. But if the foundation is strong, there is a good chance that what is built upon it will stand.

When two people trust each other completely, the relationship can grow to a level of friendship that is as rewarding as anything in life. It reaches the highest heights. Writer and chaplain to Queen Victoria, Charles Kingsley, said, "A blessed thing it is for any man or woman to have a friend, one human soul whom we can trust utterly, who knows the best and worst of us, and who loves us in spite of all our faults."

—*Winning with People*

Say what you mean and mean what you say
as you work with others today and every day.

LINK UP WITH OTHERS

Some people aren't very outgoing and simply don't think in terms of team building and team participation. As they face challenges, it never occurs to them to enlist others to achieve something.

As a people person, I find that hard to relate to. Whenever I face any kind of challenge, the very first thing I do is to think about the people I want on the team to help with it. I've been that way since I was a kid. I've always thought, *Why take the journey alone when you can invite others along with you?*

I understand that not everyone operates that way. But whether or not you are naturally inclined to be part of a team is really irrelevant. If you do everything alone and never partner with other people, you create huge barriers to your own potential. Dr. Allan Fromme quipped, "People have been known to achieve more as a result of working with others than against them." What an understatement! It takes a team to do anything of lasting value. Besides, even the most introverted person in the world can learn to enjoy the benefits of being on a team. (That's true even if someone isn't trying to accomplish something great.)

For the person trying to do everything alone, the game really is over. If you want to do something big, you must link up with others. One is too small a number to achieve greatness.

—*The 17 Indisputable Laws of Teamwork*

As you face challenges, think about who
you can enlist to come alongside you.

PEOPLE ADD THE MOST VALUE
IN THEIR STRENGTH ZONES

People often ask me what the key to my success is. And I tell them that I think it can be attributed to three things: (1) the goodness of God; (2) the excellent people around me; and (3) my ability to stay in my strength zone. It took the first five years of my professional life to figure out what my strengths were. But with the passing of years since then, I've narrowed my focus down to fewer and fewer things.

As a leader and employer, I try to help others do the same. I help them find their strength zones, and I try to position them there as much as possible. You see, a successful person finds the right place for himself. But a successful leader finds the right place for others. How do I do that?

First, I look for the best in others. Anybody can see weaknesses, mistakes, and shortcomings in others. Seeing only the good things is harder. Hall of Fame baseball player Reggie Jackson said, "A great manager has a knack for making ballplayers think they are better than they think they are. He lets you know he believes in you. And once you learn how good you really are, you never settle for playing anything less than your very best." That's true in any area of life: business, parenting, marriage, ministry, and so forth. Don't look for the flaws, warts, and blemishes in others. Look for their best.

Second, I speak up. You can think the world of others, but if you never actually tell them, then you don't really help them. I have always believed that all people have a "success seed" within them. I often look at other people and ask, "What are their success seeds?" When I discover them, I point them out to those individuals. Then I fertilize those seeds with encouragement and water them with opportunity.

—25 Ways to Win with People

LOOK FOR THE BEST IN OTHERS AND HELP THEM SEE IT TOO.

THE LAW OF SACRIFICE

If you desire to become the best leader you can be, then you need to be willing to make sacrifices in order to lead well. If that is your desire, then here are some things you need to know:

1. *There Is No Success Without Sacrifice:* Leaders must give up to go up. Talk to leaders, and you will find that they have made repeated sacrifices. Effective leaders sacrifice much that is good in order to dedicate themselves to what is best.

2. *Leaders Are Often Asked to Give Up More Than Others:* The heart of leadership is putting others ahead of yourself. It's doing what is best for the team. For that reason, I believe that leaders have to give up their rights.

3. *You Must Keep Giving Up to Stay Up:* If leaders have to give up to go up, then they have to give up even more to stay up. What gets a team to the top isn't what keeps it there. The only way to stay up is to give up even more.

4. *The Higher the Level of Leadership, the Greater the Sacrifice:* The higher you go, the more it's going to cost you. And it doesn't matter what kind of leadership career you pick. You will have to make sacrifices. You will have to give up to go up.

—*The 21 Irrefutable Laws of Leadership*

ARE YOU WILLING TO GIVE UP TO GO UP?

TAKE AN INTEREST IN PEOPLE

This may sound too simple, but it really all starts here. You have to show people that you care about them by taking an interest in them. Many leaders are so action oriented and agenda driven that they don't make people a high enough priority. If that describes you, then you need to turn that around.

I don't mean to sound crass, but it helps if you like people. If you're not a people person, that may be the first step you need to take. Look for value in every person. Put yourself in others' shoes. Find reasons to like them. You won't take an interest in people if deep down you care nothing about them. And if you care nothing about them, that flaw will always be a hindrance to your ability to lead people.

If this is an area of challenge for you, then you may want to take a look at *25 Ways to Win with People: How to Make Others Feel Like a Million Bucks*, which I coauthored with Les Parrott; or read the classic *How to Win Friends and Influence People* by Dale Carnegie. However you go about developing people skills, just remember that people always move toward someone who increases them and away from anyone who decreases them.

—The 360° Leader

TAKE INTEREST IN OTHERS BEFORE
THEY TAKE INTEREST IN YOU.

THE POSITION MYTH

If I had to identify the number one misconception people have about leadership, it would be the belief that leadership comes simply from having a position or title. But nothing could be further from the truth. You don't need to possess a position at the top of your group, department, division, or organization in order to lead. If you think you do, then you have bought into the position myth.

A place at the top will not automatically make anyone a leader. The Law of Influence in *The 21 Irrefutable Laws of Leadership* states it clearly: "The true measure of leadership is influence—nothing more, nothing less."

Because I have led volunteer organizations most of my life, I have watched many people become tied up by the position myth. When people who buy into this myth are identified as potential leaders and put on a team, they are very uncomfortable if they have not been given some kind of title or position that labels them as leaders in the eyes of other team members. Instead of working to build relationships with others on the team and to gain influence naturally, they wait for the positional leader to invest them with authority and give them a title. After a while, they become more and more unhappy, until they finally decide to try another team, another leader, or another organization.

—The 360° Leader

INSTEAD OF RELYING ON POSITION OR TITLE,
USE ONLY RELATIONAL INFLUENCE WITH OTHERS TODAY.

FEBRUARY 11

THE VALUE OF TEAMWORK

A Chinese proverb states, "Behind an able man there are always other able men." The truth is that teamwork is at the heart of great achievement. The question isn't whether teams have value. The question is whether we acknowledge that fact and become better team players. That's why I assert that one is too small a number to achieve greatness. You cannot do anything of real value alone. That is the Law of Significance.

I challenge you to think of one act of genuine significance in the history of humankind that was performed by a lone human being. No matter what you name, you will find that a team of people was involved. That is why President Lyndon Johnson said, "There are no problems we cannot solve together, and very few that we can solve by ourselves."

If you want to reach your potential or strive for the seemingly impossible, you need to become a team player. It may be a cliché, but it is nonetheless true: Individuals play the game, but teams win championships.

— *The 17 Indisputable Laws of Teamwork*

PLACE A HIGH VALUE ON TEAMWORK INSTEAD
OF ACHIEVEMENT AND YOU WILL RECEIVE
NOT ONLY TEAMWORK BUT ALSO ACHIEVEMENT.

WRITE NOTES OF ENCOURAGEMENT

I have believed in the power of written notes of encouragement for many years. Written notes don't have to come from someone famous to be encouraging. A kind word given from the heart is always well received. If you've never mastered the practice of sending handwritten notes to people, then I want to encourage you to try this often neglected way of winning with people.

In his book *The Power of Encouragement*, my friend David Jeremiah says, "Written encouragement comes directly from the heart, uninterrupted and uninhibited. That's why it's so powerful." Haven't you known that to be true?

Nineteenth-century writer Walt Whitman struggled for years to get anyone interested in his poetry. He became very discouraged. Then he received a note that read: "Dear sir, I am not blind to the worth of the wonderful gift of *Leaves of Grass*. I find it the most extraordinary piece of wit and wisdom that America has yet contributed. I greet you at the beginning of a great career." It was signed by Ralph Waldo Emerson.

I can't help but wonder what might have happened to Whitman had Emerson not invested in him by writing those kind words. That note was like fresh air to Whitman, who breathed in that encouragement and was inspired to keep writing. But you don't have to be a professional writer to make a difference in someone's life. Just taking the time to write is evidence of your willingness to invest in that person.

—*25 Ways to Win with People*

WRITE SOMEONE A NOTE OF ENCOURAGEMENT.

THE POWER OF FAILURE

Success doesn't mean avoiding failure. All of us fail. As we travel, we all hit potholes, take wrong turns, or forget to check the radiator. The only person who avoids failure altogether is the person who never leaves her driveway. So the real issue is not whether you're going to fail. It's whether you're going to fail successfully (profiting from your failure). As Nelson Boswell observed, "The difference between greatness and mediocrity is often how an individual views mistakes." If you want to continue on the success journey, you need to learn to fail forward.

Unsuccessful people are often so afraid of failure and rejection that they spend their whole lives avoiding risks or decisions that could lead to failure. They don't realize that success is based on their ability to fail and continue trying. When you have the right attitude, failure is neither fatal nor final. In fact, it can be a springboard to success. Leadership expert Warren Bennis interviewed seventy of the nation's top performers in various fields and found that none of them viewed their mistakes as failures. When talking about them, they referred to their "learning experiences," "tuition paid," "detours," and "opportunities for growth."

Successful people don't let failure go to their heads. Instead of dwelling on the negative consequences of failure, thinking of what might have been and how things haven't worked out, they focus on the rewards of success: learning from their mistakes and thinking about how they can improve themselves and their situations.

—*Your Road Map for Success*

TRY TO SEE FAILURE AS A LEARNING EXPERIENCE TODAY.

FEBRUARY 14

WHEN TO MAKE DECISIONS

M any people make decisions when things aren't going well. They look for relief in the despair of the valley instead of waiting for the clarity that comes from being on the mountaintop. Why? Because it takes a lot of effort to get to the mountaintop. And when you're experiencing the darkness of the valley, it's always tempting to make changes that you hope will relieve the discomfort.

When you are on top of the proverbial mountain, that is the time to make decisions. Here's why:

- You can see your situation more clearly.
- You are moving to something, not just from something.
- You leave those around you in a better position.
- You decide using positive data, not negative.
- You are more likely to move from peak to peak instead of valley to valley.

On the other hand, when you're in the valley, the most important thing you can do is persevere. If you keep fighting, you're likely to get your second wind, just as distance runners do. And it's said that only when runners are exhausted enough to reach that place do they find out what they can truly accomplish. If you keep persevering while you are in the valley, not only will you likely make it to higher ground where you can make better decisions, but you will also have developed character, which will serve you well throughout life.

—*The Difference Maker*

USE THE CLARITY OF MOUNTAINTOP
MOMENTS TO MAKE MAJOR DECISIONS.

LEADERSHIP IS EMPOWERMENT

How do you spot a leader? According to Robert Townsend, they come in all sizes, ages, shapes, and conditions. Some are poor administrators, while some are not overly bright. There is a clue: Since some people are mediocre, the true leader can be recognized because somehow his people consistently demonstrate superior performances.

A leader is great, not because of his or her power, but because of his or her ability to empower others. Success without a successor is failure. A worker's main responsibility is developing others to do the work.

Loyalty to the leader reaches its highest peak when the follower has personally grown through the mentorship of the leader. Why? You win people's hearts by helping them grow personally.

Years ago, one of the key players on my staff was Sheryl Fleisher. When she first joined the team, she was not a people person. I began to work closely with her until she truly became a people person. Today she successfully develops others. There is a bond of loyalty that Sheryl has given to my leadership, and we both know the reason. My time invested with her brought a positive change. She will never forget what I have done for her. Interestingly, her time invested in the lives of others greatly helped me. I will never forget what she has done for me either.

The core of leaders who surround you should all be people you have personally touched or helped to develop in some way. When that happens, love and loyalty will be exhibited by those closest to you and by those who are touched by your key leaders.

—*Developing the Leader Within You*

INVEST IN SOMEONE TODAY TO EMPOWER
HIM OR HER TO GO TO THE NEXT LEVEL.

TOUCHING A DOZEN LIVES

M ost of the time we recognize the influence we have on those who are closest to us in our lives—for good or ill. But sometimes we overlook the impact we can have on other people around us. The anonymous author of this poem probably had that in mind when he wrote,

> My life shall touch a dozen lives before this day is done,
>   Leave countless marks for good or ill ere sets the evening sun,
> This is the wish I always wish, the prayer I always pray;
>   Lord, may my life help other lives it touches by the way.

As you interact with your family, your coworkers, and the clerk at the store today, recognize that your life touches many others' lives. Certainly, your influence on your family members is greater than that on the strangers you meet. And if you have a high-profile occupation, you influence people you don't know. But even in your ordinary day-to-day interactions with people, you make an impact. You can make the few moments that you interact with a store clerk and a bank teller a miserable experience, or you can get them to smile and make their day. The choice is yours.

—*Becoming a Person of Influence*

TOUCH SOMEONE'S LIFE FOR GOOD TODAY.

GOALS CREATE A ROUTE FOR SUCCESS

What separates a motivated person from all the others? The answer is that he has goals. He has identified what he wants to accomplish to fulfill his purpose and maximize his potential. You see, on the success journey, the goals you set become your route. And to make progress, you need that—not because you're hoping or expecting to reach some final destination, but because it shows you *how to take the journey*. On the success journey, the first part of the trip is just as important as the last part. The main thing is to be constantly moving toward your destination. And setting goals is the best way to make sure that continues to happen.

—*Your Road Map for Success*

REVIEW YOUR GOALS TO BE SURE THEY ARE
ENCOURAGING YOU TO FULFILL YOUR PURPOSE
AND MAXIMIZE YOUR POTENTIAL.

MODELING SACRIFICE

If you lead a team, then you must convince your teammates to sacrifice for the good of the group. The more talented the team members, the more difficult it may be to convince them to put the team first.

Begin by modeling sacrifice. Show the team that you are:

• Willing to make financial sacrifices for the team
• Willing to keep growing for the sake of the team
• Willing to empower others for the sake of the team
• Willing to make difficult decisions for the sake of the team

Once you have modeled the willingness to pay a price for the potential of the team, you have the credibility to ask others to do the same. Then when you recognize sacrifices that teammates must make for the team, show them why and how to do it. Then praise their sacrifices to their teammates.

—*The 17 Indisputable Laws of Teamwork*

WHAT SACRIFICE WILL YOU MAKE TODAY
FOR THE SAKE OF YOUR TEAM?

ADDING VALUE TO OTHERS

The interaction between every leader and follower is a relationship, and all relationships either add to or subtract from a person's life. The bottom line in leadership isn't how far we advance ourselves but how far we advance others. That is achieved by serving others and adding value to their lives. The Law of Addition asks one simple question: *Are you making things better for the people who follow you?* That's it. We add value to others when we:

- Truly value others
- Make ourselves more valuable to others
- Know and relate to what others value
- Do things that God values

Adding value to others through service doesn't just benefit the people being served. It allows the leaders to experience:

- Fulfillment in leading others
- Leadership with the right motives
- The ability to perform significant acts as leaders
- The development of a leadership team
- An attitude of service on a team

—*The 21 Irrefutable Laws of Leadership*

ARE YOU MAKING THINGS BETTER FOR
THE PEOPLE WHO FOLLOW YOU?

GIVE PEOPLE ENERGY

Psychologist Henry H. Goddard conducted a study on energy levels in children using an instrument he called the "ergograph." His findings are fascinating. He discovered that when tired children were given a word of praise or commendation, the ergograph showed an immediate upward surge of energy in the children. When the children were criticized or discouraged, the ergograph showed that their physical energy took a sudden nosedive.

You may have already discovered this intuitively. When someone praises you, doesn't your energy level go up? And when you are criticized, doesn't that comment drag you down? Words have great power.

What kind of environment do you think you could create if you continually affirmed people when you first came into contact with them? Not only would you encourage them, but you would also become an energy carrier. Whenever you walked into a room, the people would light up! You would help to create the kind of environment everyone loves. Just your presence alone would brighten people's days.

—*25 Ways to Win with People*

DO SOMETHING TODAY TO CREATE
AN ENVIRONMENT OF AFFIRMATION.

EMBRACE COMMITMENT

The world has never seen a great leader who lacked commitment. If you want to be an effective leader, you have to be committed. True commitment inspires and attracts people. It shows them that you have conviction. They will believe in you only if you believe in your cause. People buy into the leader, then the vision. What is the true nature of commitment? Take a look at three observations.

1. *Commitment Starts in the Heart:* I am told that in the Kentucky Derby, the winning horse effectively runs out of oxygen after the first half mile, and he goes the rest of the way on heart. If you want to make a difference in other people's lives as a leader, look into your heart to see if you're really committed.

2. *Commitment Is Tested by Action:* It's one thing to talk about commitment. It's another to do something about it. The only real measure of commitment is action. Arthur Gordon acknowledged, "Nothing is easier than saying words. Nothing is harder than living them day after day."

3. *Commitment Opens the Door to Achievement:* As a leader, you will face plenty of obstacles and opposition—if you don't already. And there will be times when commitment is the only thing that carries you forward. David McNally commented, "Commitment is the enemy of resistance, for it is the serious promise to press on, to get up, no matter how many times you are knocked down."

—*The 21 Indispensable Qualities of a Leader*

HOW DO YOU MEASURE YOUR LEVEL
OF COMMITMENT AS A LEADER?

WE ARE RESPONSIBLE FOR OUR ATTITUDES

Our destinies in life will never be determined by our complaining spirits or high expectations. Life is full of surprises, and the adjustment of our attitudes is a lifelong project.

> The pessimist complains about the wind.
> The optimist expects it to change.
> The leader adjusts the sails.

We choose what attitudes we have right now. And it's a continuing choice. I am amazed at the large number of adults who fail to take responsibility for their attitudes. If they're grumpy and someone asks why, they'll say, "I got up on the wrong side of the bed." When failure begins to plague their lives, they'll say, "I was born on the wrong side of the tracks." When life begins to flatten out and others in the family are still climbing, they'll say, "Well, I was in the wrong birth order in my family." When their marriages fail, they believe they married the wrong person. When someone else gets a promotion they wanted, it's because they were in the wrong place at the wrong time.

Do you notice something? They are blaming everyone else for their problems.

The greatest day in your life and mine is when we take total responsibility for our attitudes. That's the day we truly grow up.

—*Developing the Leader Within You*

CHOOSE TO BE RESPONSIBLE FOR
HOW YOU VIEW YOUR CIRCUMSTANCES.

LET THEM FLY WITH YOU

I want to share a secret with you. It guarantees success in mentoring. Are you ready? Here it is: *Never work alone.* I know that sounds too simple, but it is truly the secret to developing others. Whenever you do anything that you want to pass along to others, take someone with you.

This isn't necessarily a natural practice for many of us. The learning model that's used in America by most people for teaching others was passed down to us from the Greeks. It's a cognitive "classroom" approach, like the one used by Socrates to teach Plato, and Plato to teach Aristotle.

But that's not the only model available for developing others. We also have one used by another ancient culture: the Hebrews. Their method was more like on-the-job training. In all the years I've been equipping and developing others, I've never found a better way to do it than this:

* **I do it.** First I learn to do the job. I have to understand the why as well as the how, and I try to perfect my craft.
* **I do it—and you watch.** I demonstrate it while you observe, and during the process, I explain what I'm doing and why.
* **You do it—and I watch.** I give you permission and authority to take over the job, but I stay with you to offer advice, correction, and encouragement.
* **You do it.** Once you're proficient, I step back and let you work alone. The learner is drawn up to a higher level, and the teacher is free to move on to higher things.

—Your Road Map for Success

AS YOU WORK TODAY, TAKE SOMEONE WITH YOU
SO THAT HE OR SHE CAN LEARN FROM YOU.

NOTHING BUT VICTORY

Have you ever thought about what separates the leaders who achieve victory from those who suffer defeat? I think that victorious leaders have one thing in common: they share an unwillingness to accept defeat. The alternative to winning is totally unacceptable to them. As a result, they figure out what must be done to achieve victory.

Whether it's a sports team, an army, a business, or a nonprofit organization, victory is possible as long as you have three components that contribute to a team's dedication to victory.

1. *Unity of Vision:* Teams succeed only when the players have a unified vision, no matter how much talent or potential there is.

2. *Diversity of Skills:* Can you imagine a whole hockey team of goalies? Or a business where there are *only* salespeople? It doesn't make sense. Every organization requires diverse talents to succeed.

3. A *Leader Dedicated to Victory and Raising Players to Their Potential:* As former football coach Lou Holtz says, "You've got to have great athletes to win, I don't care who the coach is. You can't win without good athletes, but you can lose with them. This is where coaching makes the difference."

—The 21 Irrefutable Laws of Leadership

As THE LEADER, BE UNWILLING TO ACCEPT DEFEAT,
AND LEAD YOUR TEAM TO SUCCESS.

ACHIEVERS VERSUS AVERAGE

What makes achievers excel? Why do some people skyrocket while others plummet? You know what I'm talking about. You can call it luck, blessing, or the Midas touch—call it whatever you want. But the truth is that some people just seem to achieve incredible things in spite of tremendous difficulties: They finish in the top 5 percent in nationwide sales for their company after losing key accounts. They find ingenious ways to increase profits for their department in the face of budget cuts. They earn a graduate degree while raising two children as a single parent. They discover awesome business opportunities while colleagues don't see any at all. Or they recruit winner after winner into their organization despite what looks like an anemic labor pool. It doesn't matter what kind of work they do. Wherever they are, they just seem to make things happen.

Certainly all people like to think of themselves as above average. But achievers seem to leave "average" in the dust—so far behind them that ordinary seems a distant memory.

What makes the difference? Why do some people achieve so much? Is it . . . family background? Wealth? Opportunity? High morals? The absence of hardship?

No, none of these things are the key. When it comes right down to it, I know of only one factor that separates those who consistently shine from those who don't: *The difference between average people and achieving people is their perception of and response to failure.* Nothing else has the same kind of impact on people's ability to achieve and to accomplish whatever their minds and hearts desire.

—*Failing Forward*

ACCEPT FAILURE AS THE PRICE OF SUCCESS TODAY,
AND KEEP STRIVING FORWARD.

RESISTANCE TO CHANGE

There is nothing more difficult to undertake, more perilous to conduct, or more uncertain in its success than introducing change. Many well-educated people, after being confronted with truth, have been unwilling to change their minds.

James Lind, a British naval surgeon, published a book in 1753 in which he stated explicitly that scurvy could be eliminated simply by supplying sailors with lemon juice. He cited many case histories from his experience as a naval surgeon at sea; he proved that such things as mustard cress, tamarinds, oranges, and lemons would prevent scurvy.

You might rightfully expect that Dr. Lind would have been highly honored and praised for this great contribution, but the reverse is true. He was ridiculed. In fact, My Lords of the Admiralty and other physicians ignored Dr. Lind's advice for forty years. One sea captain did take his advice—the now-famous Captain James Cook, who stocked his ships with an ample supply of fresh fruits.

The Royal Society honored Captain Cook in 1776 for his success, but the officials of the navy ignored his report. Not until 1794, the year of Dr. Lind's death, was a British navy squadron supplied with lemon juice before a voyage. On that voyage, which lasted twenty-three weeks, there was not one case of scurvy, yet another decade passed before regulations were enacted requiring sailors to drink a daily ration of lemon juice to prevent scurvy. With this enactment, scurvy disappeared from the British Navy.

Don't let your attitude toward change or your own predisposition to avoid it create detrimental hindrances to your own personal success.

—*Developing the Leader Within You*

WHAT CHANGE HAVE YOU BEEN AVOIDING
THAT IS NECESSARY FOR YOUR TEAM'S SUCCESS?

STEPPING-STONES FOR SUCCESS

The next time you find yourself envying what successful people have achieved, recognize that they have probably gone through many negative experiences that you cannot see on the surface. An old joke goes like this: "Never ask what's in a hot dog while you're eating one." The idea is that if you did know what's in it, you'd never want to eat one again. A lot of failure goes into success.

If you really want to achieve your dreams—I mean *really* achieve them, not just daydream or talk about them—you've got to get out there and fail. Fail early, fail often, but always fail forward. Turn your mistakes into stepping-stones for success.

—Failing Forward

TAKE A RISK AND BE WILLING TO FAIL FORWARD TODAY.

UNDERSTANDING PEOPLE
PAYS GREAT DIVIDENDS

The ability to understand people is one of the greatest assets anyone can ever have. It has the potential to positively impact every area of your life, not just the business arena. For example, look at how understanding people helped this mother of a preschooler. She said,

> Leaving my four-year-old son in the house, I ran out to throw something in the trash. When I tried to open the door to get back inside, it was locked. I knew that insisting that my son open the door would have resulted in an hour-long battle of the wills. So in a sad voice, I said, "Oh, too bad. You just locked yourself in the house." The door opened at once.

Understanding people certainly impacts your ability to communicate with others. David Burns, a medical doctor and professor of psychiatry at the University of Pennsylvania, observed, "The biggest mistake you can make in trying to talk convincingly is to put your highest priority on expressing your ideas and feelings. What most people really want is to be listened to, respected, and understood. The moment people see that they are being understood, they become more motivated to understand your point of view." If you can learn to understand people—how they think, what they feel, what inspires them, how they're likely to act and react in a given situation—then you can motivate and influence them in a positive way.

—Becoming a Person of Influence

MAKE UNDERSTANDING PEOPLE YOUR TOP PRIORITY TODAY.

INSTILL MOTIVATION

Vince Lombardi, the famed Green Bay Packers football coach, was a feared disciplinarian. But he was also a great motivator. One day he chewed out a player who had missed several blocking assignments. After practice, Lombardi stormed into the locker room and saw that the player was sitting at his locker, head down, dejected. Lombardi mussed his hair, patted him on the shoulder, and said, "One of these days, you're going to be the best guard in the NFL."

That player was Jerry Kramer, and Kramer says he carried that positive image of himself for the rest of his career. "Lombardi's encouragement had a tremendous impact on my whole life," Kramer said. He went on to become a member of the Green Bay Packers Hall of Fame and a member of the NFL's All-50-Year Team.

Everybody needs motivation from time to time. Motivation makes it possible to accomplish what you should accomplish. Never underestimate the power of it.

* Motivation helps people who know what they should do . . . to do it!
* Motivation helps people who know what commitment they should make . . . to make it!
* Motivation helps people who know what habit they should break . . . to break it!
* Motivation helps people who know what path they should take . . . to take it!

—25 Ways to Win with People

MOTIVATE SOMEONE IN YOUR CIRCLE OF INFLUENCE TODAY.

MARCH

MARCH 1

HELP PEOPLE WIN

Helping another person to win is one of the greatest feelings in the world. I haven't met a person yet who doesn't like to win. And everyone I know who's made the effort to help others has said that it is the most rewarding part of life.

In 1984, Lou Whittaker led the first all-American team to the summit of Mt. Everest. After months of grueling effort, five members of the team reached the final campsite at twenty-seven thousand feet. With two thousand feet to go, Whittaker had a tough decision to make: He knew how highly motivated all five climbers were to stand on the highest point on earth. But two would have to go back to the previous camp, load up food, water, and oxygen, then return to the camp where they now met. After completing this support assignment, these two climbers would be in no condition to make a try for the summit. The others would stay in the tent that day, preparing for the summit attempt.

The first decision Whittaker made was to stay at the twenty-seven-thousand-foot camp to coordinate the team's activities. The next was to send the two strongest climbers down the mountain to get the supplies; it was the tougher job. The two weaker climbers would rest, renew their strength, and receive the glory of the summit.

When asked why he didn't assign himself the summit run, his answer showed his understanding of people and the strength of his leadership. He said, "My job was to put other people on top."

Whittaker understood that when people make the right decisions that help the team to achieve its goal, everybody wins.

—*25 Ways to Win with People*

MAKE IT YOUR JOB TO PUT OTHER PEOPLE ON TOP TODAY.

MARCH 2

INCREASING YOUR PASSION

Is passion a characteristic of your life? Do you wake up feeling enthusiastic about your day? Is the first day of the week your favorite, or do you live from weekend to weekend? How long has it been since you couldn't sleep because you were too excited by an idea? You can never lead something you don't care passionately about. You can't start a fire in your organization unless one is first burning in you. To increase your passion, do the following:

Take your temperature. How passionate are you about your life and work? Does it show? Get an honest assessment by querying several coworkers and your spouse about your level of desire.

Return to your first love. Think back to when you were just starting out in your career—or even farther back to when you were a child. What really turned your crank? What could you spend hours and hours doing? Try to recapture your old enthusiasm. Then evaluate your life and career in light of those old loves.

Associate with people of passion. It sounds hokey, but birds of a feather really do flock together. If you've lost your fire, get around some firelighters. Passion is contagious. Schedule some time with people who can infect you with it.

—The 21 Indispensable Qualities of a Leader

SPEND SOME TIME WITH PASSIONATE PEOPLE TODAY.

FAILING BACKWARD VERSUS FAILING FORWARD

Look at the way any achiever approaches negative experiences, and you can learn a lot about how to fail forward. Read through these two lists, and determine which one describes your approach to failure:

Failing Backward	Failing Forward
• Blaming Others	• Taking Responsibility
• Repeating the Same Mistakes	• Learning from Each Mistake
• Expecting Never to Fail Again	• Knowing Failure Is a Part of Progress
• Expecting to Continually Fail	• Maintaining a Positive Attitude
• Accepting Tradition Blindly	• Challenging Outdated Assumptions
• Being Limited by Past Mistakes	• Taking New Risks
• Thinking, *I am a Failure*	• Believing Something Didn't Work
• Quitting	• Persevering

Think about a recent setback you experienced. How did you respond? No matter how difficult your problems were, the key to overcoming them doesn't lie in changing your circumstances. It's in changing yourself. That in itself is a process, and it begins with a desire to be teachable. If you're willing to do that, then you'll be able to handle failure. From this moment on, make a commitment to do whatever it takes to fail forward.

—*Failing Forward*

MAINTAIN A TEACHABLE ATTITUDE
IN EVERYTHING YOU DO TODAY.

IT ALL STARTS WITH PEOPLE

M any people fall into the trap of taking relationships for granted. That's not good, because our ability to build and maintain healthy relationships is the single most important factor in how we get along in every area of life. Our people skills determine our potential success.

All of life's successes come from initiating relationships with the right people and then strengthening those relationships by using good people skills. Likewise, life's failures can usually be traced back to people. Sometimes the impact is obvious. Becoming entangled with an abusive spouse, a crooked partner, or a codependent family member is going to cause great damage. Other times the trouble is less dramatic, such as alienating a coworker that you must interact with every day, failing to build a positive relationship with an important client, or missing key opportunities to encourage an insecure child. The bottom line is this: *people can usually trace their successes and failures to the relationships in their lives.*

—*Winning with People*

WHERE ARE THE RELATIONSHIPS IN YOUR LIFE TAKING YOU?

CREATE A MEMORY AND VISIT IT OFTEN

Few things bond people together like a shared memory. Soldiers who battle together, teammates who win a championship, and work teams that hit their goals share a connection that never goes away. Married couples who experience rough times can often look back on their earlier experiences together to keep them going. Families bond when they rough it on camping trips or share adventures on vacation and then love recounting their experience years later.

Some memories come as the result of circumstance, but many can be proactively created. Author Lewis Carroll wrote, "It's a poor sort of memory that only works backward." What does that mean to you and me? The richest memories are often those we plan and intentionally create.

For years parents have debated the issue of quality time versus quantity of time. As a father and grandfather, I have discovered that it takes quantity time to find quality time. If you don't carve out the time, you can't create the memory.

Haven't you found that most memories you have are with the people you spend the most time with? I know that's true for me. If you want to make memories with your family, spend more time with them. If you want to create memories with your employees, you won't do it behind the door of your office. You simply can't make memories with people if you don't take time to be with them.

—*25 Ways to Win with People*

CARVE OUT TIME TO CREATE A MEMORY
TODAY WITH SOMEONE IMPORTANT.

PROBLEM SOLVING 101

Many years ago I decided to focus on helping people solve problems rather than helping solve people's problems. These suggestions are some approaches you should find effective:

- Never allow others to think you always have the best answers. This will only make them dependent on you.
- Ask questions. Help people to think through the entire process of their problem.
- Become a coach, not a king. A coach brings out the best in others, helping them to reach deep down inside and discover their potential. A king only gives commands.
- List their solutions on paper. Integrate your ideas with theirs until they have ownership of them.
- Ask them to decide on the best solution to their problem.
- Develop a game plan.
- Ask them to take ownership and responsibility for the game plan. Let them set up a time frame and an accountability process.

Your goal should be that when the meeting is over, the other person has processed the problem, selected a solution, developed a game plan, and taken ownership of it. His or her relationship with you will not be a dependent one but a deepening one.

—Developing the Leader Within You

HELP SOMEONE TO SOLVE HIS OR HER OWN PROBLEM TODAY.

THE POWER OF RECOGNITION

A too common mistake, especially among leaders in the market-place, is failure to share recognition and show appreciation to others. For example, J. C. Staehle did an analysis of workers in America and found that the number one cause of dissatisfaction among employees was their superiors' failure to give them credit. It's difficult for people to follow someone who doesn't appreciate them for who they are and what they do. As former secretary of defense and World Bank president Robert McNamara said, "Brains are like hearts—they go where they are appreciated."

Recognition is greatly appreciated by everyone, not just people in business and industry. Even a little bit of recognition can go an incredibly long way in a person's life.

Everyone is incredibly hungry for appreciation and recognition. As you interact with people, walk slowly through the crowd. Remember people's names and take time to show them you care. Make other people a priority in your life over every other thing, including your agenda and schedule. And give others recognition at every opportunity. It will build them up and motivate them. And it will make you a person of significant influence in their lives.

—*Becoming a Person of Influence*

GIVE SOMEONE ELSE THE CREDIT TODAY.

MARCH 8

HAVE LOYALTY

A quality you should look for in people to join you on your journey is loyalty. Although this alone does not ensure success in another person, a lack of loyalty is sure to ruin your relationship with him or her. Think of it this way: When you're looking for potential leaders, if someone you're considering lacks loyalty, he is disqualified. Don't even consider taking him on the journey with you because in the end, he'll hurt you more than help you. So what does it mean for others to be loyal to you?

They love you unconditionally. They accept you with your strengths and weaknesses intact. They genuinely care for you, not just for what you can do for them.

They represent you well to others. Loyal people always paint a positive picture of you with others. They may take you to task privately or hold you accountable, but they never criticize you to others.

They are able to laugh and cry with you as you travel together. Loyal people are willing and able to share your joys and sorrows. They make the trip less lonely.

They make your dream their dream. Some people will undoubtedly share the journey with you only briefly. You help one another for a while and then go your separate ways. But a few—a special few—will want to come alongside you and help you for the rest of the journey. These people make your dream their dream. If you find people like that, take good care of them.

—Your Road Map for Success

SHOW GRATITUDE TO THE PEOPLE
IN YOUR INNER CIRCLE TODAY.

PUT PEOPLE IN THEIR STRENGTH ZONES

In *The 17 Indisputable Laws of Teamwork*, the Law of the Niche says, "All players have a place where they add the most value." When leaders really get this, the teams they lead perform at an incredible level. And it reflects positively on those leaders. I don't think it is an exaggeration to say that the success of a leader is determined more by putting people into their strength zones than by anything else.

When I was in high school, I was fortunate to have a coach who understood this. During one of our varsity basketball practices, our coach, Don Neff, decided he wanted to teach us a very important lesson about basketball. He got the first- and second-string teams out on the floor to scrimmage. That wasn't unusual—we scrimmaged all the time. Our second team had some good players, but clearly the first team was much better. This time he had us do something very different from the norm. He let the second-string players take their normal positions, but he assigned each of us starters to a different role from our usual one. I was normally a shooting guard, but for this scrimmage I was asked to play center. And as I recall, our center was put in the point-guard position.

We were instructed to play to twenty, but the game didn't take long. The second team trounced us in no time. When the scrimmage was over, Coach Neff called us over to the bench and said, "Having the best players on the floor isn't enough. You have to have the best players in the right positions."

I never forgot that lesson. It doesn't matter what kind of a team you're leading. If you don't place people in their strength zones, you're making it almost impossible for them—and you—to win.

—The 360° Leader

MAKE SURE YOUR TEAM MEMBERS
ARE IN THEIR STRENGTH ZONES.

THE FREEDOM MYTH

Sometimes I think people get the wrong idea about leadership. Many people hope that it's a ticket to freedom. It will provide a solution to their professional and career problems. But being at the top is not a cure-all. Have thoughts such as these come to mind from time to time?

* *When I get to the top, I'll have it made.*
* *When I finally finish climbing the corporate ladder,*
  I'll have time to rest.
* *When I own the company, I'll be able to do whatever I want.*
* *When I'm in charge, the sky will be the limit.*

Anybody who has owned a company or been the top leader in an organization knows that those ideas are little more than fantasies. Being the top leader doesn't mean you have no limits. It doesn't remove the lid from your potential. It doesn't matter what job you do or what position you obtain; you will have limits. That's just the way life is.

When you move up in an organization, the weight of your responsibility increases. In many organizations, as you move up the ladder, you may even find that the amount of responsibility you take on increases faster than the amount of authority you receive. When you go higher, more is expected of you, the pressure is greater, and the impact of your decisions weighs more heavily. You must take these things into account.

—*The 360° Leader*

REMIND YOURSELF THAT LEADERSHIP IS A PRIVILEGE
AND RESPONSIBILITY MORE THAN ANYTHING ELSE.

MARCH 11

REDEFINE FAILURE AND SUCCESS

On August 6, 1999, a major-league baseball player stepped up to home plate in Montreal and made another out—the 5,113th of his professional career. That's a lot of trips to the batter's box without a hit! If a player made all of those outs consecutively, and he averaged four at bats per game, he would play eight seasons (1,278 games straight) without ever reaching first base!

Was the player discouraged that night? No. You see, earlier in the same game, in his first plate appearance, that player had reached a milestone that only twenty-one other people in the history of baseball have ever achieved. He had made his 3,000th hit. That player was Tony Gwynn of the San Diego Padres.

During that game, Tony got on base with hits four times in five tries. But that's not the norm for him. Usually he *fails* to get a hit two times out of every three attempts. Those results may not sound very encouraging, but if you know baseball, you recognize that Tony's ability to succeed consistently only one time in three tries has made him the greatest hitter of his generation. And Tony recognizes that to get his hits, he has to make a lot of outs.

One of the greatest problems people have with failure is that they are too quick to judge isolated situations in their lives and label them as failures. Instead, they need to keep the bigger picture in mind. Someone like Tony Gwynn doesn't look at an out that he makes and think of failure. He sees it within the context of the bigger picture. His perspective leads to perseverance. His perseverance brings longevity. And his longevity gives him opportunities for success.

—*Failing Forward*

KEEP YOUR FAILURES WITHIN THE
CONTEXT OF THE BIGGER PICTURE.

CULTIVATING A POSITIVE ATTITUDE

English heart surgeon Martyn Lloyd-Jones asserted, "Most unhappiness in life is due to the fact that you are listening to yourself rather than talking to yourself." What kind of voices do you hear? When you face new experiences, does a voice in your head say you're going to fail? If you're hearing negative messages, you need to learn to give yourself positive mental pep talks. The best way to retrain your attitude is to prevent your mind from going down any negative forks in the road.

To improve your attitude, do the following:

Feed yourself the right "food." If you've been starved of anything positive, then you need to start feeding yourself a regular diet of motivational material. Read books that encourage a positive attitude. Listen to motivational tapes. The more negative you are, the longer it will take to turn your attitude around. But if you consume a steady diet of the right "food," you can become a positive thinker.

Achieve a goal every day. Some people get into a rut of negativity because they feel they're not making progress. If that describes you, then begin setting achievable daily goals for yourself. A pattern of positive achievement will help you develop a pattern of positive thinking.

Write it on your wall. We all need reminders to help us keep thinking right. Alex Haley used to keep a picture in his office of a turtle on a fence post to remind him that everybody needed the help of others. As incentive, people put up awards they've won, inspirational posters, or letters they've received. Find something that will work for you and put it on your wall.

—The 21 Indispensable Qualities of a Leader

ALLOW YOURSELF TO DWELL ONLY ON THE POSITIVE
AND NOT THE NEGATIVE TODAY.

EXPAND BEYOND YOUR ROUTINE

One of the greatest impediments to meeting new people is routine. We often go to the same places all the time—the same gas stations, coffee shop, grocery store, and restaurants. We employ the same providers of services. We use the same companies for our business. It's just easy. But sometimes we need to shake things up and try something new. It's all about getting outside of your comfort zone.

—*The 360° Leader*

GO OUTSIDE OF YOUR NORMAL
ROUTINE TO MEET NEW PEOPLE TODAY.

LEADERS DON'T TAKE
REJECTION PERSONALLY

When your ideas are not received well by others, do your best not to take it personally. When someone in a meeting does that, it can kill the creative process, because at that point the discussion becomes about the person whose feelings are hurt. If you can stop competing and focus your energy on creating, you will open the way for the people around you to take their creativity to the next level.

If you don't have any personal experience in the publishing world, then I'm guessing that you believe authors always select the titles of their books. While that may be the way it works for some authors, it has not been the case for me. I've written more than forty books, yet I think I've selected the titles for about a dozen of them.

A book is a pretty personal thing for an author. Why would I allow someone else to pick the title? Because I know my ideas aren't always the best ideas. I often think they are, but when everyone in the room has a different opinion, it pays to listen. That's why I've adopted the attitude that the company owner doesn't need to win—the best idea does.

Be passionate about your work and have the integrity to stand up for your ideas. Without passion you will not be taken seriously. When principle is involved, don't budge. Most matters, though, involve taste or opinion, not principle. In these areas recognize that you can compromise. If you become someone who can never compromise, you will forfeit opportunities to those who can.

—The 360° Leader

LET THE BEST IDEAS WIN TO HELP
THE ORGANIZATION MOVE FORWARD.

COMPLIMENT PEOPLE
IN FRONT OF OTHERS

The most fundamental and straightforward way of winning with people is to give them a compliment—a sincere and meaningful word of affirmation. If you want to make others feel like a million bucks, you've got to master this elementary skill. And it's essential that you learn to give your compliments in front of others as well as one-on-one. Why? Because that private compliment turned public, instantly and dramatically increases in value.

As commander of a $1 billion warship and a crew of 310, Mike Abrashoff used grassroots leadership to increase retention rates from 28 percent to 100 percent, reduce operating expenditures, and improve readiness. How did he do it? Among other things, he placed supreme importance on public compliments.

"The commanding officer of a ship is authorized to hand out 15 medals a year," he wrote. "I wanted to err on the side of excess, so I passed out 115." Nearly every time a sailor left his ship for another assignment, Captain Abrashoff gave him or her a medal. "Even if they hadn't been star players, they got medals in a public ceremony as long as they had done their best every day. I delivered a short speech describing how much we cherished the recipient's friendship, camaraderie, and hard work." Abrashoff wanted to make them feel good by complimenting them in front of others.

Whenever you have the opportunity to publicly praise another person, don't let it slip by. You can create these opportunities, as Captain Abrashoff did, but you can also find countless opportunities if you look for them.

—*25 Ways to Win with People*

COMPLIMENT SOMEONE IN
THE PRESENCE OF OTHERS TODAY.

THOSE CLOSEST TO THE LEADER

The greatest leadership principle that I have learned in more than thirty years of leadership is that those closest to the leader will determine the success level of that leader. A negative reading of this statement is also true: Those closest to the leader will determine the level of failure for that leader. The determination of a positive or negative outcome in my leadership depends upon my ability as a leader to develop those closest to me. It also depends upon my ability to recognize the value that others bring to my organization. My goal is not to draw a following that results in a crowd. My goal is to develop leaders who become a movement.

Stop for a moment and think of the five or six people closest to you in your organization. Are you developing them? Do you have a game plan for them? Are they growing? Have they been able to lift your load?

Within my organizations leadership development is continually emphasized. In their first training session, I give new leaders this principle: *As a potential leader you are either an asset or a liability to the organization.* I illustrate this truth by saying, "When there's a problem, a 'fire' in the organization, you as a leader are often the first to arrive at the scene. You have in your hands two buckets. One contains water and the other contains gasoline. The 'spark' before you will either become a greater problem because you pour the gasoline on it, or it will be extinguished because you use the bucket of water."

Every person within your organization also carries two buckets. The question a leader needs to ask is, "Am I training them to use the gasoline or the water?"

—*Developing the Leaders Around You*

HAVE YOU TRAINED THE PEOPLE CLOSEST TO YOU
IN YOUR ORGANIZATION TO BE WATER CARRIERS?

LOOK IN UNUSUAL PLACES FOR IDEAS

Good leaders are attentive to ideas; they are always searching for them. And they cultivate that attentiveness and practice it as a regular discipline. As they read the newspaper, watch a movie, listen to their colleagues, or enjoy a leisure activity, they are always on the lookout for ideas or practices they can use to improve their work and their leadership.

If you desire to find good ideas, you have to search for them. Rarely does a good idea come looking for you.

—The 360° Leader

OPEN YOUR EYES TO NEW IDEAS
EVERYWHERE YOU LOOK TODAY.

COMPETENCE

We all admire people who display high competence, whether they are precision craftsmen, world-class athletes, or successful business leaders. If you want to cultivate that quality, here's what you need to do.

1. *Show Up Every Day.* Responsible people show up when they're expected. But highly competent people take it a step farther. They come ready to play every day—no matter how they feel, what kind of circumstances they face, or how difficult they expect the game to be.

2. *Keep Improving.* All highly competent people continually search for ways to keep learning, growing, and improving. They do that by asking why. After all, the person who knows how will always have a job, but the person who knows why will always be the boss.

3. *Follow Through with Excellence.* I've never met a person I considered competent who didn't follow through. As leaders, we expect our people to follow through when we hand them the ball. They expect that and a whole lot more from us as their leaders.

4. *Accomplish More than Expected.* Highly competent people always go the extra mile. For them, good enough is never good enough. Leaders cannot afford to just make it through the day. They need to do the job, and then some, day in and day out.

5. *Inspire Others.* Highly competent leaders do more than perform at a high level. They inspire and motivate their people to do the same. While some people rely on relational skills alone to survive, effective leaders combine these skills with high competence to take their organizations to new levels of excellence and influence.

—*The 21 Indispensable Qualities of a Leader*

ARE YOU INSPIRING YOUR TEAMMATES
WITH A HIGH LEVEL OF COMPETENCE?

LEADERS ATTRACT POTENTIAL LEADERS

B irds of a feather really do flock together. I believe that it takes a leader to know a leader, grow a leader, and show a leader. I have also found that it takes a leader to attract a leader.

Attraction is the obvious first step, yet I find many people in leadership positions who are unable to accomplish this task. True leaders are able to attract potential leaders because:

+ Leaders think like them.
+ Leaders express feelings that other leaders sense.
+ Leaders create an environment that attracts potential leaders.
+ Leaders are not threatened by people with great potential.

For example, a person in a leadership position who is a "5" on a scale of 1 to 10 will not attract a leader who is a "9." Why? Because leaders naturally size up any crowd and migrate to other leaders who are at the same or higher level.

Any leader who has only followers around him will be called upon to continually draw on his own resources to get things done. Without other leaders to carry the load, he will become fatigued and burnt out. Have you asked yourself lately, "Am I tired?" If the answer is yes, you may have a good reason for it. Unless you want to carry the whole load yourself, you need to be developing leaders.

—*Developing the Leaders Around You*

WHO ARE YOU DEVELOPING TO HELP YOU CARRY THE LOAD?

MARCH 20

DON'T LET PERSONALITY OVERSHADOW PURPOSE

When someone you don't like or respect suggests something, what is your first reaction? I bet it's to dismiss it. You've heard the phrase, "Consider the source." That's not a bad thing to do, but if you're not careful, you may very likely throw out the good with the bad.

Don't let the personality of someone you work with cause you to lose sight of the greater purpose, which is to add value to the team and advance the organization. If that means listening to the ideas of people with whom you have no chemistry, or worse, a difficult history, so be it. Set aside your pride and listen. And in cases where you must reject the ideas of others, make sure you reject only the idea and not the person.

—The 360° Leader

RISE ABOVE YOUR PERSONAL PREFERENCES
FOR THE SAKE OF THE TEAM.

PROBLEM SOLVING

A uthor George Matthew Adams stated, "What you think means more than anything else in your life. More than what you earn, more than where you live, more than your social position, and more than what anyone else may think about you." Every problem introduces you to yourself. It shows you how you think and what you're made of.

When you come face-to-face with a problem, how do you react? Do you ignore it and hope it will go away? Do you feel powerless to solve it? Have you had such bad experiences trying to solve problems in the past that you've just given up? Or do you tackle them willingly? The ability to solve problems effectively comes from experience facing and overcoming obstacles. Each time you solve another problem, you get a little better at the process. But if you never try, fail, and try again, you'll never be good at it.

—The 21 Indispensable Qualities of a Leader

BE WILLING TO TACKLE A DIFFICULT PROBLEM TODAY—
EVEN IF IT MEANS YOU ARE LIKELY TO FAIL.

CHANGE REQUIRES
ADDITIONAL COMMITMENT

Time is the most precious commodity for many people. Whenever change is about to happen, we all look to see how it will affect our time. Usually we conclude that increased change will be fine if it does not increase our time commitment. Sidney Howard said that half of knowing what you want is knowing what you must give up before you get it. When the cost of change is time, many will resist the change.

When it comes to the commitment of time, the leader must determine if the person is unwilling or unable to change. Willingness deals with attitude, and there is little you can do if your followers resist change because of attitude. But ability to change deals with perspective. Many people are willing to change but, because of the way they perceive their present circumstances and responsibilities, they are unable to change. At this point, the leader can help by prioritizing tasks, eliminating nonessentials, and focusing on the consequential value of changing.

—Developing the Leader Within You

HOW CAN YOU HELP YOUR
FOLLOWERS PREPARE FOR CHANGE?

IT'S ALL IN HOW YOU LOOK AT IT

If you tend to focus on the extremes of success and failure and to fixate on particular events in your life, try to put things into perspective. When you do, you'll be able to share the philosophy of someone such as the apostle Paul, who was able to say, "I have learned in whatever state I am, to be content." And that was saying a lot, considering that Paul had been shipwrecked, whipped, beaten, stoned, and imprisoned. Throughout everything, his faith enabled him to maintain perspective. He realized that as long as he was doing what he was supposed to do, his being labeled success or failure by others really didn't matter.

Every person's life is filled with errors and negative experiences. But know this:

* Errors become mistakes when we perceive them and respond to them incorrectly.
* Mistakes become failures when we *continually* respond to them incorrectly.

People who fail forward are able to see errors or negative experiences as a regular part of life, learn from them, and then move on. They persevere in order to achieve their purpose in life.

Washington Irving once commented, "Great minds have purposes; others have wishes. Little minds are subdued by misfortunes; but great minds rise above them."

—*Failing Forward*

BRING A GOOD PERSPECTIVE AND A SENSE
OF CONTENTMENT TO YOUR TEAM AS YOU LEAD.

THE DESTINATION MYTH

If you want to succeed, you need to learn as much as you can about leadership before you have a leadership position. When I meet people in social settings and they ask me what I do for a living, some of them are intrigued when I say I write books and speak. And they often ask what I write about. When I say leadership, the response that makes me chuckle most goes something like this: "Oh. Well, when I become a leader, I'll read some of your books!" What I don't say (but want to) is: "If you'd read some of my books, maybe you'd become a leader."

Good leadership is learned in the trenches. Leading as well as they can wherever they are is what prepares leaders for more and greater responsibility. Becoming a good leader is a lifelong learning process. If you don't try out your leadership skills and decision-making process when the stakes are small and the risks are low, you're likely to get into trouble at higher levels when the cost of mistakes is high, the impact is far reaching, and the exposure is greater. Mistakes made on a small scale can be easily overcome. Mistakes made when you're at the top cost the organization greatly, and they damage a leader's credibility.

How do you become the person you desire to be? You start now to adopt the thinking, learn the skills, and develop the habits of the person you wish to be. It's a mistake to daydream about "one day when you'll be on top" instead of handling today so that it prepares you for tomorrow. As Hall of Fame basketball coach John Wooden said, "When opportunity comes, it's too late to prepare." If you want to be a successful leader, learn to lead before you have a leadership position.

—The 360° Leader

TRY OUT A NEW LEADERSHIP SKILL TODAY.

THE RESULTS OF EMPOWERMENT

If you head up any kind of organization—a business, club, church, or family—learning to empower others is one of the most important things you'll ever do as its leader. Empowerment has an incredibly high return. It not only helps the individuals you raise up by making them more confident, energetic, and productive, but it also has the ability to improve your life, give you additional freedom, and promote the growth and health of your organization.

Farzin Madjidi, program liaison for the city of Los Angeles, has expressed his beliefs concerning empowerment: "We need leaders who empower people and create other leaders. It's no longer good enough for a manager to make sure that everybody has something to do and is producing. Today, all employees must 'buy in' and take ownership of everything they're doing. To foster this, it's important that employees should make decisions that most directly affect them. That's how the best decisions are made. That's the essence of empowerment." When it comes down to it, empowering leadership is sometimes the only real advantage one organization has over another in our competitive society.

As you empower others, you will find that most aspects of your life will change for the better. Empowering others can free you personally to have more time for the important things in your life, increase the effectiveness of your organization, increase your influence with others and, best of all, make an incredibly positive impact on the lives of the people you empower.

—Becoming a Person of Influence

IF YOU ARE NOT ALREADY, BEGIN EMPOWERING
SOMEONE IN YOUR ORGANIZATION TODAY.

MARCH 26

GIVE PEOPLE HOPE

A reporter asked Prime Minister Winston Churchill, who led Britain during the dark moments of the Second World War, what was the greatest weapon his country possessed against the Nazi regime of Hitler. Without pausing for even a moment, Churchill said, "It was what England's greatest weapon has always been—hope."

Hope is one of the most powerful and energizing words in the English language. It is something that gives us power to keep going in the toughest of times. And its power energizes us with excitement and anticipation as we look toward the future.

It's been said that a person can live forty days without food, four days without water, four minutes without air, but only four seconds without hope. If you want to help people win, then become a purveyor of hope.

—25 Ways to Win with People

BE THE BRINGER OF HOPE TO YOUR TEAM TODAY.

GOALS GIVE YOU "GO"

Millionaire industrialist Andrew Carnegie said, "You cannot push anyone up the ladder unless he is willing to climb himself." The same is true of a person on the success journey: She won't go forward unless she is motivated to do so. Goals can help provide that motivation. Paul Myer commented, "No one ever accomplishes anything of consequence without a goal . . . Goal setting is the strongest human force for self-motivation."

Think about it. What is one of the greatest motivators in the world? Success. When you take a large activity (such as your dream) and break it down into smaller, more manageable parts (goals), you set yourself up for success because you make what you want to accomplish obtainable. And each time you accomplish a small goal, you experience success. That's motivating! Accomplish enough of the small goals, and you'll be taking a major step toward achieving your purpose and developing your potential.

Goals not only help you develop initial motivation by making your dreams obtainable, but they also help you continue to be motivated—and that creates momentum. Once you get going on the success journey, it will be very hard to stop you. The process is similar to what happens with a train. Getting it started is the toughest part of its trip. While standing still, a train can be prevented from moving forward by one-inch blocks of wood under each of the locomotive's drive wheels. However, once a train gets up to speed, not even a steel-reinforced concrete wall five feet thick can stop it.

—*Your Road Map for Success*

DEVELOP GOALS THAT WILL INITIATE
MOTIVATION AND CREATE MOMENTUM.

LEADERS MUST BE
ENVIRONMENTAL CHANGE AGENTS

The leaders in any organization must be the environmental change agents. They must be more like thermostats than thermometers. At first glance, a person could confuse these instruments. Both are capable of measuring heat. However, they are really quite different. A thermometer is passive. It records the temperature of its environment but can do nothing to change that environment. A thermostat is an active instrument. It determines what the environment will be. It effects change in order to create a climate.

The attitude of the leader, coupled with a positive atmosphere in the organization, can encourage people to accomplish great things. And consistent accomplishment generates momentum. Many times momentum is the only difference between a winning, positive growth climate and a losing, negative growth climate.

The next time you find it difficult to adjust the environment in your company, keep in mind this simple fact from the laws of physics: Water boils at 212 degrees, but at 211 degrees, it is still just hot water. One extra degree, an increase of less than one-half of one percent, can make the difference between a pot of languishing liquid and a bubbling caldron of power. One degree can create a full head of steam—enough power to move a train weighing tons. That one degree is usually momentum.

—*Developing the Leaders Around You*

BE A THERMOSTAT, NOT A THERMOMETER.

ASK WHY, NOT WHO

The next time you experience a failure, think about why you failed instead of *who* was at fault. Try to look at it objectively so that you can do better next time. My friend Bobb Biehl suggests a list of questions to help you analyze any failure:

* What lessons have I learned?
* Am I grateful for this experience?
* How can I turn the failure into success?
* Practically speaking, where do I go from here?
* Who else has failed in this way before, and how can that person help me?
* How can my experience help others someday to keep from failing?
* Did I fail because of another person, because of my situation, or because of myself?
* Did I actually fail, or did I fall short of an unrealistically high standard?
* Where did I succeed as well as fail?

People who blame others for their failures never overcome them. They move from problem to problem, and as a result, they never experience success. To reach your potential, you must continually improve yourself, and you can't do that if you don't take responsibility for your actions and learn from your mistakes.

—Your Road Map for Success

BE THE FIRST TO TAKE RESPONSIBILITY
WHEN THINGS GO WRONG FOR YOUR TEAM.

LOOK AT THE BIG PICTURE

E verything starts with vision. You need to have a goal. Without one you cannot have a real team. Hall of Fame catcher Yogi Berra joked, "If you don't know where you're going, you'll end up somewhere else." An individual without a goal may end up anywhere. A group of individuals without a goal can go nowhere. On the other hand, if everyone in a group embraces the vision for achieving the big picture, then the people have the potential to become an effective team.

Leaders usually have the role of capturing and communicating vision. They must see it first and then help everyone else to see it. That was what Winston Churchill did when he spoke to the coal miners during the war. That was what Dr. Martin Luther King Jr. did as he spoke to people about his dream from the steps of the Lincoln Monument in Washington, D.C. That was what GE CEO Jack Welch did when he let his people know that a division of GE that couldn't be first or second in its market wouldn't be a part of GE. The people on a team will sacrifice and work together only if they can see what they're working toward.

If you are the leader of your team, your role is to do what only you can do: Paint the big picture for your people. Without the vision they will not find the desire to achieve the goal.

—*The 17 Indisputable Laws of Teamwork*

HAVE YOU PAINTED THE BIG PICTURE FOR YOUR TEAM?

BE OPEN TO LEARNING FROM OTHERS

Have you ever met someone who felt compelled to play the expert all the time? Such people aren't much fun to be around after a while, because the only input they seem open to is their own. And as the saying goes, people won't go along with you unless they can get along with you.

If you really desire others to see you as an approachable person, go a step beyond just willingness to admit your weaknesses. Be willing to learn from them. One of the things I teach in *Winning with People* is the Learning Principle, which states, "Each person we meet has the potential to teach us something." I really believe that. If you embrace that idea, I believe you will discover two things. First, you will learn a lot, because every time you meet someone, it is a learning opportunity. Second, people will warm up to you. Complete strangers often treat me like an old friend, simply because I am open to them.

—The 360° Leader

BE OPEN TO WHAT OTHERS CAN TEACH YOU TODAY.

APRIL

APRIL 1

UNDERSTANDING PEOPLE

The first quality of a relational leader is the ability to understand how people feel and think. As you work with others, recognize that all people, whether leaders or followers, have some things in common:

- They like to feel special, so sincerely compliment them.
- They want a better tomorrow, so show them hope.
- They desire direction, so navigate for them.
- They are selfish, so speak to their needs first.
- They get low emotionally, so encourage them.
- They want success, so help them win.

Recognizing these truths, a leader must still be able to treat people as individuals. The ability to look at each person, understand him, and connect with him is a major factor in relational success. That means treating people differently, not all the same as one another. Marketing expert Rod Nichols notes that in business, this is particularly important: "If you deal with every customer in the same way, you will only close 25 percent to 30 percent of your contacts, because you will only close one personality type. But if you learn how to effectively work with all four personality types, you can conceivably close 100 percent of your contacts."

This sensitivity can be called the soft factor in leadership. You have to be able to adapt your leadership style to the person you're leading.

—*The 21 Indispensable Qualities of a Leader*

ADAPT YOUR LEADERSHIP STYLE TO
THE PERSONALITIES OF YOUR PEOPLE.

FAITH IN OTHERS

People's instincts are pretty good at knowing when others have faith in them. They can sense if your belief is genuine or phony. And truly having faith in someone can change her life. In his book *Move Ahead with Possibility Thinking*, my friend Robert Schuller, pastor of the Crystal Cathedral in Garden Grove, California, tells a wonderful story about an incident that changed his life as a boy. It occurred when his uncle had faith in him and showed it in his words and actions:

> His car drove past the unpainted barn and stopped in a cloud of summer dust at our front gate. I ran barefooted across the splintery porch and saw my uncle Henry bound out of the car. He was tall, very handsome, and terribly alive with energy. After many years overseas as a missionary in China, he was visiting our Iowa farm. He ran up to the old gate and put both of his big hands on my four-year-old shoulders. He smiled widely, ruffled my uncombed hair, and said, "Well! I guess you're Robert! I think you are going to be a preacher someday." That night I prayed secretly, "And dear God, make me a preacher when I grow up!" I believe that God made me a POSSIBILITY THINKER then and there.

As you work to become a person of influence, always remember that your goal is not to get people to think more highly of you. It's to get them to think more highly of themselves. Have faith in them, and they will begin to do exactly that.

—*Becoming a Person of Influence*

HELP SOMEONE WHO DOUBTS TO
HAVE FAITH IN HIMSELF TODAY.

EVERY GENIUS COULD
HAVE BEEN A "FAILURE"

Every successful person is someone who failed, yet never regarded himself as a failure. For example, Wolfgang Mozart, one of the geniuses of musical composition, was told by Emperor Ferdinand that his opera *The Marriage of Figaro* was "far too noisy" and contained "far too many notes." Artist Vincent van Gogh, whose paintings now set records for the sums they bring at auction, sold only one painting in his lifetime. Thomas Edison, the most prolific inventor in history, was considered unteachable as a youngster. And Albert Einstein, the greatest thinker of our time, was told by a Munich schoolmaster that he would "never amount to much."

I think it's safe to say that all great achievers are given multiple reasons to believe they are failures. But in spite of that, they persevere. In the face of adversity, rejection, and failings, they continue believing in themselves and refuse to consider themselves failures.

No matter where I fail or how many mistakes I make, I don't let it devalue my worth as a person. As the saying goes, "God uses people who fail—'cause there aren't any other kind around."

Like many people, you may have a hard time maintaining a positive mind-set and preventing yourself from feeling like a failure. But know this: It is possible to cultivate a positive attitude about yourself, no matter what circumstances you find yourself in or what kind of history you have.

—*Failing Forward*

LET YOUR POSITIVE ATTITUDE, NOT CIRCUMSTANCES
OR PAST FAILURES, DETERMINE HOW YOU VIEW YOURSELF.

APRIL 4

IT'S ALL ABOUT THE TEAM

Some sports teams seem to embrace an "everyone-for-himself" mind-set. Others weave the attitude of subordination and teamwork into the fabric of everything they do. For example, football teams such as Notre Dame and Penn State don't put the names of the players on their jerseys. Lou Holtz, former coach of the Fighting Irish, once explained why. He said, "At Notre Dame, we believed the interlocking ND was all the identification you needed. Whenever anyone complained, I told them they were lucky we allowed numbers on the uniforms. Given my druthers, I would have nothing more than initials indicating what position the wearer played. If your priority is the team rather than yourself, what else do you need?"

Winning teams have players who put the good of the team ahead of themselves. They want to play in their area of strength, but they're willing to do what it takes to take care of the team. They are willing to sacrifice their role for the greater goal.

—The 17 Indisputable Laws of Teamwork

ARE YOU WILLING TO DO WHAT IT TAKES TODAY FOR THE GOOD OF THE TEAM?

MODEL THE DESIRED STYLE OF LEADERSHIP

According to noted medical missionary Albert Schweitzer, "Example is not the main thing in influencing others . . . it is the only thing." Part of creating an appealing climate to grow potential leaders is modeling leadership. People emulate what they see modeled. Positive model—positive response. Negative model—negative response. What leaders do, potential leaders around them do. What they value, their people value. The leaders' goals become their goals. Leaders set the tone. As Lee Iacocca suggests, "The speed of the boss is the speed of the team." A leader cannot demand of others what he does not demand of himself.

As you and I grow and improve as leaders, so will those we lead. We need to remember that when people follow us, they can only go as far as we go. If our growth stops, our ability to lead will stop along with it. Neither personality nor methodology can substitute for personal growth. We cannot model what we do not possess. Begin learning and growing today, and watch those around you begin to grow. As a leader, I am primarily a follower of great principles and other great leaders.

—Developing the Leaders Around You

ASK NO MORE OF OTHERS THAN
YOU ARE ASKING OF YOURSELF.

SELF-IMPROVEMENT

A danger of teaching conferences or writing books like this one is that people start to assume you're an expert who has mastered everything you teach. Don't believe it. Like you, I'm still working on my relational and leadership skills. There are principles that I don't do well, so I'm still working to improve myself. And that will always be true for me. If I ever think I've finished growing, then I'm in trouble.

People who often experience relational difficulties are tempted to look at everyone but themselves to explain the problem. But we must always begin by examining ourselves and being willing to change whatever deficiencies we have. Critic Samuel Johnson advised that "he who has so little knowledge of human nature as to seek happiness by changing anything but his own disposition will waste his life in fruitless efforts and multiply the grief which he purposes to remove."

—*Winning with People*

WHAT MUST YOU CHANGE IN YOURSELF
TO BECOME A BETTER LEADER?

UNDERSCORING THE SCOREBOARD

Every "game" has its own rules and its own definition of what it means to win. Some teams measure their success in points scored; others in profits. Still others may look at the number of people they serve. But no matter what the game is, there is always a scoreboard. And if a team is to accomplish its goals, it has to know where it stands. It has to look at itself in light of the scoreboard. Why? Because the game is constantly changing. You see, the game plan tells what you want to happen. But the scoreboard tells what is happening.

If you lead the team, you have primary responsibility for checking the scoreboard and communicating the team's situation to its members. That doesn't necessarily mean you have to do it all by yourself. But you do need to make sure that team members continually evaluate, adjust, and make decisions as quickly as possible. That's the key to winning.

Do you have a system to make sure that happens? Or do you generally rely on your intuition? Using intuition is fine—as long as you have some fail-safe backups to make sure you don't let the team down.

Evaluate how consistently and effectively you consult your scoreboard. If you're not doing it as well as you should, then create a system that helps you to do it or empowers the leaders on your team to share the responsibility.

—*The 17 Indisputable Laws of Teamwork*

DON'T BE SO FOCUSED ON THE MOMENT
THAT YOU FORGET TO CHECK THE SCOREBOARD.

APRIL 8

SLOW DOWN

Most people who want to lead are naturally fast. But if you want to become a better leader, you actually need to slow down. You can move faster alone. You can garner more individual honors alone. But to lead others, you need to slow down enough to connect with them, engage them, and take them with you.

If you have children, you instinctively understand this. The next time you need to get something done around the house, try doing it two ways. First, have your kids help. That means you need to enlist them. You need to train them. You need to direct them. You need to supervise them. You need to redirect them. You need to recapture and reenlist them when they wander off. It can be pretty exhausting, and even when the work is completed, it may not be to the standard you'd like.

Then try doing the task alone. How much faster can you go? How much better is the quality of the work? How much less aggravation is there to deal with?

Working alone is faster (at least in the beginning), but it doesn't have the same return. If you want your children to learn, grow, and reach their potential, you need to pay the price and take the time and trouble to lead them through the process. It's similar with employees. Leaders aren't necessarily the first to cross the finish line—people who run alone are the fastest. Leaders are the first to bring all of their people across the finish line. The payoff to leadership—at work or home—comes on the back end.

—*The 360° Leader*

SLOW DOWN AND CONNECT WITH OTHERS TODAY.

APRIL 9

DEVELOPING COMPETENCY

A competent person does what he does well, continually persevering and distilling what's best—and he stops doing what he doesn't do well. Does that describe you? Do you focus your energy on what you can do well so that you become highly competent at it? Can your teammates depend on you to deliver in such a way that it brings the entire team success? If not, you may need to get better focused and develop the skills you need so that you can do your job and do it well.

To improve your competence . . .

Focus yourself professionally. It's hard to develop competence if you're trying to do everything. Pick an area in which to specialize. What is the one thing that brings together your skills, interests, and opportunities? Whatever it is, seize it.

Sweat the small stuff. Too many people don't take their work as far as they can. To do that, you need to develop an ability to get all the details right. That doesn't mean becoming a micromanager or control freak. It means doing the last 10 percent of whatever job you're doing. Try doing that on the next project or big task that is your responsibility.

Give more attention to implementation. Since implementation is often the most difficult part of any job, give it greater attention. How can you improve the gap between coming up with ideas and putting them into practice? Get your teammates together and discuss how you can improve the process.

—*The 17 Essential Qualities of a Team Player*

BRING EXCEPTIONAL FOCUS TO YOUR WORK TODAY.

EMBRACE RESPONSIBILITY

Good leaders never embrace a victim mentality. They recognize that who and where they are remain their responsibility—not that of their parents, their spouses, their children, the government, their bosses, or their coworkers. They face whatever life throws at them and give it their best, knowing that they will get an opportunity to lead the team only if they've proved that they can carry the ball.

Gilbert Arland offers this advice: "When an archer misses the mark he turns and looks for the fault within himself. Failure to hit the bull's-eye is never the fault of the target. To improve your aim, improve yourself."

Are you on target when it comes to responsibility? Do others see you as a finisher? Do people look to you to carry the ball in pressure situations? Are you known for excellence? If you haven't been performing at the highest level, you may need to cultivate a stronger sense of responsibility.

—The 21 Indispensable Qualities of a Leader

REMEMBER THAT A LEADER CAN DELEGATE
ANYTHING EXCEPT RESPONSIBILITY.

APRIL 11

SELF-IMAGE

A uthor Sydney J. Harris observed, "If you're not comfortable with yourself, you can't be comfortable with others." I would take that one step further. If you do not believe in yourself, you will sabotage relationships.

For years I have taught a concept called the Law of the Lid, which is found in *The 21 Irrefutable Laws of Leadership*. It states, "Leadership ability determines a person's level of effectiveness." Here's what I mean by that: no matter how hard you work, you can only go so far professionally if you are a poor leader. A company, department, or team will always be held back by a weak leader.

When it comes to relationships, self-image works in a similar way. It is the relational lid. Your image of yourself restricts your ability to build healthy relationships. A negative self-image will even keep a person from being successful. And even when a person with a poor self-image does somehow achieve success, it won't last because he will eventually bring himself down to the level of his own expectations.

Psychologist and *New York Times* best-selling author Phil McGraw states, "I always say that the most important relationship you will ever have is with yourself. You've got to be your own best friend first." How can you be "best friends" with someone you don't know or don't like? You can't. That's why it's so important to find out who you are and work to become someone you like and respect.

—*Winning with People*

INVEST IN BUILDING A HEALTHY SELF-IMAGE
BY LEARNING TO LIKE AND RESPECT WHO YOU ARE.

FOCUS ON THE POTENTIAL LEADER'S NEEDS

People often associate great achievement with a number of things: luck, timing, circumstance, or natural talent. The secret to a person's success often appears to be an elusive quality. The University of Chicago did a five-year study of leading artists, athletes, and scholars to determine what made them successful. Conducted by Dr. Benjamin Bloom, the research was based on anonymous interviews with the top twenty performers in various fields. Included were a variety of professionals such as concert pianists, Olympic swimmers, tennis players, sculptors, mathematicians, and neurologists. Bloom and his team of researchers probed for clues as to how these high achievers developed. For a more complete picture, they also interviewed their families and teachers. The report stated conclusively that drive, determination, and desire, not great natural talent, led to the extraordinary success of these individuals.

Great leaders know the desires of the people they lead. As much as potential leaders respect the knowledge and ability of their leaders, these are secondary matters to them. They don't care how much their leaders *know* until they know how much their leaders *care* . . . about their needs, their dreams, their desires. Once a leader is genuinely interested in the well-being of those around him, the determination and drive of the people in that group are activated in a remarkable way. The starting point of all achievement is drive, determination, and desire.

—Developing the Leaders Around You

TAKE A GENUINE INTEREST IN THE NEEDS, DREAMS,
AND DESIRES OF THE POTENTIAL LEADERS AROUND YOU.

SEPARATE WHAT YOU CAN
DO FROM WHO YOU ARE

Haven't you known people who should have risen to the top but didn't? They had all the talent they should ever need, but they still didn't succeed. Philosopher Ralph Waldo Emerson must have known people like that, too, because he said, "Talent for talent's sake is a bauble and a show. Talent working with joy in the cause of universal truth lifts the possessor to a new power as a benefactor."

So is talent ever enough? Yes, but only in the very beginning. Novelist Charles Wilson says, "No matter the size of the bottle, the cream always rises to the top." Talent stands out. It gets you noticed. In the beginning, talent separates you from the rest of the pack. It gives you a head start on others. For that reason, natural talent is one of life's greatest gifts. But the advantage it gives lasts only a short time. Songwriter Irving Berlin understood this truth when he said, "The toughest thing about success is that you've got to keep on being a success. Talent is only a starting point in business. You've got to keep working that talent."

Too many talented people who start with an advantage over others lose that advantage because they rest on their talent instead of raising it. They assume that talent alone will keep them out front. They don't realize the truth: if they merely wing it, others will soon fly past them. Talent is more common than they think. Mega-best-selling author Stephen King asserts that "talent is cheaper than table salt. What separates the talented individual from the successful one is a lot of hard work." Clearly, more than just talent is needed for anyone who wants to achieve success.

—Talent Is Never Enough

BE PREPARED TO PAY THE PRICE IN OTHER AREAS TO
DEVELOP YOUR TALENT TO ITS POTENTIAL.

DEPENDABILITY

A re your teammates able to depend on you? Can they trust your motives? Do you make good decisions that others can rely on? And do you perform consistently, even when you don't feel like it? Are you a go-to player, or do your teammates work around you when crunch time comes?

To improve your dependability . . .

Check your motives. If you haven't committed goals to paper before, stop and do it before reading any farther. Now, look at those goals. How many of them benefit the teams you're part of—your family, the organization you work for, your fellow volunteers, the other players on your ball team? How many benefit only you personally? Spend some time working to align your personal priorities with those of your team.

Discover what your word is worth. Approach five teammates with this question: "When I say that I intend to do something, how reliable am I? Rate me on a scale of one to ten." Include a superior and a subordinate in your survey, if possible. If the answers you get don't match your expectations, don't defend yourself. Simply ask for examples in a nonthreatening way. If the average answer is lower than a nine or ten, then start writing down your commitments as you make them from that day forward, and track your follow-through for one month.

Find someone to hold you accountable. You are more likely to follow through and develop dependability if you have a partner to help you. Find someone you respect to help you keep your commitments.

—*The 17 Essential Qualities of a Team Player*

TAKE STEPS TO IMPROVE YOUR DEPENDABILITY TODAY,
AND FIND SOMEONE TO HELP HOLD YOU ACCOUNTABLE.

APRIL 15

THE POWER OF PERSPECTIVE

Success can bring many things: power, privilege, fame, wealth. But no matter what else it brings, with success come options. How we use those options reveals our character. Wealthy people can use their resources to benefit others or only themselves. Famous people can use their notoriety to model good character or to selfishly serve themselves. Leaders can make decisions that affect others positively or negatively. It's up to them.

At the heart of the matter is whether people desire to use their power to put others in their place or to put themselves in others' place. Educator and agricultural chemist George Washington Carver made an incredible observation: "How far you go in life depends on your being tender with the young, compassionate with the aged, sympathetic with the striving and tolerant of the weak and strong. Because someday in life you will have been all of these." Our treatment of others results from our perspective of them.

—Winning with People

PUT YOURSELF IN SOMEONE ELSE'S PLACE
BEFORE LEADING HIM OR HER.

A CHECKLIST FOR CHANGE

Below are the questions you should review before attempting changes within an organization.

YES	NO	
____	____	Will this change benefit the followers?
____	____	Is this change compatible with the purpose of the organization?
____	____	Is this change specific and clear?
____	____	Are the top 20 percent (the influencers) in favor of this change?
____	____	Is it possible to test this change before making a total commitment to it?
____	____	Are physical, financial, and human resources available to make this change?
____	____	Is this change reversible?
____	____	Is this change the next obvious step?
____	____	Does this change have both short- and long-range benefits?
____	____	Is the leadership capable of bringing about this change?
____	____	Is the timing right?

The last question is the ultimate consideration for implementing change. Success in bringing about change will happen only if the timing is right.

—*Developing the Leader Within You*

TAKE THE STEPS NECESSARY BEFORE TRYING
TO IMPLEMENT CHANGE TO BE SUCCESSFUL

BECOME A BETTER MOTIVATOR

E verything rises and falls on leadership. There are two ways you can get others to do what you want: You can compel them to do it, or you can persuade them. Compulsion is the method of slavery; persuasion is the method of free men.

Persuading requires an understanding of what makes people tick and what motivates them, that is, a knowledge of human nature. Great leaders possess that knowledge.

In a recent survey, seventy psychologists were asked: "What is the most essential thing for a supervisor to know about human nature?" Two-thirds said that motivation—an understanding of what makes people think, feel, and act as they do—is uppermost.

If you understand what motivates people, you have at your command the most powerful tool for dealing with them.

—Developing the Leader Within You

SEEK TO UNDERSTAND WHAT
MOTIVATES YOUR EMPLOYEES TODAY.

SEE FAILURES AS ISOLATED INCIDENTS

Author Leo Buscaglia once talked about his admiration for cooking expert Julia Child: "I just love her attitude. She says, 'Tonight we're going to make a soufflé!' And she beats this and whisks that, and she drops things on the floor . . . and does all these wonderful human things. Then she takes the soufflé and throws it in the oven and talks to you for a while. Finally, she says, 'Now it's ready!' But when she opens the oven, the soufflé just falls flat as a pancake. But does she panic or burst into tears? No! She smiles and says, 'Well, you can't win them all. Bon appetit!'"

When achievers fail, they see it as a momentary event, not a lifelong epidemic. It's not personal. If you want to succeed, don't let any single incident color your view of yourself.

—Failing Forward

KEEP YOUR MISTAKES AND FAILURES IN
PERSPECTIVE AS YOU TRY TO MOVE FORWARD.

SECURITY

During the term of President Ronald Reagan, leaders of seven industrial nations were meeting at the White House to discuss economic policy. During the meeting Canadian Prime Minister Pierre Trudeau strongly upbraided British Prime Minister Margaret Thatcher, telling her that she was all wrong and that her policies wouldn't work. She stood there in front of him with her head up, listening until he was finished. Then she walked away.

Reagan went up to her and said, "Maggie, he should never have spoken to you like that. He was out of line, just entirely out of line. Why did you let him get away with that?"

Thatcher looked at Reagan and answered, "A woman must know when a man is being simply childish."

That story surely typifies Margaret Thatcher. She appeared to have no doubts about herself or her beliefs—and she was absolutely secure in her leadership as a result. That is the case for all great leaders.

Secure leaders are able to believe in others because they believe in themselves. They aren't arrogant; they know their own strengths and weaknesses and respect themselves. When their people perform well, they don't feel threatened. They go out of their way to bring the best people together and then build them up so that they will perform at the highest level. And when a secure leader's team succeeds, it brings him great joy. He sees that as the highest compliment he can receive.

—The 21 Indispensable Qualities of a Leader

DO YOU BELIEVE IN YOURSELF ENOUGH TO
GRACIOUSLY TAKE THE HEAT AS A LEADER?

CHARACTER DRIVEN
VERSUS EMOTIONAL DRIVEN

Successful people are willing to do things unsuccessful people will not do. My observation is that one of those things that makes a difference is this issue of being character driven instead of emotion driven. This is the difference:

Character-Driven People	Emotion-Driven People
• Do right, then feel good	• Feel good, then do right
• Are commitment driven	• Are convenience driven
• Make principle-based decisions	• Make popular based decisions
• Let action control attitude	• Let attitude control action
• Believe it, then see it	• See it, then believe it
• Create momentum	• Wait for momentum
• Ask, "What are my responsibilities?"	• Ask, "What are my rights?"
• Continue when problems arise	• Quit when problems arise
• Are steady	• Are moody
• Are leaders	• Are followers

The late Louis L'Amour is one of the best-selling authors of all time. Nearly 230 million copies of his books are in print worldwide, and every one of his more than one hundred books is still in print. When asked the key to his writing style, he responded, "Start writing, no matter what. The water does not flow until the faucet is turned on."

—*Developing the Leader Within You*

RELY ON YOUR CHARACTER, NOT YOUR EMOTIONS,
TO DO THE DIFFICULT TASKS OF LEADERSHIP.

GROWTH IS A CHOICE

Most people fight against change, especially when it affects them personally. As novelist Leo Tolstoy said, "Everyone thinks of changing the world, but no one thinks of changing himself." The ironic thing is that change is inevitable. Everybody has to deal with it. On the other hand, growth is optional. You can choose to grow or fight it. But know this: People unwilling to grow will never reach their potential.

In one of his books, my friend Howard Hendricks asks the question, "How have you changed . . . lately? In the last week, let's say? Or the last month? The last year? Can you be *very specific?*" He knows how people tend to get into a rut when it comes to growth and change. Growth is a choice, a decision that can really make a difference in a person's life.

Most people don't realize that successful and unsuccessful people do not differ substantially in their abilities. They vary in their desires to reach their potential. And nothing is more effective when it comes to reaching potential than commitment to personal growth.

—Your Road Map for Success

IN WHAT SPECIFIC WAYS HAVE YOU CHANGED
LATELY TO REACH YOUR POTENTIAL?

APRIL 22

LEAD (DON'T MANAGE) WITH VISION

An important part of leadership involves casting vision. Some leaders forget to cast vision because they get caught up in managing. True leaders recognize a difference between leaders and managers. Managers are maintainers, tending to rely on systems and controls. Leaders are innovators and creators who rely on people. Creative ideas become reality when people who are in a position to act catch the vision of their innovative leader.

An effective vision provides guidance. It gives direction for an organization . . . direction that cannot effectively result from rules and regulations, policy manuals, or organizational charts. True direction for an organization is born with a vision. It begins when the leader accepts it. It gains acceptance when the leader models it. And it becomes reality when the people respond to it.

—Developing the Leaders Around You

ARE YOU LEADING YOUR TEAM OR MERELY MANAGING THEM?

GIVE OTHERS A REPUTATION TO UPHOLD

One of the best ways to inspire others and make them feel good about themselves is to show them who they could be. Years ago, a manager for the New York Yankees wanted rookie players to know what a privilege it was to play for the team. He used to tell them, "Boys, it's an honor just to put on the New York pinstripes. So when you put them on, play like world champions. Play like Yankees. Play proud."

When you give someone a reputation to uphold, you give him something good to shoot for. It's putting something that was beyond his reach within his grasp. By speaking to their potential, you help the people around you to "play proud," as the Yankees do. Why is that important? Because people will go farther than they thought they could when someone they respect tells them they can.

—25 Ways to Win with People

GIVE SOMEONE A REPUTATION TO UPHOLD TODAY.

APRIL 24

DISCIPLINED EMOTIONS

People have just two choices when it comes to their emotions: they can master their emotions or be mastered by them. That doesn't mean that to be a good team player, you have to turn off your feelings. But it does mean that you shouldn't let your feelings prevent you from doing what you should or drive you to do things you shouldn't.

A classic example of what can happen when a person doesn't discipline his emotions can be seen in the life of golf legend Bobby Jones. Like today's Tiger Woods, Jones was a golf prodigy. He began playing in 1907 at age five. By age twelve, he was scoring below par, an accomplishment most golfers don't achieve in a lifetime of playing the game. At age fourteen, he qualified for the U.S. Amateur Championship. But Jones didn't win that event. His problem can be best described by the nickname he acquired: "club thrower." Jones often lost his temper—and his ability to play well.

An older golfer that Jones called Grandpa Bart advised the young man, "You'll never win until you can control that temper of yours." Jones took his advice and began working to discipline his emotions. At age twenty-one, Jones blossomed and went on to be one of the greatest golfers in history, retiring at age twenty-eight after winning the grand slam of golf. Grandpa Bart's comment sums up the situation: "Bobby was fourteen when he mastered the game of golf, but he was twenty-one when he mastered himself."

—*The 17 Essential Qualities of a Team Player*

HAVE YOU MASTERED YOUR EMOTIONS,
OR ARE YOU MASTERED BY THEM?

COMPLIMENTS AFFIRM PEOPLE

To affirm is to make firm. An affirmation is a statement of truth you make firm in a person's heart when you utter it. As a result, it cultivates conviction. For example, when you compliment a person's attitude, you reinforce it and make it more consistent. Because you notice it in a positive way, he will be more likely to demonstrate that same attitude again.

Likewise, when you affirm people's dreams, you help their dreams become more real than their doubts. Like the repetition of a weight-lifting regimen, routine compliments build up people's qualities and strengthen their personalities.

"There are high spots in all of our lives," wrote author George Matthew Adams, "and most of them have come about through encouragement from someone else. I don't care how great, how famous or successful a man or woman may be, each hungers for applause. Encouragement is oxygen to the soul. Good work can never be expected from a worker without encouragement. No one can ever have lived without it."

—*25 Ways to Win with People*

Affirm and encourage your followers today.

DEVELOP THE TALENT YOU HAVE,
NOT THE ONE YOU WANT

One thing I teach people at my conferences is to stop working on their weaknesses and start working on their strengths. (By this I mean abilities, not attitude or character issues, which *must* be addressed.) It has been my observation that people can increase their ability in an area by only 2 points on a scale of 1 to 10. For example, if your natural talent in an area is a 4, with hard work you may rise to a 6. In other words, you can go from a little below average to a little above average. But let's say you find a place where you are a 7; you have the potential to become a 9, maybe even a 10, if it's your greatest area of strength and you work exceptionally hard! That helps you advance from 1 in 10,000 talent to 1 in 100,000 talent—but only if you do the other things needed to maximize your talent.

—*Talent Is Never Enough*

FIND YOUR STRENGTHS AND START WORKING IN THEM.

PAY THE PRICE THAT ATTRACTS LEADERS

Success always comes at a price. That is a lesson I learned a long time ago. My father taught me that a person can pay now and play later, or he can play now and pay later. Either way, he is going to pay.

Creating a climate for potential leaders also requires a leader to pay a price. It begins with personal growth. The leader must examine himself, ask himself the hard questions, and then determine to do the right thing regardless of atmosphere or mood. There are few ideal and leisurely settings for the disciplines of growth. Most of the significant things done in the world were done by persons who were either too busy or too sick to do them. Emotion-based companies allow the atmosphere to determine the action. Character-based companies allow the action to determine the atmosphere.

Successful leaders recognize that personal growth and the development of leadership skills are lifetime pursuits. Warren Bennis and Burt Nanus, in *Leaders: The Strategies for Taking Charge,* did a study of ninety top leaders in all fields. They found that "it is the capacity to develop and improve their skills that distinguishes leaders from their followers." They came to the conclusion that "leaders are perpetual learners."

— *Developing the Leaders Around You*

BE WILLING TO PAY THE PRICE TO BE A PERPETUAL LEARNER.

WHAT IS ATTITUDE?

When you hear the word *attitude*, what do you think about? I think of attitude as an inward feeling expressed by outward behavior. People always project on the outside what they feel on the inside. Some people try to mask their attitude, and they can fool others for a while. But that cover-up doesn't last long. Attitude always wiggles its way out.

Your attitude colors every aspect of your life. It is like the mind's paintbrush. It can paint everything in bright, vibrant colors—creating a masterpiece. Or it can make everything dark and dreary. Attitude is so pervasive and important that I've come to think of it like this:

It is the vanguard of your true self.
Its root is inward but its fruit is outward.
It is your best friend or worst enemy.
It is more honest and consistent about you than your words.
It is your outward look based on your past experiences.
It is what draws people to you or repels them.
It is never content until it is expressed.
It is the librarian of your past.
It is the speaker of your present.
It is the prophet of your future.

There is not a single part of your current life that is not affected by your attitude. And your future will definitely be influenced by the attitude you carry with you from today forward.

—The Difference Maker

DETERMINE TO POSSESS A POSITIVE ATTITUDE TODAY.

APRIL 29

COURAGE

L arry Osborne offers this observation: "The most striking thing about highly effective leaders is how little they have in common. What one swears by, another warns against. But one trait stands out: the willingness to risk."

Fear limits a leader. Roman historian Tacitus wrote, "The desire for safety stands against every great and noble enterprise." But courage has the opposite effect. It opens doors, and that's one of its most wonderful benefits. Perhaps that's why British theologian John Henry Newman said, "Fear not that your life will come to an end but that it will never have a beginning." Courage not only gives you a good beginning, but it also provides a better future.

What's ironic is that those who don't have the courage to take risks and those who do, experience the same amount of fear in life. The only difference is that those who don't take chances worry about trivial things. If you're going to have to overcome your fear and doubts anyway, you might as well make it count.

Eleanor Roosevelt acknowledged, "You gain strength, courage, and confidence by every experience in which you really stop to look fear in the face. You are able to say to yourself, 'I lived through this horror. I can take the next thing that comes along.' You must do the thing you think you cannot do."

—The 21 Indispensable Qualities of a Leader

FOR THE BENEFIT OF THE TEAM,
DO SOMETHING YOU'RE AFRAID OF TODAY.

THE POTENTIAL MYTH

How many kids say, "Someday I want to grow up to be vice president of the United States"? Probably none. If a child has political aspirations, he wants to be president. If she has a bent toward business, she wants to be a company owner or CEO. Few people aspire to reach the middle.

Yet the reality is that most people will never be the top leader in an organization. They will spend their careers somewhere in the middle. Is that okay? Or should everybody play career "king of the hill" and try to reach the top?

I believe that people should strive for the top of their game, not the top of the organization. An excellent example of that is Vice President Dick Cheney. He has enjoyed a remarkable career in politics: White House chief of staff to President Gerald Ford, six-term congressman from Wyoming, secretary of defense to President George H. W. Bush, and vice president to the second President Bush. He possesses all the credentials one would need to run for president of the United States. Yet he knows that the top position is not his best role.

Mary Kay Hill, a longtime aide to former Wyoming senator Alan Simpson, who worked with Cheney on Capitol Hill, said, "You plug him in, and he works anywhere. He just has a real good way of fitting in and working his environment." Cheney appears to be an excellent example of a 360-Degree Leader, someone who knows how to influence others from whatever position he finds himself in.

—The 360° Leader

LEARN TO INFLUENCE OTHERS FROM
WHEREVER YOU ARE IN YOUR ORGANIZATION.

MAY

MAY 1

MOVING INTO ACTION

German poet and novelist Johann Wolfgang von Goethe once said, "Thinking is easy, acting is difficult, and to put one's thoughts into action is the most difficult thing in the world." Maybe that's why so few people follow through and act on their goals. According to Gregg Harris, two-thirds of people surveyed (sixty-seven of one hundred) set goals for themselves. But of those sixty-seven, only ten have made realistic plans to reach their goals. And out of those ten, only two follow through and actually make them happen.

The trick to acting on your goals is getting started. President Franklin D. Roosevelt remarked, "It is common sense to take a method and try it. If it fails, admit it frankly and try another. But above all, try something." That's good advice. You don't have to be perfect; you only need to make progress. Or as the Chinese proverb asserts, "Be not afraid of going slowly; be only afraid of standing still."

—Your Road Map for Success

TAKE A CONCRETE STEP TOWARD AN IMPORTANT GOAL TODAY.

IDENTIFYING POTENTIAL LEADERS

There is something much more important and scarce than ability: it is the ability to recognize ability. One of the primary responsibilities of a successful leader is to identify potential leaders. It's not always an easy job, but it is critical.

Dale Carnegie was a master at identifying potential leaders. Once asked by a reporter how he had managed to hire forty-three millionaires, Carnegie responded that the men had not been millionaires when they started working for him. They had become millionaires as a result. The reporter next wanted to know how he had developed these men to become such valuable leaders. Carnegie replied, "Men are developed the same way gold is mined. Several tons of dirt must be moved to get an ounce of gold. But you don't go into the mine looking for dirt," he added. "You go in looking for the gold." That's exactly the way to develop positive, successful people. Look for the gold, not the dirt; the good, not the bad. The more positive qualities you look for, the more you are going to find.

—Developing the Leaders Around You

HAVE YOU MADE IT A PRIORITY TO FIND
POTENTIAL LEADERS AND DEVELOP THEM?

LEAD EVERYONE DIFFERENTLY

One of the mistakes rookie leaders often make is that they try to lead everyone the same way. But let's face it. Everyone doesn't respond to the same kind of leadership. You should try to be consistent with everyone. You should treat everyone with kindness and respect. But don't expect to use the same strategies and methods with everyone.

You have to figure out what leadership buttons to push with each individual person on your team. One person will respond well to being challenged; another will want to be nurtured. One will need the game plan drawn up for him; another will be more passionate if she can create the game plan herself. One will require consistent, frequent follow-up; another will want breathing room. If you desire to be an effective leader, you need to take responsibility for conforming your leadership style to what your people need, not expecting them to adapt to you.

—*The 360° Leader*

HOW HAVE YOU BEEN LEADING POORLY, AND HOW CAN
YOU CHANGE TO GET THE BEST FROM YOUR TEAM?

BECOME COMFORTABLE WITH THE MIDDLE

We often think leadership is easier at the top. The reality is that it's actually easier to lead from the middle—if a really good leader is above you. Good leaders at the top break ground for their people. They create momentum for the entire organization. Haven't you seen average or even below-average leaders succeed because they were part of an organization that was led well overall?

When you have excellent leaders, you don't need as much skill and energy to make things happen. You benefit from everything they do. So why not enjoy it—and learn from them too? I've long admired the following poem by Helen Laurie:

> How often I've been put to the test
> To make the best of second-best,
> Only to wake one day and see
> That second-best is best for me.

Being in the middle can be a great place—as long as you have bought into the vision and believe in the leader.

So how do you get comfortable with the middle? Comfort is really a function of expectations. The wider the gap between what you imagine to be and reality, the more disappointed you are likely to be. Talk things out with your boss. The more you know about what's expected of you, what's normal in the organization, and how much authority you have, the more comfortable you will be.

—*The 360° Leader*

BE CONTENT WITH WHERE YOU ARE,
AND GIVE YOUR WORK YOUR BEST.

SELF-DISCIPLINE

Author H. Jackson Brown Jr. quipped, "Talent without discipline is like an octopus on roller skates. There's plenty of movement, but you never know if it's going to be forward, backwards, or sideways." If you know you have talent, and you've seen a lot of motion—but little concrete results—you may lack self-discipline.

Sort out your priorities. Think about which two or three areas of life are most important to you. Write them down, along with the disciplines that you must develop to keep growing and improving in those areas. Develop a plan to make the disciplines a daily or weekly part of your life.

List the reasons. Take the time to write out the benefits of practicing the disciplines you've just listed. Then post the benefits someplace where you will see them daily. On the days when you don't want to follow through, reread your list.

Get rid of excuses. Write down every reason why you might not be able to follow through with your disciplines. Read through them. You need to dismiss them as the excuses they are. Even if a reason seems legitimate, find a solution to overcome it. Don't leave yourself any reasons to quit. Remember, only in the moment of discipline do you have the power to achieve your dreams.

A nursery in Canada displays this sign on its wall: "The best time to plant a tree is twenty-five years ago . . . The second best time is today." Plant the tree of self-discipline in your life today.

—The 21 Indispensable Qualities of a Leader

BEGIN A ROUTINE OF REGULARLY
SCHEDULED ACTIONS OF SELF-DISCIPLINE.

REMOVE THE "YOU" FROM FAILURE

If you've been thinking of yourself as a failure, you can break yourself out of that negative thinking pattern. Look at an area of your life where you have repeatedly failed, and do the following:

Examine your expectations for that area. Write them down. Are they realistic? Do you expect to do everything perfectly? Do you expect to succeed on the first try? How many mistakes should you expect to make before you succeed? Adjust your expectations.

Find new ways to do your work. Brainstorm at least twenty new approaches, and then try at least half of them.

Focus on your strengths. How can you use your best skills and personal strengths to maximize your effort?

Vow to bounce back. No matter how many times you fall down, pick yourself up and keep going.

Don't wait until you feel positive to move forward. Act your way into feeling good. That's the only way to start thinking more positively about yourself.

—*Failing Forward*

REMEMBER THAT EVEN IF SOMEONE
FAILS, HE IS NOT A FAILURE.

ENTHUSIASM

There is no substitute for enthusiasm. When the members of a team are enthusiastic, the whole team becomes highly energized. And that energy produces power. Industrialist Charles Schwab observed, "People can succeed at almost anything for which they have enthusiasm."

You cannot win if you do not begin. That's one of the reasons why you need to act your way into feeling. You can't break a cycle of apathy by waiting to feel like doing it. I addressed an issue similar to this in *Failing Forward*:

> People who want to get out of the fear cycle often . . . believe that they have to eliminate [their fear] to break the cycle. But . . . you can't wait for motivation to get you going. To conquer fear, you have to feel the fear and take action anyway . . . You've got to get yourself moving. The only way to break the cycle is to face your fear and take action—no matter how small or seemingly insignificant that action might seem. To get over fear, you've got to get started.

Likewise, if you want to be enthusiastic, you need to start acting that way. If you wait for the feeling before acting, you may never become enthusiastic.

—The 17 Essential Qualities of a Team Player

No matter how you feel,
ACT ENTHUSIASTIC ABOUT LIFE TODAY.

FIGHTING MEDIOCRITY

In *Inc.* magazine, marketing expert I. Martin Jacknis identifies a trend he has seen in hiring. He terms it the *Law of Diminishing Expertise.* Simply stated, leaders tend to hire people whose ability and expertise are beneath their own. As a result, when organizations grow and more people are hired, the number of people with low expertise far exceeds the leaders who have great expertise.

Fortunately, there are ways to combat the trend toward mediocrity:

1. Make hiring the responsibility of a highly developed leader.
2. Hire the most highly developed leaders you can get.
3. Commit to modeling leadership.
4. Commit to developing those around you.

I would say that David Ogilvy, founder of the giant advertising agency Ogilvy and Mather, understood the law of diminishing expertise, based on the information Dennis Waitley gives about him in *The New Dynamics of Winning.* He states that Ogilvy used to give each new manager in his organization a Russian doll. The doll contained five progressively smaller dolls. A message inside the smallest one read: "If each of us hires people who are smaller than we are, we shall become a company of dwarfs. But if each of us hires people who are bigger then we are, Ogilvy and Mather will become a company of giants." Commit to finding, hiring, and developing giants.

—Developing the Leaders Around You

REMEMBER THAT THE BEST LEADER SHOULD
BE RESPONSIBLE FOR HIRING OTHER LEADERS.

THE ALL-OR-NOTHING MYTH

What are the prospects for your getting to the top of your organization, of someday becoming *the* leader? The reality for most people is that they will never be the CEO. Does that mean they should just give up leading altogether?

That's what some people do. They look at an organization, recognize they will not be able to make it to the top, and give up. Their attitude is, "If I can't be the captain of the team, then I'll take my ball and go home."

Others enter the process of leadership but then become frustrated by their position in an organization. Why? Because they define *success* as being "on top." As a result, they believe that if they are not on top, they are not successful. If that frustration lasts long enough, they can become disillusioned, bitter, and cynical. If it gets to that point, instead of being a help to themselves and their organization, they become a hindrance.

But what good can people do if they sit on the sidelines?

You do not need to be the top dog to make a difference. Leadership is not meant to be an all-or-nothing proposition. If being someplace other than the top has caused you great frustration, please don't throw in the towel. Why? Because you can make an impact from wherever you are in an organization.

I believe that individuals can become better leaders wherever they are. Improve your leadership, and you can impact your organization. You can change people's lives. You can be someone who adds value. You can learn to influence people at every level of the organization—even if you never get to the top. By helping others, you can help yourself.

—*The 360° Leader*

RECOGNIZE THE VALUE OF WHERE
YOU ARE IN THE ORGANIZATION.

PAY NOW, PLAY LATER

There are two paths that people can take. They can either play now and pay later, or pay now and play later. Regardless of the choice, one thing is certain. Life will demand a payment.

My father taught me this important discipline. Each week he would lay out the chores for the next seven days. Many of them could be done anytime during the week. Our goal was to complete them by Saturday noon. If completed, we could do something fun with the family. If not completed, fun was forfeited and that individual stayed home to complete the chore. I needed to miss my deadline only a couple of times to realize that I needed to "pay up front" and finish my work on time.

This lesson has been valuable to me, and I taught it to my children, Elizabeth and Joel Porter, when they were growing up. I wanted them to realize that there is no such thing as a "free lunch," that life is not a gift—it is an investment. The sooner they could take control of their desires and submit them to life's demands, the more successful they would become. John Foster said, "A man without decision of character can never be said to belong to himself. He belongs to whatever can make captive of him." My friend Bill Klassen reminded me that "when we pay later, the price is greater!"

"I've never known a man worth his salt who in the long run, deep down in his heart, didn't appreciate the grind, the discipline," said Vince Lombardi. "I firmly believe that any man's finest hour—this greatest fulfillment to all he holds dear—is that moment when he has worked his heart out in a good cause and lies exhausted on the field of battle—victorious."

—*Developing the Leader Within You*

ARE YOU INVESTING IN YOUR LIFE BY
PAYING THE PRICE NEEDED TO SUCCEED?

MANAGING THE REVOLVING DOOR

If you lead your team, you are responsible for making sure the revolving door moves in such a way that the players who are joining the team are better than those who are leaving. One way you can facilitate that is to place high value on the good people already on the team.

Every team has three groups of players. The first is the starters, who directly add value to the organization or who directly influence its course. The second is the bench players, who indirectly add value to the organization or who support the starters. The third group is a core group within the starters that I call the inner-circle members. Without these people the team would fall apart. Your job is to make sure each group is continually developed so that bench players are able to step up to become starters, and starters are able to step up to become inner-circle members.

If you're not sure who the inner-circle members are on your team, then try this exercise: Write the names of the people on your team who are starters. Now determine the people you could most easily do without. One by one, check off the names of the people whose loss would hurt the team least if they left. At some point you will end up with a smaller group of people without whom the team would be dead. That's your inner circle. (You can even rank the remaining people in order of importance.)

It's a good exercise to remind you of the value of people on the team. And by the way, if your treatment of those people doesn't match their value, you run the risk of losing them and having your revolving door work against you.

—*The 17 Indisputable Laws of Teamwork*

DOES YOUR TREATMENT OF YOUR INNER-CIRCLE
MEMBERS MATCH THEIR VALUE?

BE THE FIRST TO HELP

My friend Zig Ziglar said, "You can get everything in life you want if you will just help enough other people get what they want." Zig is certainly living proof of that. He has helped so many people, and he has been a success as a result.

I like helping people. I think it's one of the reasons God put us here on earth. But helping others does more than benefit others. It also helps you win with them. I say that because whenever you are quick to help others, it makes a statement. It's like leaving a calling card they will never forget.

—25 Ways to Win with People

BE ALERT AND TRY TO BE THE FIRST
TO HELP PEOPLE ON YOUR TEAM.

HAVE YOU FOUND YOUR NICHE?

Have you found your niche? As you fulfill your responsibilities, do you find yourself thinking something like, *There's no place like this place anywhere near this place, so this must be the place?* If so, then stay the course and keep growing and learning in your area of expertise. If not, you need to get on track.

If you know what your niche is but aren't working in it, start planning a transition. It could be as simple as a change in duties or as complex as a change of career. No matter whether it will require six weeks or six years, you need a transition plan and a timetable for completing it. Once you're certain of your course, have the courage to take the first step.

If you have no idea what you should be doing, you need to do some research. Talk to your spouse and close friends about your strengths and weaknesses. Ask for your leader's assessment. Take personality or temperament tests. Look for recurring themes in your life. Try to articulate your life purpose. Do whatever it takes to find clues concerning where you should be. Then try new things related to your discoveries. The only way to find your niche is to gain experience.

— *The 17 Indisputable Laws of Teamwork*

IF YOU HAVEN'T ALREADY, FIND YOUR
NICHE AND BEGIN GROWING WITHIN IT.

MAY 14

THE FRUSTRATION CHALLENGE

Few things can be more maddening to a good leader in the middle than working for an ineffective leader. A normal reaction to the Frustration Challenge is to fix or replace the leader you're working for, but that is usually not an option for leaders in the middle. Even if it were, it would be inappropriate. No matter what our circumstances, our greatest limitation isn't the leader above us—it's the spirit within us.

What should you do when you find yourself following a leader who is ineffective? It may not be easy, but it is possible to survive—and even flourish—in a situation like this. Here is what I recommend:

1. Develop a solid relationship with your leader.
2. Identify and appreciate your leader's strengths.
3. Commit yourself to adding value to your leader's strengths.
4. Get permission to develop a game plan to complement your leader's weaknesses.
5. Expose your leader to good leadership resources.
6. Publicly affirm your leader.

It's hard to find a downside to adding value to your leader and organization, especially if you maintain a long view. In time, people will recognize your talent. Others will value your contribution. They will admire your ability to succeed and to help others—even those less talented than you—succeed.

—*The 360° Leader*

DETERMINE TO HAVE A SPIRIT OF COOPERATION
AND TEAMWORK DESPITE NEGATIVE CIRCUMSTANCES.

WHEN FAILURE GETS YOU BY THE HEART

Let's face it. Failure can be very painful—sometimes physically and more often emotionally. Seeing part of your vision fall flat really hurts. And if people heap ridicule on top of your hurt feelings, you feel even worse. *The first important step in weathering failure is learning not to personalize it—making sure you know that your failure does not make you a failure.* But there's more to it than that. For many people the pain of failure leads to fear of failure. And they become like the person who says, "I'm too old to cry, but it hurts too much to laugh." That's when many people get stuck in the fear cycle. And if fear overcomes you, it's almost impossible to fail forward.

Playwright George Bernard Shaw asserted, "A life spent in making mistakes is not only more honorable but more useful than a life spent doing nothing." To overcome fear and break the cycle, you have to be willing to recognize that you will spend much of your life making mistakes. The bad news is that if you've been inactive for a long time, getting started is hard to do. The good news is that as soon as you start moving, it gets easier.

If you can take action and keep making mistakes, you gain experience. (That's why President Theodore Roosevelt said, "He who makes no mistakes makes no progress.") That experience eventually brings competence, and you make fewer mistakes. As a result, your fear becomes less paralyzing. But the whole cycle-breaking process starts with action. You must act your way into feeling, not wait for positive emotions to carry you forward.

—*Failing Forward*

PAY THE PRICE OF MAKING MISTAKES TO
DEVELOP EXPERIENCE AND CONFIDENCE.

TEACHABILITY

Leaders face the danger of contentment with the status quo. After all, if a leader already possesses influence and has achieved a level of respect, why should he keep growing? The answer is simple:

- Your growth determines who you are.
- Who you are determines who you attract.
- Who you attract determines the success of your organization.

If you want to grow your organization, you have to remain teachable. When I was a kid growing up in rural Ohio, I saw this sign in a feed store: "If you don't like the crop you are reaping, check the seed you are sowing." Though the sign was an ad for seeds, it contained a wonderful principle.

What kind of crop are you reaping? Do your life and leadership seem to be getting better day after day, month after month, year after year? Or are you constantly fighting just to hold your ground? If you're not where you hoped you would be by this time in your life, your problem may be lack of teachability. When was the last time you did something for the first time? When was the last time you made yourself vulnerable by diving into something for which you weren't the expert?

—The 21 Indispensable Qualities of a Leader

IF YOU'RE NOT ATTRACTING THE LEADERS YOU DESIRE,
SPEND MORE TIME DEVELOPING YOURSELF.

DISCONTENT WITH THE STATUS QUO

I've told my staff before that *status quo* is Latin for "the mess we're in." Leaders see what is, but more important, they have vision for what could be. They are never content with things as they are. To be leading, by definition, is to be in front, breaking new ground, conquering new worlds, moving away from the status quo. Donna Harrison states, "Great leaders are never satisfied with current levels of performance. They constantly strive for higher and higher levels of achievement." They move beyond the status quo themselves, and they ask the same of those around them.

Dissatisfaction with the status quo does not mean a negative attitude or grumbling. It has to do with willingness to be different and take risks. A person who refuses to risk change fails to grow. A leader who loves the status quo soon becomes a follower. Raymond Smith, former CEO and Chairman of the Bell Atlantic Corporation, once remarked, "Taking the safe road, doing your job, and not making any waves may not get you fired (right away, at least), but it sure won't do much for your career or your company over the long haul. We're not dumb. We know that administrators are easy to find and cheap to keep. Leaders—risk takers—are in very short supply. And ones with vision are pure gold."

Risk seems dangerous to people more comfortable with old problems than new solutions. The difference between the energy and time that it takes to put up with the old problems and the energy and time it takes to come up with new solutions is surprisingly small. The difference is attitude.

—*Developing the Leaders Around You*

ARE YOU CONTENT WITH THE STATUS QUO,
OR ARE YOU WILLING TO TAKE RISKS TO
GAIN HIGHER LEVELS OF ACHIEVEMENT?

DO YOU MAKE OTHERS BETTER?

How do your teammates see you? Are you an enlarger? Do you make them better than they are alone through your inspiration and contribution? Do you know what your teammates value? Do you capitalize on those things by adding value to them in those areas?

Becoming an enlarger of others isn't always easy. First, it takes a secure person to add value to others. If you believe deep down that helping others somehow hurts you or your opportunities for success, then you'll have a hard time enlarging others. But as Henry Ward Beecher insisted, "No man is more cheated than the selfish man." When a team member unselfishly enlarges others, he also enlarges himself.

—*The 17 Essential Qualities of a Team Player*

MAKE ENLARGING OTHERS YOUR PRIMARY AGENDA TODAY.

HIRE FOR SKILL AND EXPERIENCE

Back when I thought that attitude was everything, I tried to hire people with the best attitudes and figured I could get them up to speed in their skills. Now that I am older and more experienced, I realize that I had things backward. Now I hire primarily for skill and experience. Here's why: When it comes to talent and skill, a person can grow only a limited amount. On a scale from one to ten, most people can improve in a skill area only about two points. So, for example, if you are naturally a 6 as a leader, you may be able to grow to an 8 if you work at it. However, if you are a 2, you can work as hard as you want and you will never reach even average. The old saying of coaches is true: You can't get out what God didn't put in.

Attitude, however, is a different matter. There is no growth ceiling. Even a person with a 2 attitude can grow to become a 10. So even someone whose attitude isn't the best can turn that around.

On the day that I decided as a leader to hire only people with successful track records to key positions in my organization, my professional life changed. The entire team became more productive, and my organization began going to another level. That's not to say that I began hiring people with bad attitudes; I didn't. It wasn't an either/or decision. It was a both/and decision. Competence, experience, and positive attitude are a winning combination.

—The Difference Maker

COACH ANYONE ON YOUR TEAM WHO NEEDS IT TO
HAVE A BETTER ATTITUDE, BECAUSE THE POTENTIAL
FOR GROWTH IN THAT AREA IS UNLIMITED.

TAKING A LOOK IN THE MIRROR

A few years ago when I traveled to New Zealand to do a conference, I stayed in a hotel in Christchurch. One evening I was thirsty and started looking for a Coke machine. When I couldn't find one and I saw a door marked "Staff," I figured I'd go in and see if anyone in there could help me. I didn't find a hotel worker or a drink machine there, but I did observe something interesting. As I approached the door to go back out into the hall, I found that the door had a full-length mirror with the following words: "Take a good look at yourself. This is what the customer sees." The hotel's management was reminding employees that to fulfill their purpose, they needed to take a look at themselves.

And that's true for us too. Psychotherapist Sheldon Kopp believes "all the significant battles are waged within the self." As we examine ourselves, we discover what those battles are. And then we have two choices. The first is to be like the man who visited his doctor and found out he had serious health issues. When the doctor showed him his X-rays and suggested a painful and expensive surgery, the man asked, "Okay, but how much would you charge to just touch up the X-rays?"

The second choice is to stop blaming others, look at ourselves, and do the hard work of resolving the issues that are causing us problems. If you want to have better relationships with others, then stop, look in the mirror, and start working on yourself.

—Winning with People

TAKE A GOOD LOOK IN THE MIRROR TODAY.

HAVE A HIGH OPINION OF PEOPLE

The opinions you have of people in your life affect them profoundly. Dr. J. Sterling Livingston, formerly of the Harvard Business School and founder of the Sterling Institute management consulting firm, observed, "People perform consistently as they perceive you expect them to perform."

A reputation is something that many people spend their entire lives trying to live down or live up to. So why not help others up instead of pushing them down? All people possess both value and potential. You can find those things if you try.

—25 Ways to Win with People

LOOK FOR THE VALUE AND POTENTIAL
IN THOSE AROUND YOU TODAY.

START SMALL

What you are going to be tomorrow, you are becoming today. It is essential to begin developing self-discipline in a small way today in order to be disciplined in a big way tomorrow.

1. List five areas in your life that lack discipline.
2. Place them in order of your priority for conquering them.
3. Take them on, one at a time.
4. Secure resources, such as books and tapes, that will give you instruction and motivation to conquer each area.
5. Ask a person who models the trait you want to possess to hold you accountable for it.
6. Spend fifteen minutes each morning getting focused in order to get control of this weak area in your life.
7. Do a five-minute checkup on yourself at midday.
8. Take five minutes in the evening to evaluate your progress.
9. Allow sixty days to work on one area before you go to the next.
10. Celebrate with the one who holds you accountable as you show continued success.

Remember, having it all doesn't mean having it all at once. It takes time. Start small and concentrate on today. The slow accumulation of disciplines will one day make a big difference.

—*Developing the Leader Within You*

CHOOSE ONE AREA FROM YOUR LIST AND
TAKE A STEP OF DISCIPLINE TO IT TODAY.

EXPECT THE BEST

Your attitude toward life determines life's attitude toward you. How you think affects your approach to the success journey in a powerful way.

> What I believe about life determines
> How I perceive life, which determines
> What I receive from life.

If you expect the worst, you will certainly get it. If you expect the best, even when negative circumstances come your way—and they will because a positive attitude doesn't stop them—you can make the best of it and keep going.

If you talk to people in the top organizations across the country, the higher you go, the better the attitudes you'll discover. A Fortune 500 study found that 94 percent of all the executives surveyed attributed their success more to attitude than any other factor. That just goes to show you that if you want to go far, have a good attitude.

A good attitude makes it possible for you to be successful. It gives you fuel so that you want to pursue your purpose, grow to your potential, and sow seeds benefiting others. It can give you the staying power to improve. But it also makes the journey more enjoyable along the way—no matter where it takes you. As former UCLA basketball coach John Wooden said, "Things turn out the best for the people who make the best of the way things turn out."

—Your Road Map for Success

GO INTO TODAY EXPECTING ONLY THE BEST.

BREAKING FREE OF FAILURE

Business professors Gary Hamel and C. K. Prahalad have written about an experiment that was conducted with a group of monkeys.

Four monkeys were placed in a room that had a tall pole in the center. Suspended from the top of that pole was a bunch of bananas. One of the hungry monkeys started climbing the pole to get something to eat, but just as he reached out to grab a banana, he was doused with a torrent of cold water. Squealing, he scampered down the pole and abandoned his attempt to feed himself. Each monkey made a similar attempt, and each one was drenched with cold water. They finally gave up.

Then researchers removed one of the monkeys from the room and replaced him with a new monkey. As the newcomer began to climb the pole, the other three grabbed him and pulled him down. After trying to climb the pole several times and being dragged down by the others, he finally gave up.

The researchers replaced the original monkeys, one by one, and each time a new monkey was brought in, he would be dragged down by the others before he could reach the bananas. In time, the room was filled with monkeys who had never received a cold shower. None of them would climb the pole, but not one of them knew why.

Unfortunately people who have gotten used to failure can be a lot like those monkeys. They make the same mistakes again and again, yet they are never quite sure why.

—*Failing Forward*

IF YOU ARE ON THE FAILURE FREEWAY,
GET OFF BY TRYING SOMETHING NEW.

CHOOSE A LEADERSHIP MODEL

Give careful thought to which leaders you will follow because they will determine your course. I have developed six questions to ask myself before picking a model to follow:

Does my model's life deserve a following? This question relates to quality of character. I will become like the people I follow, and I don't want models with flawed character.

Does my model's life have a following? This question looks at credibility. If the person has no following, he or she may not be worth following.

What is the main strength that influences others to follow my model? What does the model have to offer me? What is his best? Also note that strong leaders have weaknesses as well as strengths. I don't want to inadvertently emulate the weaknesses.

Does my model produce other leaders? The answer to this question will tell me whether the model's leadership priorities match mine in regard to developing new leaders.

Is my model's strength reproducible in my life? If I can't reproduce his strength in my life, his modeling will not benefit me. But don't be too quick to say that a strength is not reproducible. Most are.

If my model's strength is reproducible in my life, what steps must I take to develop and demonstrate that strength? If you only answer the questions and never implement a plan to develop those strengths in yourself, you are only performing an intellectual exercise.

—Developing the Leaders Around You

BE SURE YOU HAVE A MENTOR WORTHY OF YOUR FOLLOWING.

MANAGING YOUR ATTITUDE

I grew up in small-town rural Ohio, and there were plenty of farms nearby. I once heard a farmer say that the hardest thing about cows is that they never stay milked. A similar thing can be said about a good attitude. The hardest thing about having a good attitude is that it doesn't stay that way on its own.

If you're like most people, just getting to work in the morning is a test of your attitude. I live in the Atlanta area, which is notorious for its bad traffic. The latest report I read stated that we had the fourth worst traffic in the nation behind Los Angeles, San Francisco, and Washington, D.C. So every time I get in my car, I remind myself, *Today I am going to have a great attitude!*

That doesn't mean I always succeed. I have to remain sensitive to my personal attitude indicators. If I notice myself getting impatient—which is by far my greatest attitude challenge—I try to remind myself to have a good attitude. If I hear myself making cynical remarks, I check my attitude. If I find myself wanting to throw in the towel and stop developing people because they're not catching on quickly enough, I make an attitude correction. And my fail-safe attitude indicator is Margaret, my wife. If it's starting to get out of line, she tells me!

In my book *Today Matters*, one of the concepts I write about is that most people overrate decision making, and they underrate decision managing. It's pretty easy to say to yourself, *From now on, I'm going to have a great attitude.* It's much harder to actually follow through with it. That's why I believe one of the best things you can do for yourself is make the daily *management* of your attitude one of your objectives.

—*The Difference Maker*

MANAGE YOUR ATTITUDE TODAY.

MAKE CHOICES THAT
WILL ADD VALUE TO TALENT

What creates the effectiveness necessary for converting talent into results? It comes from the choices you make. Orator, attorney, and political leader William Jennings Bryan said, "Destiny is not a matter of chance, it is a matter of choice; it is not a thing to be waited for, it is a thing to be achieved." I've discovered thirteen key choices that can be made to maximize any person's talent:

1. Belief lifts your talent.
2. Passion energizes your talent.
3. Initiative activates your talent.
4. Focus directs your talent.
5. Preparation positions your talent.
6. Practice sharpens your talent.
7. Perseverance sustains your talent.
8. Courage tests your talent.
9. Teachability expands your talent.
10. Character protects your talent.
11. Relationships influence your talent.
12. Responsibility strengthens your talent.
13. Teamwork multiplies your talent.

Make these choices, and you can become a talent-plus person. If you have talent, you stand alone. If you have talent *plus*, you stand out.

—*Talent Is Never Enough*

TO YOUR TALENT, BEGIN WORKING ON
ADDING ONE OF THE ABOVE QUALITIES.

BECOMING MORE DISCIPLINED

How are you doing when it comes to discipline? Do you take on mental and physical challenges just for the practice? Or are you constantly seeking a way to stay in your comfort zone? Do you sometimes regret that you've been unable to get yourself to do what you know to be right? Or most of the time do you believe that you do the best that you can? And how do you react under pressure? Do the people on your team expect extra effort or a sudden explosion from you when things go wrong? Your answers to those questions will give insight into whether you are winning the battle for discipline.

To become a more disciplined team player . . .

Strengthen your work habits. Discipline means doing the right things at the right time for the right reason. Review your priorities and follow-through to see if you're on track. And do something necessary but unpleasant every day to keep yourself disciplined.

Take on a challenge. To strengthen your mind and resolve, pick a task or project that will put you in over your head. Doing that will require you to think sharply and act with discipline. Keep doing that and you will find yourself capable of more than you imagined.

Tame your tongue. If you sometimes overreact emotionally, a first step to improvement is to stop yourself from saying things you shouldn't. The next time you want to lash out, hold your tongue for five minutes, and give yourself a chance to cool down and look at things more rationally. Use this strategy repeatedly and you will find yourself in better command of your emotions.

—*The 17 Essential Qualities of a Team Player*

WHAT KIND OF EXAMPLE ARE YOU SETTING FOR YOUR TEAM?

IMPROVING YOUR ENTHUSIASM

Microsoft chairman Bill Gates remarked, "What I do best is share my enthusiasm." Obviously that ability has brought the people in his organization immense success. If asked, would your teammates say that you have a similar effect on them? Enthusiasm increases a person's accomplishments while apathy increases his alibis. Which are people more likely to discover in you?

To improve your enthusiasm . . .

Show a sense of urgency. A good way to fire up your own furnace is to do things with greater urgency. Identify a project that you are currently less enthusiastic about than you should be. Give yourself deadlines for completing its steps that are a little more ambitious than you feel comfortable with. Doing that should help you be more focused and energized.

Be willing to do more. One way to demonstrate enthusiasm with your teammates is to go the extra mile with others. This week when someone asks you to do something, do what's required and then some. Then quietly observe its impact on the team's atmosphere.

Strive for excellence. Elbert Hubbard said, "The best preparation for good work tomorrow is to do good work today." Nothing breeds enthusiasm like a job well done. If you've allowed yourself to ease off when it comes to your work standards, redouble efforts to do things according to your highest levels of excellence.

—*The 17 Essential Qualities of a Team Player*

MAKE YOUR ENTHUSIASM INFECTIOUS
WITH YOUR TEAMMATES TODAY.

KEEPING MISTAKES IN PERSPECTIVE

To leave the road of continual failure, a person must first utter the three most difficult words to say: "I was wrong." He has to open his eyes, admit his mistakes, and accept complete responsibility for his current wrong actions and attitudes. Every failure you experience is a fork in the road. It's an opportunity to take the right action, learn from your mistakes, and begin again.

Leadership expert Peter Drucker says, "The better a man is, the more mistakes he will make, for the more new things he will try. I would never promote to a top-level job a man who was not making mistakes . . . otherwise he is sure to be mediocre." Mistakes really do pave the road to achievement.

Here is an acronym I created to help me keep mistakes in perspective. Mistakes are:

M – messages that give us feedback about life.
I – interruptions that should cause us to reflect and think.
S – signposts that direct us to the right path.
T – tests that push us toward greater maturity.
A – awakenings that keep us in the game mentally.
K – keys that we can use to unlock the next door of opportunity.
E – explorations that let us journey where we've never been before.
S – statements about our development and progress.

—Failing Forward

LOOK FOR WAYS TO PRAISE YOUR PEOPLE'S MISTAKES
AND HELP YOUR TEAM LEARN FROM THEM TODAY.

THE VALUE OF LISTENING

E dgar Watson Howe once joked, "No man would listen to you talk if he didn't know it was his turn next." Unfortunately, that accurately describes the way too many people approach communication—they're too busy waiting for their turn to really listen to others. But people of influence understand the incredible value of becoming a good listener. For example, when Lyndon B. Johnson was a junior senator from Texas, he kept a sign on his office wall that read, "You ain't learnin' nothin' when you're doin' all the talkin'." And Woodrow Wilson, the twenty-eighth American president, once said, "The ear of the leader must ring with the voices of the people."

The ability to skillfully listen is one key to gaining influence with others. Consider these benefits to listening that we've found:

* Listening shows respect.
* Listening builds relationships.
* Listening increases knowledge.
* Listening generates ideas.
* Listening builds loyalty.

Roger G. Imhoff urged, "Let others confide in you. It may not help you, but it surely will help them." At first glance, listening to others may appear to benefit only them. But when you become a good listener, you put yourself in a position to help yourself too. You have the ability to develop strong relationships, gather valuable information, and increase your understanding of yourself and others.

—*Becoming a Person of Influence*

FOCUS ON LISTENING TO OTHERS TODAY.

JUNE

JUNE 1

BUILD TRUST

I have learned that trust is the single most important factor in building personal and professional relationships. Warren Bennis and Burt Nanus call trust "the glue that binds followers and leaders together." Trust implies accountability, predictability, and reliability. More than anything else, followers want to believe in and trust their leaders. They want to be able to say, "Someday I want to be like him or her." People first must believe in you before they will follow your leadership.

Trust must be built day by day. It calls for consistency. Some of the ways a leader can betray trust include: breaking promises, gossiping, withholding information, and being two-faced. These actions destroy the environment of trust necessary for the growth of potential leaders. And when a leader breaks trust, he must work twice as hard to regain it.

People will not follow a leader they do not trust. It is the leader's responsibility to actively develop that trust in him from the people around him. Trust is built on many things:

Time. Take time to listen and give feedback on performance.
Respect. Give someone respect and he will return it with trust.
Unconditional Positive Regard. Show acceptance of the person.
Sensitivity. Anticipate feelings and needs of the potential leader.
Touch. Give encouragement—handshake, high five, pat on the back.

Once people trust their leader as a person, they become able to trust his leadership.

—*Developing the Leaders Around You*

TAKE RESPONSIBILITY FOR EARNING
TRUST WITH YOUR FOLLOWERS.

SAY THE RIGHT WORDS
AT THE RIGHT TIME

Most people recognize that words have incredible power. Editor and theologian Tyron Edwards observed, "Words are both better and worse than thoughts; they express them, and add to them; they give them power for good or evil; they start them on an endless flight, for instruction and comfort and blessing, or for injury, sorrow and ruin." But saying the right words is not enough. Timing is crucial.

Sometimes the best thing we can do for someone else is to hold our tongue. When tempted to give advice that's not wanted, to show off, to say "I told you so," or to point out another's error, the best policy is to say nothing. As nineteenth-century British journalist George Sala advised, we should strive "not only to say the right thing in the right place, but far more difficult, to leave unsaid the wrong thing at the tempting moment."

—25 Ways to Win with People

USE DISCERNMENT IN CHOOSING
YOUR WORDS AND THEIR TIMING TODAY.

JUNE 3

IT ALL BEGINS WITH A DREAM

If you live your dream and successfully share it, others will buy into it. People have a desire to follow a leader with a great dream. Now more than ever, people are looking for heroes. Unfortunately, many are looking in places that are likely to leave them disappointed: sports, music, movies, and television. But real heroes are leaders who can help others achieve success, people who take others with them. And it all begins with a dream. As Winifred Newman said, "Vision is the world's most desperate need. There are no hopeless situations, only people who think hopelessly."

—Your Road Map for Success

SHARE YOUR VISION WITH SOMEONE TODAY.

CATCH THEM DOING SOMETHING RIGHT

If you desire to see everyone as a "10" and help them believe in themselves, you need to encourage them by catching them doing something right. And that is really countercultural. We are trained our whole lives to catch people doing something wrong. If our parents and teachers caught us doing something, you can bet it was something wrong. So we tend to think in those same terms.

When you focus on the negative and catch people doing something wrong, it has no real power to make them any better. When we catch people doing something wrong, they become defensive. They make excuses. They evade. On the other hand, if we catch people doing something right, it gives them positive reinforcement. It helps them tap into their potential. It makes them want to do better.

Make it part of your daily agenda to look for things going right. They don't have to be big things, though of course you want to praise those things as well. It can be almost anything, as long as you are sincere in your praise.

—The 360° Leader

CATCH SOMEONE DOING SOMETHING RIGHT
TODAY AND PRAISE THEM FOR IT.

BE INTENTIONAL

W hat does it mean to be intentional? It means working with purpose—making every action count. It's about focusing on doing the right things, moment to moment, day to day, and then following through with them in a consistent way.

Successful individuals are intentional. They aren't scattered or haphazard. They know what they're doing and why they're doing it. For a team to be successful, it needs intentional people who are able to remain focused and productive, people who make every action count.

How intentional are you? As you proceed through your day, do you have a plan and a purpose for everything you do? Do you know where you're going and why you're doing what you're doing? Or are you simply drifting down the stream of life? If your teammates don't detect a sense of intentionality in you, they won't know what to expect from you, and they will be unlikely to count on you when it really counts.

—*The 17 Essential Qualities of a Team Player*

BE INTENTIONAL TODAY. MAKE EVERY ACTION COUNT.

HOW YOU SEE IS WHAT YOU GET

You're probably familiar with Murphy's Law, which says, "If anything bad can happen, it will—and at the worst possible time." And then there's the Peter Principle, which says, "People always rise to the level of their incompetence." A similar saying is the law of human behavior: "Sooner or later we get just what we expect."

Is the law of human behavior optimistic or pessimistic? Stop and think about your answer. I say that because your response reveals your attitude. If you expect the worst out of life, then you probably said the law was written by a pessimist. If you have a positive outlook, then you probably answered "optimist" because the prospect of getting what you expect is encouraging to you. Your attitude determines your outlook.

Let's face it. Not everyone is naturally optimistic. Some people are born seeing the glass half empty rather than half full. But no matter what your natural bent is, you can become a more optimistic person. How do you cultivate optimism? By learning the secret of contentment. If you can learn that, then no matter what happens to you, you can weather the storm and build on the good you find in any situation.

Contentment is not a popular concept. Our culture actually discourages the idea. People are continually bombarded with the message, "What you have isn't enough. You need more—a bigger house, a better car, a larger salary, whiter teeth, sweeter breath, nicer clothes . . ." The list is endless. But the truth is that possessing healthy contentment is essential to being able to withstand failure.

—*Failing Forward*

DECIDE TODAY THAT WHAT YOU HAVE IS ENOUGH.

JUNE 7

A LITTLE EXTRA TIME

Successful people practice harder and practice longer than unsuccessful people do. Success expert Peter Lowe, who has gleaned success secrets from hundreds of people who are at the top of their profession, says, "The most common trait I have found in all successful people is that they have conquered the temptation to give up."

Giving a little extra time requires more than just perseverance. It requires patience. The Law of Process in my book *The 21 Irrefutable Laws of Leadership* says, "Leadership develops daily, not in a day." That can be said of any talent we try to cultivate and improve.

As you work to give a little extra time to your efforts, it is wise to maintain a longer view of the process of improvement. Such a perspective really helps. Gutzon Borglum, the sculptor who created the memorial to the American presidents at Mount Rushmore, was asked if he considered his work to be perfect. It's said he replied, "Not today. The nose of Washington is an inch too long. It's better that way, though. It will erode to be exactly right in 10,000 years." Now that's patience!

—Talent Is Never Enough

GIVE JUST A LITTLE BIT MORE TIME, EFFORT, AND
PATIENCE TO A DIFFICULT TASK OR PROBLEM TODAY.

A GREAT ATTITUDE IS
YOUR GREATEST ASSET

What usually separates the best from the rest? Have you ever thought about that? What separates the gold medalist from the silver medalist in the Olympics? What separates the successful entrepreneur from the one who doesn't make it? What makes it possible for one person to thrive after a debilitating accident while another gives up and dies? It's attitude.

As Denis Waitley said in *The Winner's Edge*, "The winner's edge is not in a gifted birth, a high IQ, or in talent. The winner's edge is all in the attitude, not aptitude. Attitude is the criterion for success. But you can't buy an attitude for a million dollars. Attitudes are not for sale."

For years I have tried to live by the following statement: I cannot always choose what happens to me, but I can always choose what happens in me. Some things in life are beyond my control. Some things are within it. My attitude in the areas beyond my control *can* be the difference maker. My attitude in the areas that I do control *will* be the difference maker. In other words, the greatest difference my difference maker can make is within me, not others. That is why your attitude is your greatest asset or liability. It makes you or breaks you. It lifts you up or brings you down. A positive mental attitude will not let you do *everything*. But it can help you do *anything* better than you would if your attitude were negative.

—*The Difference Maker*

MAKE YOUR ATTITUDE YOUR GREATEST ASSET TODAY.

TAKE OTHERS TO A HIGHER LEVEL

I believe that deep down everyone—even the most negative person—wants to be a lifter. We all want to be a positive influence in the lives of others. And we can be. If you want to lift people up and add value to their lives, keep the following in mind:

Lifters commit themselves to daily encouragement. Roman philosopher Lucius Annaeus Seneca observed, "Wherever there is a human being, there is an opportunity for kindness." Encourage others and do it daily.

Lifters know the little difference that separates hurting and helping. The little things you do every day have a greater impact on others than you might think. You hold the power to make another person's life better or worse by the things you do today.

Lifters initiate the positive in a negative environment. It's one thing to be positive in a positive or neutral environment. It's another to be an instrument of change in a negative environment. Sometimes that requires a kind word, other times it takes a servant's action, and occasionally it calls for creativity.

Lifters understand life is not a dress rehearsal. People who lift others don't wait until tomorrow or some other "better" day to help people. They act now!

Everyone is capable of becoming a person who lifts up others. You don't have to be rich. You don't have to be a genius. You don't have to have it all together. You do have to care about people and initiate lifting activities. Doing that will positively change the relationships you already have and open you up to many more.

—*Winning with People*

BRING THE MINDSET OF LIFTING UP
OTHERS INTO YOUR DAY TODAY.

JUNE 10

LOOK WITHIN YOU

Theodore Hesburgh said, "The very essence of leadership is that you have a vision. It's got to be a vision you can articulate clearly and forcefully on every occasion. You can't blow an uncertain trumpet." An "uncertain trumpet" is usually the result of an individual who either lacks a vision or is trying to lead with someone else's dream. There is a vast difference between a person with a vision and a visionary person.

- ♦ A person with a vision talks little but does much.
- ♦ A visionary person does little but talks much.
- ♦ A person with a vision finds strength from inner convictions.
- ♦ A visionary person finds strength from outward conditions.
- ♦ A person with vision continues when problems arise.
- ♦ A visionary person quits when the road becomes difficult.

Demosthenes, the greatest orator of the ancient world, stuttered! Julius Caesar was an epileptic. Napoleon was of humble parentage and far from being a born genius. Beethoven was deaf, as was Thomas Edison. Charles Dickens was lame; so was Handel. Homer was blind; Plato was a hunchback; Sir Walter Scott was paralyzed.

What gave these great individuals the stamina to overcome severe setbacks and become successful? Each person had an inner dream that lit a fire that could not be extinguished. Great visions begin as an "inside job." Napoleon Hill said, "Cherish your visions and dreams as they are the children of your soul: the blueprints of your ultimate achievements."

—*Developing the Leader Within You*

BE SURE TO "BLOW A CERTAIN TRUMPET"
TODAY WITH YOUR PEOPLE.

JUNE 11

GENEROSITY

Nothing speaks to others more loudly or serves them better than generosity from a leader. True generosity isn't an occasional event. It comes from the heart and permeates every aspect of a leader's life, touching his time, money, talents, and possessions. Effective leaders, the kind that people want to follow, don't gather things just for themselves; they do it in order to give to others. Cultivate the quality of generosity in your life. Here's how:

Give something away. Find out what kind of hold your possessions have on you. Take something you truly value, think of someone you care about who could benefit from it, and give it to him. If you can do it anonymously, even better.

Put your money to work. If you know someone with the vision to do something really great—something that will positively impact the lives of others—provide resources for him to accomplish it. Put your money to work for something that will outlive you.

Find someone to mentor. Once you reach a certain level in your leadership, the most valuable thing you have to give is yourself. Find someone to pour your life into. Then give him time and resources to become a better leader.

Indian poet Rabindranath Tagore wrote, "All that is not given is lost."

—*The 21 Indispensable Qualities of a Leader*

WHAT ARE YOU CURRENTLY LOSING BY HOLDING ON TO IT?

THINGS EVERYBODY NEEDS TO
UNDERSTAND ABOUT PEOPLE

Knowing what people need and want is the key to understanding them. And if you can understand them, you can influence them and impact their lives in a positive way. If we were to boil down all the things we know about understanding people and narrow them down to a short list, we would identify these five things:

1. *Everybody wants to be somebody.* There isn't a person in the world who doesn't have the desire to be someone, to have significance.

2. *Nobody cares how much you know until he knows how much you care.* To be an influencer, you have to love people before you try to lead them.

3. *Everybody needs somebody.* Contrary to popular belief, there are no such things as self-made men and women. Everybody needs friendship, encouragement, and help.

4. *Everybody can be somebody when somebody understands and believes in her.* Once you understand people and believe in them, they really can become somebody.

5. *Anybody who helps somebody influences a lot of bodies.* What you give to one person overflows into the lives of all the people that person impacts. The nature of influence is to multiply.

—*Becoming a Person of Influence*

TRY TO LET EVERYBODY YOU ENCOUNTER TODAY
KNOW THAT YOU BELIEVE THEY ARE SOMEBODY.

ENCOURAGE THE DREAMS OF OTHERS

I consider it a great privilege when people share their dreams with me. It shows a great deal of courage and trust. And at that moment, I'm conscious that I have great power in their lives. That's no small matter. A wrong word can crush a person's dream; the right word can inspire him or her to pursue it.

If someone thinks enough of you to tell you about his or her dreams, take care. Actress Candice Bergen commented, "Dreams are, by definition, cursed with short life spans." I suspect she said that because there are people who don't like to see others pursuing their dreams. It reminds them of how far they are from living their own dreams. As a result, they try to knock down anyone who is shooting for the stars. By talking others out of their dreams, critical people excuse themselves for staying in their comfort zones.

Never allow yourself to become a dream killer. Instead, become a dream releaser. Even if you think another person's dream is far-fetched, that's no excuse for criticizing them.

—25 Ways to Win with People

ASK SOMEONE TO SHARE THEIR DREAM WITH YOU TODAY.

ADD SIGNIFICANCE

Moishe Rosen teaches a one-sentence mental exercise that is an effective tool in helping a person identify his dream. He asks a person to fill in the blanks:

If I had _____,
I would _____.

The idea is that if you had anything you wanted—unlimited time, unlimited money, unlimited information, unlimited staff (all the resources you could ask for)—what would you do? Your answer to that question is your dream.

Everyone has heard the story of Isaac Newton's discovery of the law of gravity after observing the fall of an apple. What few people know is that Edmund Halley, the astronomer who discovered Halley's Comet, is almost single-handedly responsible for Newton's theories becoming known. Halley challenged Newton to think through his original notions. He corrected Newton's mathematical errors and prepared geometrical figures to support his work. Not only did he encourage Newton to write his great work, *Mathematical Principles of Natural Philosophy*, but he edited the work, supervised its publication, and financed its printing, even though Newton could easily afford the printing costs.

Halley encouraged Newton to act on his dream, and it added immeasurable significance to Newton's life. Halley received little credit, but he must have gained great satisfaction in knowing he had inspired revolutionary ideas in the advancement of scientific thought.

—*Developing the Leaders Around You*

WHAT WOULD YOU DO IF THERE
WERE NO LIMITS ON YOUR LIFE?

DEALING WITH THE WEAK LINK

If you're a team leader, you cannot ignore the issues created by a weak link. For the various kinds of teams, different solutions are appropriate. If the team is a family, then you don't simply "trade" weak people. You lovingly nurture them and try to help them grow, but you also try to minimize the damage they can cause to other family members. If the team is a business, then you have responsibilities to the owner or stockholders. If you've offered training without success, then a "trade" might be in order. If the team is a ministry and training has made no impact, then it might be appropriate to ask the weak people to sit on the sidelines for a while. Or they might need some time away from the team to work on emotional or spiritual issues.

No matter what kind of situation you face, remember that your responsibilities to people come in the following order: to the organization, to the team, and then to the individual. Your own interests—and comfort—come last.

—*The 17 Indisputable Laws of Teamwork*

IF YOU ARE THE LEADER, IT IS YOUR RESPONSIBILITY TO ADDRESS THE PROBLEM OF A WEAK LINK ON YOUR TEAM.

FAILURE IS AN INSIDE JOB

In our culture, too many people believe that contentment comes from attaining material possessions or positions of power. But they aren't the keys to contentment either. If you are tempted to believe that they are, remember the words of John D. Rockefeller. When a journalist asked him how much wealth was enough, the millionaire, who was at the time one of the richest and most powerful men in the world, answered, "Just a little more."

Contentment comes from having a positive attitude. It means:

+ Expecting the best in everything—not the worst
+ Remaining upbeat—even when you get beat up
+ Seeing solutions in every problem—not problems in every solution
+ Believing in yourself—even when others believe you've failed
+ Holding on to hope—even when others say it's hopeless

No matter what happens to you, a positive attitude comes from within. Your circumstances and your contentment are unrelated.

—*Failing Forward*

RELY ON A POSITIVE ATTITUDE TODAY TO
GET YOU THROUGH DIFFICULT CIRCUMSTANCES.

LIFE GIVES YOU WHAT YOU EXPECT

The happiest people in life don't necessarily *have* the best of everything. They just try to *make* the best of everything. They're like the person in a remote village going to a well every day to get water who says, "Every time I come to this well, I come away with my bucket full!" instead of, "I can't believe I have to keep coming back to this well to fill up my bucket!"

A person's attitude has a profound influence on his approach to life. Ask a coach before a big game whether his attitude and that of his players will make a difference in the outcome of the game. Ask a surgeon if the patient's attitude matters when she's trying to save that life in an emergency room. Ask a teacher if students' attitudes have an impact before they take a test.

One of the things I've learned is that life often gives you whatever you expect from it. If you expect bad things, those are what you get. If you expect good things, you often receive them. I don't know why it works that way, but it does. If you don't believe me, try it out. Give yourself thirty days in which you expect the best of everything: the best parking place, the best table in the restaurant, the best interaction with clients, the best treatment from service people. You'll be surprised by what you encounter, especially if you give your very best to others in every situation as well.

—The Difference Maker

BEGIN YOUR THIRTY-DAY TRIAL OF
EXPECTING THE BEST OF EVERYTHING.

THE POWER OF RIGHT CHOICES

Life is a matter of choices, and every choice you make makes you. What will you do for your career? Who will you marry? Where will you live? How much education will you get? What will you do with today? But one of the most important choices you will make is *who will you become!* Life is not merely a matter of holding and playing a good hand as you would hope to do in a card game. What you start with isn't up to you. *Talent* is God-given. Life is playing the hand you have been dealt well. That is determined by your choices.

The talent-plus people are the ones who maximize their talent, reach their potential, and fulfill their destiny.

I was reading a book by Dr. Seuss to my grandchildren called *Oh, The Places You'll Go!* In it, I found a wonderful truth. It said,

> You have brains in your head.
> You have feet in your shoes.
> You can steer yourself
> Any direction you choose.

I believe that with all my heart. My prayer is that you steer yourself in the right direction and make right choices that will empower you to become a talent-plus person, build upon the foundation of your abilities, and live your life to its fullest potential.

—*Talent Is Never Enough*

MAXIMIZE YOUR TALENT BY STEERING
YOUR ENTIRE LIFE IN THE RIGHT DIRECTION.

GIVE ENCOURAGEMENT

Too many leaders expect their people to encourage themselves. But most people require outside encouragement to propel them forward. It is vital to their growth. Physician George Adams found encouragement to be so vital to a person's existence that he called it "oxygen to the soul."

New leaders need to be encouraged. When they arrive in a new situation, they encounter many changes and undergo many changes themselves. Encouragement helps them reach their potential; it empowers them by giving them energy to continue when they make mistakes.

Use lots of positive reinforcement with your people. Don't take acceptable work for granted; thank people for it. Praise a person every time you see improvement. And personalize your encouragement any time you can. Remember, what motivates one person may leave another cold or even irritated. Find out what works with each of your people and use it.

UCLA basketball coach John Wooden told players who scored to give a smile, wink, or nod to the player who gave them a good pass. "What if he's not looking?" asked a team member. Wooden replied, "I guarantee he'll look." Everyone values encouragement and looks for it—especially when his leader is a consistent encourager.

—*Developing the Leaders Around You*

LOOK FOR OPPORTUNITIES TO
ENCOURAGE YOUR TEAM TODAY.

MAKE YOUR TEACHABLE MOMENTS COUNT

Even people who are strategic about seeking teachable moments can miss the whole point of the experience. I say this because for thirty years I've been a speaker at conferences and workshops—events that are designed to help people learn. But I've found that many people walk away from an event and do very little with what they heard after closing their notebooks.

We tend to focus on learning events instead of the learning process. Because of this, I try to help people take action steps that will help them implement what they learn. I suggest that in their notes, they use a code to mark things that jump out at them:

T indicates you need to spend some time thinking on that point.

C indicates something you need to change.

☺ means you are doing that thing particularly well.

A indicates something you need to apply.

S means you need to share that information with someone else.

After the conference I recommend that they create to-do lists based on what they marked, then schedule time to follow through.

—*Talent Is Never Enough*

FIND WAYS TO CREATE ACTION STEPS, AND
FOLLOW THROUGH ON SOMETHING YOU LEARN TODAY.

MANAGE YOUR EMOTIONS

I once heard that people with emotional problems are 144 percent more likely to have auto accidents than those who don't have them. The same study evidently found that one out of five victims of fatal accidents had been in a quarrel with another person in the six hours preceding the accident.

It's important for everybody to manage emotions. Nobody likes to spend time around an emotional time bomb who may "go off" at any moment. But it's especially critical for leaders to control their emotions because whatever they do affects many other people.

Good leaders know when to display emotions and when to delay them. Sometimes they show them so that their people can feel what they're feeling. It stirs them up. Is that manipulative? I don't think so, as long as the leaders are doing it for the good of the team and not for their own gain. Because leaders see more than others and ahead of others, they often experience the emotions first. By letting the team know what you're feeling, you're helping them to see what you're seeing.

Other times leaders have to hold their feelings in check. When I say that leaders should delay their emotions, I'm not suggesting that they deny them or bury them. The bottom line in managing your emotions is that you should put others—not yourself—first in how you handle and process them. Whether you delay or display your emotions should not be for your own gratification.

—The 360° Leader

WHEN FACED WITH AN EMOTIONAL DECISION,
ASK YOURSELF, *WHAT DOES THE TEAM NEED?*
NOT, *WHAT WILL MAKE ME FEEL BETTER?*

DON'T LOSE YOUR MARBLES

My friend Dwight Bain sent me a story of a ham radio operator who overheard an older gentleman giving advice to a younger man.

"It's a shame you have to be away from home and your family so much," he said. "Let me tell you something that has helped me keep a good perspective on my own priorities. You see, one day I sat down and did a little arithmetic. The average person lives about seventy-five years. Now then, I multiplied 75 times 52 and came up with 3,900, which is the number of Saturdays that the average person has in his lifetime.

"It took me until I was fifty-five years old to think about all this in any detail," he continued, "and by that time I had lived through over 2,800 Saturdays. I got to thinking that if I lived to be seventy-five, I only had about a thousand of them left to enjoy."

He went on to explain that he bought 1,000 marbles and put them in a clear plastic container in his favorite work area at home. "Every Saturday since then," he said, "I have taken one marble out and thrown it away. I found that by watching the marbles diminish, I focused more on the really important things in life. There's nothing like watching your time here on this earth run out to help get your priorities straight."

Then the older gentleman finished, "Now let me tell you one last thought before I sign off and take my lovely wife out to breakfast. This morning, I took the very last marble out of the container. I figure if I make it until next Saturday, then I have been given a little extra time."

We can't choose whether we will get any more time, but we can choose what we do with it.

—*The 17 Essential Qualities of a Team Player*

BE INTENTIONAL WITH YOUR TIME.

DEVELOP A PERSONAL RELATIONSHIP
WITH THE PEOPLE YOU EQUIP

All good mentoring relationships begin with a personal relationship. As your people get to know and like you, their desire to follow your direction and learn from you will increase. If they don't like you, they will not want to learn from you, and the equipping process slows down or even stops.

To build relationships, begin by listening to people's life stories, their journeys so far. Your genuine interest in them will mean a lot to them. It will also help you to know their personal strengths and weaknesses. Ask them about their goals and what motivates them. Find out what kind of temperaments they have. You certainly don't want to equip and develop a person whose greatest love is numbers and financial statements for a position where he would be spending 80 percent of his time dealing with disgruntled customers.

One of the best ways to get to know people is to see them outside of the business world. People are usually on their guard at work. They try to be what others want them to be. By getting to know them in other settings, you can get to know who they really are. Try to learn as much as you can about the people and do your best to win their hearts. If you first find their hearts, they'll be glad to give you their hands.

—*Developing the Leaders Around You*

MAKE AN APPOINTMENT TO GET TO KNOW
SOMEONE ON YOUR TEAM TODAY.

MAKE THE MOST OF YOUR GIFTS
AND OPPORTUNITIES

More than thirty years ago I memorized a quote that has shaped the way I live: "My potential is God's gift to me. What I do with my potential is my gift to Him." I believe I am accountable to God, others, and myself for every gift, talent, resource, and opportunity I have in life. If I give less than my best, then I am shirking my responsibility. I believe UCLA coach John Wooden was speaking to this idea when he said, "Make every day your masterpiece." If we give our very best all the time, we can make our lives into something special. And that will overflow into the lives of others.

There's a story I love about President Dwight Eisenhower. He once told the National Press Club that he regretted not having a better political background so that he would be a better orator. He said his lack of skill in that area reminded him of his boyhood days in Kansas when an old farmer had a cow for sale. The buyer asked the farmer about the cow's pedigree, butterfat production, and monthly production of milk. The farmer said, "I don't know what a pedigree is, and I don't have an idea about butterfat production, but she's a good cow, and she'll give you all the milk she has." That's all any of us can do—give all that we have. That's always enough.

—*25 Ways to Win with People*

STRIVE TO MAKE THE MOST OF YOUR POTENTIAL TODAY.

DEFINING THE TEAM

We've all seen teams that have a common goal yet lack common values. Everyone on the team has different ideas about what's important. The result is chaos. Eventually the team breaks down if everyone tries to do things his own way. That's why team members need to be on the same page. Just as personal values influence and guide an individual's behavior, organizational values influence and guide the team's behavior.

If you want to add value to your team and help it reach its potential, then you need to share in its values. First, make sure that you know what they are. Then, examine your values and goals in comparison to them. If you can wholeheartedly buy into the team's values, commit yourself to aligning yourself with them. If you can't, then your misalignment will be a constant source of frustration to you and your teammates. And you might want to think about finding a different team.

—The 17 Indisputable Laws of Teamwork

ARE YOU AND YOUR TEAMMATES ON THE
SAME PAGE WHEN IT COMES TO VALUES?

JUNE 26

ENCOURAGING ANOTHER'S DREAM

Because dreams are at the center of our souls, we must do everything in our power to help turn dreams into reality. That is one of the greatest gifts we can ever give. How can you do it? Follow these six steps:

1. *Ask them to share their dream with you.* Everyone has a dream, but few people are asked about it.

2. *Affirm the person as well as the dream.* Let the person know that you not only value his or her dream but that you also recognize traits in that individual that can help him or her achieve it.

3. *Ask about the challenges they must overcome to reach their dream.* Few people ask others about their dreams; even fewer try to find out what kinds of hurdles the person is up against to pursue them.

4. *Offer your assistance.* No one achieves a worthwhile dream alone. You'll be amazed by how people light up when you offer to help them achieve their dream.

5. *Revisit their dream with them on a consistent basis.* If you really want to help others with their dreams, don't make it a one-time activity you mark off your list. Check in with them to see how they're doing and to lend assistance.

6. *Determine daily to be a dream booster, not a dream buster.* Everyone has a dream, and everyone needs encouragement. Set your mental radar to pick up on others' dreams and help them along.

—*25 Ways to Win with People*

BEGIN THE FIRST STEP OF HELPING ANOTHER
PERSON TURN HIS DREAM INTO REALITY.

IT'S A STATE OF MIND

Failure is an inside job. So is success. If you want to achieve, you have to win the war in your thinking first. You can't let the failure outside you get inside you. You certainly can't control the length of your life—but you can control its width and depth. You can't control the contour of your face—but you can control its expression. You can't control the weather—but you can control the atmosphere of your mind. Why worry about things you can't control when you can keep yourself busy controlling the things that depend on you?

I read an article that highlighted the strength, courage, and resilience of the Norwegian people. Some of the toughest explorers in history have come from Norway. It doesn't matter how harsh the climate or how difficult the circumstances; they always seem to persevere.

That ability has become a part of their culture. They are a nation of outdoor enthusiasts—living on the edge of the Arctic Circle. The Norwegians have a saying that I think captures their attitude: "There is no such thing as bad weather, only bad clothing."

—*Failing Forward*

HOW CAN YOU "CHANGE CLOTHING" TO OVERCOME
ANY BAD WEATHER YOUR ORGANIZATION IS EXPERIENCING?

VISION STATEMENTS

What you see is what you can be. This deals with your potential. I have often asked myself, does the vision make the leader? Or, does the leader make the vision?

I believe the vision comes first. I have known many leaders who lost the vision and, therefore, lost their power to lead. People do what people see. That is the greatest motivational principle in the world. Stanford Research says that 89 percent of what we learn is visual, 10 percent of what we learn is auditory, and 1 percent of what we learn is through other senses.

In other words, people depend on visual stimulation for growth. Couple a vision with a leader willing to implement that dream, and a movement begins. People do not follow a dream in itself. They follow the leader who has that dream and the ability to communicate it effectively. Therefore, vision in the beginning will make a leader, but for that vision to grow and demand a following, the leader must take responsibility for it.

Hubert H. Humphrey is an example of "what you see is what you can be." During a trip to Washington, D.C., in 1935, he wrote this in a letter to his wife: "Honey, I see how someday, if you and I just apply ourselves and make up our minds to work for bigger and better things, we can someday live here in Washington and probably be in government, politics, or service . . . Oh, gosh, I hope my dream comes true—I'm going to try anyhow."

—*Developing the Leader Within You*

ARE YOU COMMUNICATING VISION
AND PURSUING IT WITH PASSION?

GIVE THEM THE "10" TREATMENT

It's been my observation that people usually rise to the leader's expectations—if they like the leader. If you have built solid relationships with your employees and they genuinely like and respect you, they will work hard and give their best.

I've learned a lot of things about leadership from many leaders over the years, but the one I still admire most is my father, Melvin Maxwell. In December 2004, I visited my parents in the Orlando area, and while I was there, I was scheduled to participate in a conference call. Because I needed a quiet place to do it, my dad graciously let me use his office. As I sat at his desk, I noticed a card next to the phone with the following words written in my father's hand:

#1 Build people up by encouragement.
#2 Give people credit by acknowledgment.
#3 Give people recognition by gratitude.

I knew in a second why it was there. My father had written it to remind him of how he was to treat people as he spoke on the phone with them. And I was instantly reminded that Dad, more than anyone else, taught me to see everyone as a "10." Begin today to see and lead people as they can be, not as they are, and you will be amazed by how they respond to you.

—The 360° Leader

TREAT SOMEONE LIKE A "10" TODAY AND
WATCH THEM RISE TO YOUR EXPECTATIONS.

MANAGE YOUR ENERGY

Some people have to ration their energy so that they don't run out. Up until a few years ago, that wasn't me. When people asked me how I got so much done, my answer was always, "High energy, low IQ." From the time I was a kid, I was always on the go.

Now I do have to pay attention to my energy level. In *Thinking for a Change*, I shared one of my strategies for managing my energy. When I look at my calendar every morning, I ask myself, *What is the main event?* That is the one thing to which I cannot afford to give anything less than my best. That one thing can be for my family, my employees, a friend, my publisher, the sponsor of a speaking engagement, or my writing time. I always make sure I have the energy to do it with focus and excellence.

Even people with high energy can have that energy sucked right out of them under difficult circumstances. Leaders in the middle of an organization often have to deal with what I call "the ABCs energy-drain."

Activity Without Direction—doing things that don't seem to matter
Burden Without Action—not being able to do things that really matter
Conflict Without Resolution—not being able to deal with what's
    the matter

If you find that you are in an organization where you often must deal with these ABCs, then you will have to work extra hard to manage your energy well. Either that or you need to look for a new place to work.

—*The 360° Leader*

EXAMINE THE ABCs. WHERE DO
YOU NEED TO MANAGE YOUR ENERGY?

JULY

BEING MISSION-CONSCIOUS

Do you and your teammates keep the big picture in mind? Or do you tend to get so bogged down in the details of your responsibilities that you lose sight of the big picture? If you in any way hinder the bigger team—your organization—because of your desire to achieve personal success or even the success of your department, then you may need to take steps to improve your ability to keep the team's mission in mind.

Check to see if your team focuses on its mission. Start by measuring the clarity of the mission. Does your team or organization have a mission statement? If not, work to get the team to create one. If it does, then examine whether the goals of the team match its mission. If the values, mission, goals, and practices of a team don't match up, you're going to have a tough time as a team player.

Find ways to keep the mission in mind. If you're a strong achiever, the type of person who is used to working alone, or you tend to focus on the immediate rather than the big picture, you may need extra help being reminded of the mission of the team. Write down the mission and place it somewhere you can see it. Keep it in front of you so that you are always conscious of the team's mission.

Contribute your best as a team member. Once you're sure of the team's mission and direction, determine to contribute your best in the context of the team, not as an individual. That may mean taking a behind-the-scenes role for a while. Or it may mean focusing your inner circle in a way that contributes more to the organization, even if it gives you and your people less recognition.

—*The 17 Essential Qualities of a Team Player*

AVOID GETTING BOGGED DOWN IN DETAILS
AND KEEP THE BIG PICTURE IN MIND TODAY.

JULY 2

SET GOALS FOR GROWTH

The greatest achievers in life are people who set goals for themselves and then work hard to reach them. What they *get* by reaching the goals is not nearly as important as what they *become* by reaching them. When you help people set goals, use the following guidelines:

Make the goals appropriate. Always keep in mind the job you want the people to do and the desired result: the development of your people into effective leaders. Identify goals that will contribute to that larger goal.

Make the goals attainable. Ian MacGregor, former AMAX Corporation chairman of the board, said, "I work on the same principle as people who train horses. You start with low fences, easily achieved goals, and work up."

Make the goals measurable. Your potential leaders will never know when they have achieved their goals if they aren't measurable. When they are measurable, the knowledge that they have been attained will give them a sense of accomplishment.

Clearly state the goals. When goals have no clear focus, neither will the actions of the people trying to achieve them.

Make the goals require a "stretch." As I mentioned before, goals have to be achievable. On the other hand, when goals don't require a stretch, the people achieving them won't grow.

Put the goals in writing. When people write down their goals, it makes them more accountable for those goals.

It is also important to encourage your potential leaders to review their goals and progress. Ben Franklin set aside time every day to review two questions. In the morning he asked himself, "What good shall I do today?" In the evening he asked, "What good have I done today?"

—*Developing the Leaders Around You*

HELP SOMEONE ON YOUR TEAM TO SET GOALS TODAY.

JULY 3

THE PEOPLE YOU ATTRACT

Effective leaders are always on the lookout for good people. What will determine whether the people you want are the people you get? It's determined by who you *are*. If you have recruited and hired a staff, you will probably find that you and the people who follow you share common ground in several key areas.

- Generation: Most organizations reflect the characteristics of their key leaders, and that includes their age.
- Attitude: People with good attitudes tend to make people around them feel more positive. Terrible attitudes bring others down.
- Background: People attract—and are attracted to—others of similar background. This natural magnetism is so strong that organizations that value diversity have to fight against it.
- Values: Whether shared values are positive or negative, the character you possess is what you will likely find in the people who follow you.
- Energy: It's a good thing that people with similar levels of energy are attracted to one another, because when you pair a high-energy person with a low-energy person and ask them to work closely together, they can drive one another crazy.
- Giftedness: People are attracted to talent and excellence and are most likely to respect and follow one who possesses their kind of talent.
- Leadership Ability: Who you are is what you attract. The leaders you attract will be similar in style and ability to you.

—The 21 Irrefutable Laws of Leadership

WHO YOU ARE IS WHO YOU ATTRACT—GROW ACCORDINGLY.

ATTITUDE TOWARD CHALLENGES

I once heard a lecturer say that no society has ever developed tough men during times of peace. The old adage is true: What doesn't kill you makes you stronger. Think back to the times in your life when you have grown the most. I'm willing to bet that you grew as the result of overcoming difficulties. The better your attitude, the more likely you will be to overcome difficulties, grow, and move forward.

I've been told that in the Chinese language two words are often combined to create another word with a very different meaning. For example, when the symbol for the word meaning *man* is combined with the symbol for the word meaning *woman*, the resulting word means *good*.

Possessing a positive attitude can have a similar effect. When a problem comes into contact with someone who has a positive attitude, the result is often something wonderful. Out of the turmoil that problems cause can emerge great statesmen, scientists, authors, or businesspeople. Every challenge has an opportunity. And every opportunity has a challenge. A person's attitude determines how she handles those.

— *The Difference Maker*

LET YOUR POSITIVE ATTITUDE TRANSFORM
EVERY CHALLENGE INTO AN OPPORTUNITY.

DEVELOP AND FOLLOW YOUR PRIORITIES

There's an old saying that if you chase two rabbits, both will escape. Unfortunately that is what many people seem to do. They don't focus their attention, and as a result, they become ineffective. Perhaps the reason is that people in our culture have too many choices—nearly unlimited options. Management expert Peter Drucker recognized this phenomenon. He said, "Concentration is the key to economic results. No other principle of effectiveness is violated as constantly today as the basic principle of concentration . . . Our motto seems to be, 'Let's do a little bit of everything.'"

If you want to develop your talent, you need to focus. If you're going to focus, you need to work on knowing what your true priorities are and then following them. This is something I have learned to do over time. I love options. I like to have the freedom to pursue the best course of action at any given moment. When I was in my twenties, I spent a lot of time doing things that had little return. In my thirties, I did better, but I still wasn't as focused as I should have been. It wasn't until I reached forty that I started to become highly selective about where I spent my time and energy. Today I filter just about everything I do through my top priority: *Am I adding value to people?* For me, it all comes down to that.

—*Talent Is Never Enough*

WHAT IS YOUR TOP PRIORITY?

THE PAST IMPACTS THE PRESENT

A few years ago, I heard my friend Chuck Swindoll tell the story of Chippie the parakeet. He said the bird's problems began when the woman who owned him decided to clean up the seeds and loose feathers from the bottom of his cage using a vacuum. When the phone rang, the owner turned to pick it up, and—you guessed it—with a thud and a whoosh, Chippie was gone.

The owner quickly turned off the vacuum and unzipped the bag. There was Chippie. He was stunned but breathing.

Seeing that he was covered with black dust, his owner rushed Chippie to the bathtub, where she turned on the faucet full blast and held the bird under the icy water.

At that point she realized that she'd done even more damage, and she quickly cranked up her blow dryer and gave the wet, shivering little parakeet a blast. Chuck finished the story by saying, "Chippie doesn't sing much anymore . . ."

People who are unable to overcome the past are a little like Chippie. They allow their negative experiences to color the way they live.

It may sound as if I'm making light of what may have happened to you in the past. I'm not. I know that people suffer genuine tragedies in this imperfect world. They lose children, spouses, parents, and friends—sometimes under horrible circumstances. People contract cancer, multiple sclerosis, AIDS, and other debilitating diseases. They suffer unspeakable abuses at the hands of others. But tragedies don't have to stop a person from possessing a positive outlook, being productive, and living life to the fullest. No matter how dark a person's past is, it need not color his present permanently.

—*Failing Forward*

In what way is your past coloring your present?

JULY 7

IMPROVING YOUR PREPAREDNESS

A re you used to winging it? Do you try to fake it 'til you make it? Or is solid preparation part of your regular routine? If you continually let your teammates down, you're probably playing in the wrong position or not spending enough time and energy preparing to meet challenges. To improve your preparedness . . .

Become a process thinker. Getting ready requires thinking ahead so that you recognize now what you will need later. Create a system or list for yourself that will help you mentally walk through any process ahead of time, breaking tasks down into steps. Then determine what preparation will be required to complete each step.

Do more research. People in just about every profession utilize some kind of research to improve themselves. Become more familiar with the research tools of your trade and make yourself an expert at using them.

Learn from your mistakes. The greatest preparation tool can often be a person's own experience. Think about the mistakes you recently made while completing a project or executing a challenge. Write them down, study them, and determine what you can do differently the next time you face a similar situation.

—*The 17 Essential Qualities of a Team Player*

FOCUS ON SOLID PREPARATION TODAY.

JULY 8

BE WILLING TO DO WHAT OTHERS WON'T

It's said that an aid group in South Africa once wrote to missionary and explorer David Livingstone, "Have you found a good road to where you are? If so, we want to know how to send other men to join you."

Livingstone replied, "If you have men who will come only if they know there is a good road, I don't want them. I want men who will come even if there is no road at all." That's what top leaders want from the people working for them: they want individuals who are willing to do what others won't.

Few things gain the appreciation of a top leader more quickly than an employee with a whatever-it-takes attitude. They must be willing and able to think outside of their job description, to be willing to tackle the kinds of jobs that others are too proud or too frightened to take on.

Few things are more frustrating for a leader than having someone refuse to do a task because it is "not his job." (In moments like those, most of the top leaders I know are tempted to invite such people to be without a job altogether!) Good leaders don't think in those terms. They understand the Law of the Big Picture from *The 21 Irrefutable Laws of Leadership*: "The goal is more important than the role."

A 360-Degree Leader's goal is to get the job done, to fulfill the vision of the organization and its leader. That often means doing whatever it takes. As a leader "moves up," that more often takes the form of hiring someone to get it done, but leaders in the middle often don't have that option. So instead, they jump in and get it done themselves.

—The 360° Leader

CULTIVATE A WHATEVER-IT-TAKES ATTITUDE.

CREATE A GROWTH ENVIRONMENT

Just as the growth of tropical fish is limited by the size of the aquarium in which they live, you are affected by your environment. That's why it's crucial to create an environment of growth around you. That kind of place should look like this:

Others are ahead of you: When you surround yourself with people from whom you can learn, you are more likely to grow.

You are still challenged: Complacency kills growth.

Your focus is forward: If you're thinking more about the past than the future, your growth has probably stopped.

The atmosphere is affirming: Industrialist Charles Schwab said, "I have yet to find the man . . . who did not do better work and put forth greater effort under a spirit of approval than under a spirit of criticism."

You are out of your comfort zone: Growth requires risk. Ronald E. Osborne stated, "Unless you do something beyond what you've already mastered, you will never grow."

Others are growing: When it comes to growth, it's better to swim in a school than to try to do everything on your own.

There is a willingness to change: Clayton G. Orcutt declared, "Change itself is not progress, but change is the price that we pay for progress."

Growth is modeled and expected: In the best possible environment, growth is not only allowed, but leaders model it and expect it from everyone. And when that happens, everyone's potential is off the charts.

—*Your Road Map for Success*

TAKE RESPONSIBILITY FOR CREATING AN
ENVIRONMENT OF GROWTH FOR YOUR TEAM MEMBERS.

THE POWER OF THOUGHTS

The human mind has a tremendous amount of power in our lives. That which holds our attention determines our actions. Because of that, where we are today is the result of the dominating thoughts in our minds. And the way we think determines what our attitudes are. The good news is that you and I can change that. You can control your thoughts, and because of that, you can control your attitude.

Let's do an experiment that will show you what I mean. Take a moment to think about the place where you live. No problem. You decided to think about it, and you did it. Next, imagine for a moment that the place where you live has burned to the ground, and everything in it is gone. What kind of emotional response did you have? Maybe you were sad because many irreplaceable things would have been lost in a fire. Maybe you were happy because your current living situation is terrible and a fresh start would do you good. The point is that your thinking prompts your emotion. That's key, and here's why:

Major premise: We can control our thoughts.
Minor premise: Our feelings come from our thoughts.
Therefore: We can control our feelings by changing how we think.

Why is that important? Because your attitude is your emotional approach to life. It's the framework through which you see events, other people, even yourself. That's why I believe the saying, "You are not what you think you are, but what you think . . . you are."

—*The Difference Maker*

HOW ARE THE DOMINATING THOUGHTS
OF YOUR MIND AFFECTING YOUR ATTITUDE?

PREPARATION FOR TOMORROW
BEGINS TODAY

R ecently, a few friends and I were privileged to have dinner with former New York City mayor Rudy Giuliani and his wife, Judith, in
Orlando after a speaking engagement. I found the mayor to be a very
warm and personable man who was an easy conversationalist. During our
conversation, I of course asked him about his experience during 9/11. He
talked about his impressions from that day and how the event impacted
him as a leader. He said that leaders need to be ready for anything. They
need to study, acquire skills, and plan for every kind of situation.

"Your success will be determined by your ability to prepare," he said.
He went on to explain that when a situation like that on September 11
occurs—for which there was no plan in place—leaders must take action
and rely on whatever preparation had taken place. In his case, it was the
emergency drills they had followed. Both helped during the crisis.

Preparation doesn't begin with what you do. It begins with what you
believe. If you believe that your success tomorrow depends on what you
do today, then you will treat today differently. What you receive tomorrow depends on what you believe today. If you are *preparing* today,
chances are, you will not be *repairing* tomorrow.

—Talent Is Never Enough

FOCUS ON PREPARING TODAY SO THAT
YOU CAN EXPERIENCE SUCCESS TOMORROW.

COURAGEOUS LEADERSHIP

When I began my leadership career, I was very ineffective as a leader. I believed I had talent. But when I got out into the real world, I fell far short of my expectations. How did I turn things around? By making small decisions that were difficult. With each one, I gained more confidence and more courage, and I began to change. The process took me four years. At the end of that time, I had learned many valuable lessons, and I wrote the following to help me cement what I had learned:

> Courageous Leadership Simply Means I've Developed:
> 1. Convictions that are stronger than my fears.
> 2. Vision that is clearer than my doubts.
> 3. Spiritual sensitivity that is louder than popular opinion.
> 4. Self-esteem that is deeper than self-protection.
> 5. Appreciation for discipline that is greater than my desire for leisure.
> 6. Dissatisfaction that is more forceful than the status quo.
> 7. Poise that is more unshakeable than panic.
> 8. Risk taking that is stronger than safety seeking.
> 9. Right actions that are more robust than rationalization.
> 10. A desire to see potential reached more than to see people appeased.

You don't have to be great to become a person of courage. You just need to want to reach your potential and to be willing to trade what seems good in the moment for what's best for your potential. That's something you can do regardless of your level of natural talent.

—Talent Is Never Enough

MAKE A SMALL DECISION TODAY THAT WILL INCREASE
YOUR CONFIDENCE AND LEADERSHIP COURAGE.

VISION

My observation over the last twenty years has been that all effective leaders have a vision of what they must accomplish. That vision becomes the energy behind every effort and the force that pushes through all the problems. With vision, the leader is on a mission and a contagious spirit is felt among the crowd until others begin to rise alongside the leader. Unity is essential for the dream to be realized. Long hours of labor are given gladly to accomplish the goal. Individual rights are set aside because the whole is much more important than the part. Time flies, morale soars upward, heroic stories are told, and commitment is the watchword. Why? Because the leader has a vision!

The word *vision* has perhaps been overused in the last few years. The first goal of many a management workshop is to develop a statement of purpose for the organization. Others will look at you oddly if you cannot recite your organization's purpose by memory and produce a card with the statement of purpose printed on it.

Why all the pressure to develop a purpose for your organization? There are two reasons. First, vision becomes the distinctive, rallying cry of the organization. It is a clear statement in a competitive market that you have an important niche among all the voices clamoring for customers. It is your real reason for existence. Second, vision becomes the new control tool, replacing the 1,000-page manual that is boxy and constrains initiative. In an age when decentralization all the way to the front line is required to survive, the vision is the key that keeps everyone focused.

—*Developing the Leader Within You*

RELY ON VISION INSTEAD OF RULES AND
PROCEDURES TO GUIDE YOU AND YOUR TEAM.

JULY 14

SELF-IMPROVING

We live in a society with destination disease. Too many people want to do enough to "arrive," and then they want to retire. My friend Kevin Myers says it this way: "Everyone is looking for a quick fix, but what they really need is fitness. People who look for fixes stop doing what's right when pressure is relieved. People who pursue fitness do what they should no matter what the circumstances are."

People who are constantly improving themselves make three processes an ongoing cycle in their lives:

1. *Preparation:* Self-improving team players think about how they can improve today—not some far-off time in the future. When they get up in the morning, they ask themselves, *What are my potential learning moments today?* Then they try to seize those moments. At the end of the day, they ask themselves, *What have I learned today that I need to learn more about tomorrow?*

2. *Contemplation:* I recently came across the following statement: "If you study the lives of the truly great individuals who have influenced the world, you will find that in virtually every case, they spent considerable amounts of time alone—contemplating, meditating, listening." Time alone is essential to self-improvement.

3. *Application:* Applying what you've learned is sometimes difficult because it requires change. Most people change only when one of three things happens: they hurt enough that they have to, they learn enough that they want to, or they receive enough that they are able to. Your goal is to keep learning so that you want to change for the better every day.

—*The 17 Essential Qualities of a Team Player*

LEARN SOMETHING NEW TODAY, REFLECT ON WHAT YOU
HAVE LEARNED, AND APPLY IT AS SOON AS POSSIBLE.

BREAKTHROUGH

Every major difficulty you face in life is a fork in the road. You choose which track you will head down, toward breakdown or breakthrough. Dick Biggs, a consultant who helps Fortune 500 companies improve profits and increase productivity, writes that all of us have unfair experiences; as a result, some people merely exist and adopt a "cease and desist" mentality. He continues,

> One of the best teachers of persistence is your life's critical turning points. Expect to experience 3–9 turning points or "significant changes" in your life. These transitions can be happy experiences . . . or unhappy times such as job losses, divorce, financial setbacks, health problems and the death of loved ones. Turning points can provide perspective, which is the ability to view major changes within the larger framework of your lifetime and let the healing power of time prevail. By learning from your turning points, you can grow at a deeper level within your career and life.

If you've been badly hurt, then start by acknowledging the pain and grieving any loss you may have experienced. Then forgive the people involved—including yourself, if needed. Doing that will help you move on. Just think, *today* may be your day to turn the hurts of your past into a breakthrough for the future.

—Failing Forward

DON'T ALLOW ANYTHING FROM YOUR PERSONAL
HISTORY TO KEEP HOLDING YOU HOSTAGE.

JULY 16

THE POWER OF A DREAM

I believe that each of us has a dream placed in the heart. I'm not talking about wanting to win the lottery. That kind of idea comes from a desire to escape our present circumstances, not to pursue a heartfelt dream. I'm talking about a vision deep inside that speaks to the very soul. It's the thing we were born to do. It draws on our talents and gifts. It appeals to our highest ideals. It sparks our feelings of destiny. It is inseparably linked to our purpose in life. The dream starts us on the success journey.

A dream does many things for us:

- A dream gives us direction.
- A dream increases our potential.
- A dream helps us prioritize.
- A dream adds value to our work.
- A dream predicts our future.

Oliver Wendell Holmes noted, "The great thing in this world is not so much where we are but in what direction we are moving." This is also one of the great things about having a dream. You can pursue your dream no matter where you are today. And what happened in the past isn't as important as what lies ahead in the future. As the saying goes, "No matter what a person's past may have been, his future is spotless." You can begin pursuing your dream today!

—*Your Road Map for Success*

DARE TO DREAM AND ACT ON THAT DREAM.

DO THE RIGHT THING

Doing the right thing doesn't come naturally to any of us. As America's first president, George Washington, said, "Few men have virtue enough to withstand the highest bidder." Yet that is what we must do to develop the kind of character that will sustain us.

It's not easy to do the right thing when the wrong thing is expedient. Molière commented, "Men are alike in their promises. It is only in their deeds that they differ. The difference in their deeds is simple: People of character do what is right regardless of the situation."

One way that I've tried to control my natural bent to do wrong is to ask myself some questions (adapted from questions written by business ethicist Dr. Laura Nash):

1. Am I hiding something?
2. Am I hurting anyone?
3. How does it look from the other person's point of view?
4. Have I discussed this face-to-face?
5. What would I tell my child to do?

If you do the right thing—and keep doing it—even if it doesn't help you move ahead with your talent in the short term, it will protect you and serve you well in the long term. Character builds—and it builds you. Or as Dr. Dale Bronner, a board member of my nonprofit organization EQUIP, puts it, "Honesty is not something you do; honesty is who you are."

—*Talent Is Never Enough*

DETERMINE TO DO THE RIGHT THING, EVEN WHEN IT HURTS.

PREPARATION

In 1946, entertainer Ray Charles heard that Lucky Millinder's band was coming to town. Charles managed to arrange an audition, and that excited him. If he could get on with Millinder, he would be in the big time.

When his opportunity came, the young musician played the piano and sang his heart out. Being blind, Charles couldn't see Millinder's reaction to his performance, so when he was finished, Charles waited patiently for his response. Finally he heard the band leader say, "Ain't good enough, kid." Charles went back to his room and cried.

"That was the best thing that ever happened to me," Charles later recalled. "After I got over feeling sorry for myself, I went back and started practicing so nobody would ever say that to me again." No one has. As the saying goes, "You can claim to be surprised once; after that, you're unprepared." Charles's preparation has paid him dividends for more than half a century, and he has played with some of the most talented musicians in the world. Preparation may not guarantee a win, but it sure puts you in position for one.

—*The 17 Essential Qualities of a Team Player*

TO YOUR TALENT, ADD PREPARATION.

BE A CATALYST

How are you when it comes to crunch time on your team? Do you want the ball, or would you rather it was in someone else's hands? If there are more talented and effective catalysts on your team, then you should not want to be the go-to player in a pinch. In those cases, the best thing you can do is get an "assist" by helping to put those people into position to benefit the team. But if you avoid the spotlight because you are afraid or because you haven't worked as hard as you should to improve yourself, then you need to change your mind-set.

Start to put yourself on the road to improvement by doing the following things:

- *Find a mentor.* Players become catalysts only with the help of people better than themselves. Find someone who makes things happen to help you along the way.
- *Begin a growth plan.* Put yourself on a program that will help you develop your skills and talents. You cannot take the team to a higher level if you haven't gotten there.
- *Get out of your comfort zone.* You won't know what you're capable of until you try to go beyond what you've done before.

If you follow these three guidelines, you still may not become a catalyst, but you will at least become the best you can be—and that's all that anyone can ask of you.

—*The 17 Indisputable Laws of Teamwork*

TAKE ONE OF THESE STEPS TOWARD GROWTH TODAY.

DISCOVER PEOPLE'S TRUE STRENGTHS

M ost people do not discover their strengths on their own. They often get drawn into the routine of day-to-day living and simply get busy. They rarely explore their strengths or reflect on their successes or failures. That's why it is so valuable for them to have a leader who is genuinely interested in them help them to recognize their strengths.

There are many helpful tools available that you can use to aid people in the process of self-discovery. Marcus Buckingham and Donald O. Clifton's book *Now, Discover Your Strengths* and the Strengths Finder material on their Web site can be helpful. So can personality tests such as DISC or Myers-Briggs. And there are many vocational tests as well. Whatever works in the context of your organization can be helpful. But don't limit yourself to tests. Often the most valuable help you can give will be based on your personal observations.

—The 360° Leader

COMMIT TO HELPING YOUR PEOPLE
RECOGNIZE THEIR STRENGTHS.

SHARE A SECRET WITH SOMEONE

A Sicilian proverb says, "Only the spoon knows what is stirring in the pot." When you allow another person to know what is stirring within you, giving him a "taste" of a plan or idea, you instantly make a meaningful connection with him. Who doesn't want to know what's going on in the mind of someone they care about?

You might think that sharing a secret with someone always has to be a big deal with life-changing ramifications. It doesn't. Of course, when you let people in on something impacting, it makes quite an impression. But you can make sharing a secret part of your everyday life using everyday things. The first time you share something with others, aren't you sharing something that has been secret up to that moment? Why not let the person to whom you're talking know that you're revealing it for the first time? That makes him feel special.

Sharing a secret with someone is really a matter of two things: reading the context of a situation and desiring to build up the other person. If you do those two things, you can learn this skill.

—25 Ways to Win with People

SHARE WHAT'S STIRRING WITHIN YOU TODAY
TO MAKE A MEANINGFUL CONNECTION.

ARE YOU A SPLATTER OR BOUNCER?

If only life could become easier with every day of living! But that's not reality, is it? As you get older, truly some things get harder, but others also get easier. In every stage of life, there are good aspects and bad. The key is to focus on the good and learn to live with the bad. Of course, not everyone does that. In fact, I've found that there are really only two kinds of people in this world when it comes to dealing with discouragement: splatters and bouncers. When splatters hit rock bottom, they fall apart, and they stick to the bottom like glue. On the other hand, when bouncers hit bottom, they pull together and bounce back.

Paul J. Meyer, founder of the Success Motivation Institute, says, "Ninety percent of those who fail are not actually defeated. They simply quit." That's what discouragement can do to you if you don't handle it the right way—it can cause you to quit. Since you *will* become discouraged at some point, the question is, *Are you going to give up or get up?*

—*The Difference Maker*

MAKE THE DECISION TO GET UP AND BOUNCE BACK TODAY.

PASSION INCREASES WILLPOWER

One of my roles as a motivational teacher is to try to help people reach their potential. For years, I tried to inspire passion in audiences by going about it the wrong way. I used to tell people about what made me passionate, what made me want to get out and do my best. But I could see that it wasn't having the effect I desired—people just didn't respond. I couldn't ignite others' passion by sharing my own.

I decided to change my focus. Instead of sharing my passion, I started helping others discover their passion. To do that, I ask these questions:

+ What do you sing about?
+ What do you cry about?
+ What do you dream about?

The first two questions speak to what touches you at a deep level today. The third answers what will bring you fulfillment tomorrow. The answers to these questions can often help people discover their true passion.

While everybody can possess passion, not everyone takes the time to discover it. And that's a shame. Passion is fuel for the will. Passion turns your have-to's into want-to's. What we accomplish in life is based less on what we want and more on how much we want it. The secret to willpower is what someone once called *wantpower*. People who want something enough usually find the willpower to achieve it.

You can't help people become winners unless they want to win. Champions become champions from within, not from without.

—Talent Is Never Enough

ASK PEOPLE ON YOUR TEAM WHAT
THEY SING, CRY, AND DREAM ABOUT.

GIVE PEOPLE THE BENEFIT OF THE DOUBT

When you were a child, perhaps you were taught the Golden Rule: "Do unto others as you would have them do unto you." I've often found that when my intentions were right but my action turned out wrong, I wanted others to see me in light of the Golden Rule. In other words, I wanted others to give me the benefit of the doubt. Why shouldn't I try to extend the same courtesy to others?

Frank Clark commented, "What great accomplishments we would have in the world if everybody had done what they intended to do." While I'd agree that's true, I'd also add, "What great relationships we would have if everybody was appreciated for what they intended to do—in spite of what they may have done." When you give someone the benefit of the doubt, you are following the most effective interpersonal rule that has ever been written.

—25 Ways to Win with People

GIVE SOMEONE THE BENEFIT OF THE DOUBT TODAY.

FIVE-STEP PROCESS OF TRAINING

The best type of training takes advantage of the way people learn. I have found the best training method to be a five-step process:

Step 1: I model. The process begins with my doing the tasks while the person being trained watches. When I do this, I try to give the person an opportunity to see me go through the whole process. When people see the task performed correctly and completely, it gives them something to try to duplicate.

Step 2: I mentor. I continue to perform the task, but this time the person I'm training comes alongside me and assists in the process. I also take time to explain not only the *how* but also the *why* of each step.

Step 3: I monitor. The trainee performs the task and I assist and correct. It's especially important during this phase to be positive and encouraging. Work with him until he develops consistency. Once he's gotten down the process, ask him to explain it to you.

Step 4: I motivate. I take myself out of the task at this point and let the trainee go. My task is to make sure he knows how to do it without help and to keep encouraging him. At this time the trainee may want to make improvements to the process. Encourage him to do it, and at the same time learn from him.

Step 5: I multiply. This is my favorite part of the whole process. Once the new leaders do the job well, it becomes their turn to teach others how to do it. As teachers know, the best way to learn something is to teach it.

—*Developing the Leaders Around You*

FOLLOW THE FIVE-STEP TRAINING
PROCESS WITH SOMEONE TODAY.

GET OVER YOURSELF

M any people believe that touching the lives of others can be done only by some elite group of specially gifted people. But that's not the case. Any ordinary person can make a positive impact on the lives of others.

Some unsuccessful people tell themselves that as soon as they achieve considerable success or discover some unseen talent, they will turn their attention to making a difference in the lives of others. But I have news for them. Many people who struggle with chronic failure do so *because* they think of no one but themselves. They worry about what other people think of them. They scramble to make sure no one gets the better of them. They continually focus on protecting their turf.

If you continually focus all your energy and attention on yourself, I have a message for you: *Get over yourself—everyone else has.*

If you have a history of repeated failure *and* you dedicate most of your time and energy to looking out for number one, you may need to learn a new way of thinking—where others come first.

—*Failing Forward*

IN WHAT WAY MUST YOU GET OVER YOURSELF
TO PUT YOUR FOCUS ON OTHERS?

TELL LEADERS WHAT THEY *NEED* TO HEAR

Because of their intuition, good leaders often see more than others see, and they see things before others do. Why? Because they see everything from a leadership bias. But if the organization they lead gets large, they often lose their edge. They become disconnected. What is the remedy to this problem? They ask the people in their inner circle to see things for them.

Most good leaders want the perspective of people they trust. Sales expert Burton Bigelow said, "Very few big executives want to be surrounded by 'yes' men. Their greatest weakness often is the fact that 'yes' men build up around the executive a wall of fiction, when what the executive wants most of all is plain facts."

One of the ways to become a person whom leaders trust is to tell them the truth. If you've never spoken up to your leaders and told them what they need to hear, then it will take courage. As World War II general and later president Dwight D. Eisenhower said, "A bold heart is half the battle." But if you are willing to speak up, you can help your leaders and yourself. Start small and be diplomatic. If your leader is receptive, become more frank over time. If you get to the point where your leader is not only willing to hear from you but actually wants your perspective, then remember this: Your job is to be a funnel, not a filter. Be careful to convey information without "spinning" it. Good leaders want the truth—even if it hurts.

—*The 360° Leader*

HAVE A BOLD HEART, START SMALL, AND DIPLOMATICALLY
BEGIN TELLING YOUR LEADER WHAT HE NEEDS TO HEAR.

GETTING A GOOD READ ON THINGS

People born with natural leadership ability are especially strong in the area of leadership intuition. Others have to work hard to develop and hone it. But either way, intuition comes from two things: the combination of natural ability, which comes in a person's areas of strength, and learned skills. It is an informed intuition, and it causes leadership issues to jump out to a leader in a way that they don't with others.

Leaders are readers of their situation. In all kinds of circumstances, leaders pick up on details that might elude others. They don't need to sift through stats, read reports, or examine a balance sheet. They know the situation *before* they have all the facts.

Leaders are readers of their resources. Leaders focus on mobilizing people and leveraging resources to achieve their goals rather than on using their own individual efforts.

Leaders are readers of trends. Intuitive leaders can "smell out" when something is happening, when conditions are changing, and when trouble or opportunity is coming. They can look years, even decades ahead.

Leaders are readers of people. Reading people is perhaps the most important intuitive skill leaders can possess. After all, if what you are doing doesn't involve people, it's not leadership. And if you aren't persuading people to follow, you aren't really leading.

Leaders are readers of themselves. Leaders must know not only their own strengths and blind spots, skills and weaknesses, but also their current state of mind. Why? Because leaders can hinder progress just as easily as they can help create it.

—*The 21 Irrefutable Laws of Leadership*

WHAT DO YOU NEED TO LEARN TO READ BETTER
TO IMPROVE YOUR LEADERSHIP INTUITION?

LEADERSHIP THAT'S REWARDING

Educational psychologist E. L. Thorndyke did work in behavior modification around the turn of the century. It led him to discover what he called the Law of Effect. Simply stated, it is this: "Behaviors immediately rewarded increase in frequency; behaviors immediately punished decrease in frequency."

Several years ago I developed a list of behaviors and qualities that I expect from the people in my organization, and I determined to reward those behaviors. I call it the RISE program:

> Rewards
> Indicating
> Staff
> Expectations

In other words, I decided to give rewards to staff members to indicate they were meeting or exceeding expectations. The qualities I value most highly and reward are a positive attitude, loyalty, personal growth, leadership reproduction, and creativity. Notice that personal growth is on the list. You will find that once you set up a positive reward system for achieving the right goals, your people will become their own best managers, and they will develop as leaders.

—Developing the Leaders Around You

REWARD YOUR PEOPLE ACCORDING TO
THE QUALITIES YOU VALUE.

GIVING THE TEAM A HEAD START

In essence, leadership is like a running head start for the team. Leaders see farther than their teammates. They see things more quickly than their teammates. They know what's going to happen and can anticipate it. As a result, they get the team moving in the right direction ahead of time, and for that reason, the team is in a position to win. Even an average runner can win a 100-meter race against a world-class sprinter if he has a 50-meter head start.

The greater the challenge, the greater the need for the many advantages that leadership provides. And the more leaders a team develops, the greater the edge from leadership.

The edge gained from good leadership is quite evident in sports, but the power of leadership carries over into every field. The business that is run by a top-notch leader often finds its market niche first and outperforms its rivals, even if the rivals possess greater talent. The nonprofit organization headed by strong leaders recruits more players, equips them to lead, and serves a greater number of people as a result. Even in a technical area such as engineering or construction, leadership is invaluable in ensuring the team is successful.

— The 17 Indisputable Laws of Teamwork

TRAIN PLAYERS ON THE TEAM TO BECOME BETTER LEADERS.

MANAGE YOUR WORDS

David McKinley, a 360-Degree Leader in a large organization in Plano, Texas, told me a story about something that happened in his first job after graduate school. He was preparing to make an important call on someone, and he decided that he should ask the top leader to go with him. When they got there, David, in his enthusiasm, just wouldn't stop talking. He didn't give his leader a chance to do anything but watch until the very end of their visit.

As they returned to the car, David's boss told him, "I might as well have stayed at the office." He went on to explain how his presence was superfluous. David told me, "I learned a huge lesson that day about staying 'in bounds' when I was with the senior leader. His honest counsel and correction strengthened our relationship and has served me well throughout my life." If you have something worthwhile to say, say it briefly and well. If you don't, sometimes the best thing to do is remain silent.

—*The 360° Leader*

KNOW WHEN TO SPEAK UP AND WHEN TO OBSERVE.

AUGUST

INTEGRITY IS A HARD-WON ACHIEVEMENT

Integrity is not a given factor in everyone's life. It is a result of self-discipline, inner trust, and a decision to be relentlessly honest in all situations in our lives. Unfortunately in today's world, strength of character is a rare commodity. As a result, we have few contemporary models of integrity. Our culture has produced few enduring heroes, few models of virtue. We have become a nation of imitators, but there are few leaders worth imitating.

The meaning of integrity has been eroded. Drop the word into conversations in Hollywood, on Wall Street, even on Main Street, and you'll get blank stares in return. For most Americans, the word conjures up ideas of prudishness or narrow-mindedness. In an age when the meanings of words are manipulated, foundational values such as integrity can be pulverized overnight.

Integrity is antithetical to the spirit of our age. The overarching philosophy of life that guides our culture revolves around a materialistic, consumer mentality. The craving need of the moment supersedes consideration of values that have eternal significance.

Billy Graham said, "Integrity is the glue that holds our way of life together. We must constantly strive to keep our integrity intact.

—Developing the Leader Within You

ARE YOU WILLING TO BE A PERSON
OF INTEGRITY AT ALL COSTS?

AUGUST 2

WORKING IN OBSCURITY

I think very highly of the importance of leadership. I guess that's obvious for a guy whose motto is "Everything rises and falls on leadership." Occasionally someone will ask me about how ego fits into the leadership equation. They'll want to know what keeps a leader from having a huge ego. I think the answer lies in each leader's pathway to leadership. If people paid their dues and gave their best in obscurity, ego is usually not a problem.

One of my favorite examples of this occurred in the life of Moses in the Old Testament. Though born a Hebrew, he lived a life of privilege in the palace of Egypt until he was forty years old. But after killing an Egyptian, he was exiled to the desert for forty years. There God used him as a shepherd and father, and after four decades of faithful service in obscurity, Moses was called to leadership. Scripture says by that time he was the most humble man in the world. Bill Purvis, the senior pastor of a large church in Columbus, Georgia, said, "If you do what you can, with what you have, where you are, then God won't leave you where you are, and He will increase what you have."

English novelist and poet Emily Bronte said, "If I could I would always work in silence and obscurity, and let my efforts be known by their results." Not everyone wants to be out of the spotlight as she did. But it's important for a leader to learn to work in obscurity because it is a test of personal integrity. The key is being willing to do something because it matters, not because it will get you noticed.

—*The 360° Leader*

GIVE YOUR BEST REGARDLESS IF ANYONE IS WATCHING.

FOCUS ON THE PRESENT

Just as you should keep your focus off yesterday, you shouldn't have it on tomorrow. If you're always thinking about tomorrow, then you'll never get anything done today. Your focus needs to remain in the one area where you have some control—today. What's ironic is that if you focus on today, you get a better tomorrow.

I try to do certain things every day to help me in this area. I read daily to grow in my personal life. I listen to others daily to broaden my perspective. I spend time thinking daily to apply what I am learning. And I try to write daily so that I can remember what I've learned. I also try to share those lessons with others. (Today's lessons become tomorrow's books.) Every day I read aloud to myself the daily dozen list from my book *Today Matters* to help me focus and have the right mind-set.

You should do something similar. You can't change yesterday. You can't count on tomorrow. But you can choose what you do today.

—Talent Is Never Enough

GIVE TODAY YOUR FOCUS AND
REAP THE BENEFITS TOMORROW.

BE A PART OF THE VISION

What is the vision for your team? You'd be surprised how many individuals are part of a group that works together but isn't clear about why. For example, that was the case when I became the leader of Skyline Church in the San Diego area. The church's board was comprised of twelve people. When I asked each member to articulate the church's vision the first time we met, I got eight different answers. A team can't move forward in confidence if it has no compass!

As a member of your team, you need a clear understanding of its vision. If the team doesn't have one, then help it to develop one. If the team has already found its compass and course, then you need to examine yourself in light of it to make sure there is a good match. If there isn't, you and your teammates are going to be frustrated. And everyone will probably be best served by a change.

—The 17 Indisputable Laws of Teamwork

ASK YOUR TEAMMATES TO ARTICULATE YOUR ORGANIZATION'S
VISION TO MAKE SURE EVERYONE IS ON THE SAME PAGE.

BECOMING BETTER AND BETTER

There is nothing noble in being superior to someone else; progress is becoming superior to your previous self. Is that something you strive for? Do you try to become better than you were last year, last month, or last week? George Knox was right: "When you cease to be better, you cease to be good."

To become self-improving . . .

Become highly teachable. Pride is a serious enemy of self-improvement. For a month, put yourself in learning roles whenever possible. Instead of talking in meetings when people ask for advice, listen. Tackle a new discipline, even if it makes you feel inadequate. And ask questions anytime you don't understand something. Adopt the attitude of a learner, not an expert.

Plan your progress. Determine how you will learn on two levels. First, pick an area where you want to improve. Plan what books you will read, conferences you will attend, and experts you will interview for the next six months. Second, find learning moments wherever you can every day so that not a day passes without your experiencing improvement of some kind.

Value self-improvement above self-promotion. King Solomon of ancient Israel said, "Let instruction and knowledge mean more to you than silver or the finest gold. Wisdom is worth much more than precious jewels or anything else you desire." Make your next career move based on how it will improve you personally rather than how it will enhance you financially.

—*The 17 Essential Qualities of a Team Player*

WHAT SPECIFICALLY ARE YOU DOING
TO CONTINUALLY GET BETTER?

COMMIT TO PAY THE PRICE FOR CHANGE

American dramatist and screenwriter Sidney Howard remarked, "One half of knowing what you want is knowing what you must give up before you get it." Change always costs you something, if not monetarily, then in time, energy, and creativity. In fact, if change doesn't cost you anything, then it isn't real change!

As you consider how to make the changes needed to improve and grow, it is important to measure the cost of change compared to the cost of the status quo. You have to do your homework. That often makes the difference between:

Change = Growth
and
Change = Grief

What will the changes you desire really cost you?

Management expert Tom Peters gives a perspective on this. He suggests, "Don't rock the boat. Sink it and start over." If you desire to be creative and do something really innovative, that's sometimes what it takes. You must destroy the old to create something new. You cannot allow yourself to be paralyzed by the idea of change.

—*The Difference Maker*

IS WHAT YOU WANT WORTH WHAT
YOU MUST GIVE UP TO GET IT?

PUT THE TEAM FIRST

Great developers of leaders think of the welfare of the team before thinking of themselves. Bill Russell was a gifted basketball player. Many consider him to be one of the best team players in the history of professional basketball. Russell observed, "The most important measure of how good a game I played was how much better I'd made my teammates play." That's the attitude necessary to become a great reproducer of leaders. The team has to come first.

Do you consider yourself to be a team player? Answer each of the following questions to see where you stand when it comes to promoting the good of the team:

1. Do I add value to others?
2. Do I add value to the organization?
3. Am I quick to give away the credit when things go right?
4. Is our team consistently adding new members?
5. Do I use my "bench" players as much as I could?
6. Do many people on the team consistently make important decisions?
7. Is our team's emphasis on creating victories more than
   producing stars?

If you answered no to a few of these questions, you may want to reevaluate your attitude toward the team. It has been said, "The ultimate leader is one who is willing to develop people to the point that they eventually surpass him or her in knowledge and ability." That should be your goal as you multiply your influence by developing leaders.

—Becoming a Person of Influence

DEVELOP A LIFESTYLE OF EMPOWERING
LEADERS. PUT THEM FIRST.

INTEGRITY BUILDS A SOLID REPUTATION

Image is what people think we are. Integrity is what we really are.
Two old ladies were walking around a somewhat overcrowded English
country churchyard and came upon a tombstone. The inscription said:
"Here lies John Smith, a politician and an honest man."

"Good heavens!" said one lady to the other. "Isn't it awful that they
had to put two people in the same grave!"

All of us have known those who were not the same on the outside as
they were inside. Sadly, many who have worked harder on their images
than on their integrity don't understand when they suddenly "fall." Even
friends who thought they knew them are surprised.

Your answers to the following questions will determine if you are into
image-building instead of integrity-building:

- Consistency: Are you the same person no matter who you
  are with?
- Choices: Do you make decisions that are best for others when
  another choice would benefit you?
- Credit: Are you quick to recognize others for their efforts and
  contributions to your success?

Thomas Macauley said, "The measure of a man's real character is
what he would do if he would never be found out." Life is like a vise; at
times it will squeeze us. At those moments of pressure, whatever is inside
will be found out. We cannot give what we do not have. Image promises
much but produces little. Integrity never disappoints.

—Developing the Leader Within You

ARE YOU IMAGE-FOCUSED OR INTEGRITY-FOCUSED?

AUGUST 9

KEEP YOUR EYES OFF THE MIRROR

The Big Picture Principle states, "The entire population of the world
—with one minor exception—is composed of other people." If
you've never thought of life in those terms, then it's time to give it a try.
I've never met a person that truly wins with other people who has not
mastered the ability to keep his eyes off the mirror and serve others with
dignity.

I'm told that psychological research shows that people are better
adjusted and more likely to feel content if they serve others. Serving
others actually cultivates health and brings about happiness. People have
instinctively known that for centuries—even before the science of psychology was formally developed. For example, look at the wisdom (and
humor) found in this Chinese proverb:

> If you want happiness for an hour—take a nap.
> If you want happiness for a day—go fishing.
> If you want happiness for a month—get married.
> If you want happiness for a year—inherit a fortune.
> If you want happiness for a lifetime—help others.

You can actually *help yourself* by helping others. Remember that, and
it will help you to take—and keep—your eyes off the mirror.

—25 Ways to Win with People

OPEN YOUR EYES TO THE PEOPLE
AROUND YOU AND SERVE THEM WELL TODAY.

STOP TAKING YOURSELF TOO SERIOUSLY

In my seminars, I work with a lot of leaders. And I've found that many of them take themselves much too seriously. Of course, they're not alone. I meet people in every walk of life who have too much doom and gloom in their attitudes. They need to lighten up. No matter how serious your work is, that's no reason to take *yourself* seriously.

Most of us think that we are more important than we really are. On the day I die, one of my good pastor friends will give me a wonderful eulogy and tell funny stories about me, but twenty minutes later the most important thing he'll have on his mind will be trying to find the potato salad at my reception.

You need to have a sense of humor about these things—especially if you work with people. Comedian Victor Borge summed it up: "Laughter is the shortest distance between two people."

—Failing Forward

TAKE YOURSELF LESS SERIOUSLY AND RECOGNIZE
THAT LAUGHTER BREEDS RESILIENCE.

A CHECKLIST FOR CHANGE

L aw 19 in *The 21 Irrefutable Laws of Leadership* states, "When to lead is as important as what to do and where to go." I developed the following checklist to help me navigate the process:

+ Will this benefit the followers?
+ Is this change compatible with the purpose of the organization?
+ Is this change specific and clear?
+ Are the top 20 percent (the influencers) in favor of this change?
+ Is it possible to test this change before making a total commitment to it?
+ Are physical, financial, and human resources available to make this change?
+ Is this change reversible?
+ Is this change the next obvious step?
+ Does this change have both short- and long-range benefits?
+ Is the leadership capable of bringing about this change?
+ Does everything else indicate the timing is right?

Before implementing a big change, I run through this checklist and answer each question with a yes or no. If too many questions have a no by them, then I conclude that the timing may not be right.

—The Difference Maker

PAY EXTRA ATTENTION TO TIMING, NOT
JUST MAKING THE RIGHT DECISIONS.

AUGUST 12

BELIEF DETERMINES EXPECTATION

If you want your talent to be lifted to its highest level, then you don't begin by focusing on your talent. You begin by harnessing the power of your mind. Your beliefs control everything you do. Accomplishment is more than a matter of working harder or smarter. It's also a matter of believing positively. Someone called it the "sure enough" syndrome. If you expect to fail, sure enough, you will. If you expect to succeed, sure enough, you will. You will become on the outside what you believe on the inside.

Personal breakthroughs begin with a change in your beliefs. Why? Because your beliefs determine your expectations, and your expectations determine your actions. A belief is a habit of mind in which confidence becomes a conviction that we embrace. In the long run, a belief is more than an idea that a person possesses. It is an idea that possesses a person. You need to expect to succeed. Does that mean you always will? No. You will fail. You will make mistakes. But if you expect to win, you maximize your talent, and you keep trying.

Attorney Kerry Randall said, "Contrary to popular opinion, life does not get better by chance, life gets better by change. And this change always takes place inside; it is the change of thought that creates the better life." Improvement comes from change, but change requires confidence. For that reason, you need to make confidence in yourself a priority. President Franklin Delano Roosevelt asserted, "The only limit to our realization of tomorrow will be our doubts of today." Don't let your doubts cause your expector to expire.

—*Talent Is Never Enough*

HOW ARE YOUR BELIEFS EFFECTING YOUR EXPECTATIONS?

PRIORITIZE YOUR LIFE
ACCORDING TO YOUR PASSION

People who have passion but lack priorities are like individuals who find themselves in a lonely log cabin deep in the woods on a cold snowy night and then light a bunch of small candles and place them all around the room. They don't create enough light to help them see, nor do they produce enough heat to keep them warm. At best, they merely make the room seem a bit more cheerful. On the other hand, people who possess priorities but no passion are like those who stack wood in the fireplace of that same cold cabin but never light the fire. But people who have passion with priorities are like those who stack the wood, light the fire, and enjoy the light and heat that it produces.

In the early 1970s, I realized that my talent would be maximized and my potential realized only if I matched my passion with my priorities. I was spending too much of my time doing tasks for which I possessed neither talent nor passion. I had to make a change—to align what I felt strongly about with what I was doing. It made a huge difference in my life. It didn't eliminate my troubles or remove my obstacles, but it empowered me to face them with greater energy and enthusiasm. For more than thirty years, I have worked to maintain that alignment of priorities and passion. And as I have, I've kept in mind this quote by journalist Tim Redmond, which I put in a prominent place for a year to keep me on track: "There are many things that will catch my eye, but there are only a few that catch my heart. It is those I consider to pursue."

—*Talent Is Never Enough*

MAKE SURE YOUR PASSION AND
PRIORITIES ARE ALIGNED TODAY.

FOCUS ON THE BENEFITS
OF COMPLETING A TASK

It is extremely difficult to be successful if you are forever putting things off. Procrastination is the fertilizer that makes difficulties grow. When you take too long to make up your mind about an opportunity that presents itself, you will miss out on seizing it. To become effective and make progress in your area of talent or responsibility, you can't spend your valuable time on unimportant or unnecessary tasks. So I'm going to make an assumption that if you do procrastinate about a task, it is a necessary one. (If it's not, don't put it off; eliminate it.) To get yourself over the hump, focus on what you'll get out of it if you get it done. Will completing the task bring a financial benefit? Will it clear the way for something else you would *like* to do? Does it represent a milestone in your development or the completion of something bigger? At the very least, does it help to clear the decks for you emotionally? If you seek a positive reason, you are likely to find one.

Once you find that idea, start moving forward and act decisively. U.S. admiral William Halsey observed, "All problems become smaller if you don't dodge them, but confront them. Touch a thistle timidly, and it pricks you; grasp it boldly, and its spines crumble."

— *Talent Is Never Enough*

EITHER ELIMINATE OR ACT UPON THE
THINGS YOU HAVE BEEN PUTTING OFF.

SUCCEEDING WITH DIFFICULT PEOPLE

People working at the bottom of an organization usually have no choice concerning whom they work with. As a result, they often have to work with difficult people. In contrast, people at the top almost never have to work with difficult people because they get to choose who they work with. If someone they work with becomes difficult, they often let that person go or move him or her out.

For leaders in the middle, the road is different. They have some choice in the matter, but not complete control. They may not be able to get rid of difficult people, but they can often avoid working with them. But good leaders—ones who learn to lead up, across, and down—find a way to succeed with people who are hard to work with. Why do they do it? Because it benefits the organization. How do they do it? They work at finding common ground and connect with them. And instead of putting these difficult people in their place, they try to put themselves in their place.

—The 360° Leader

CONNECT WITH DIFFICULT PEOPLE, AND LOOK
FOR REASONS TO LIKE AND RESPECT THEM.

MANAGE YOUR THINKING

Poet and novelist James Joyce said, "Your mind will give back to you exactly what you put into it." The greatest enemy of good thinking is busyness. And middle leaders are usually the busiest people in an organization.

I encouraged readers in *Thinking for a Change* to have a place to think, and I wrote about the "thinking chair" I have in my office. I don't use that chair for anything else other than my think-time. I've discovered since the book's publication that I didn't explain clearly enough how to correctly use the thinking chair. People at conferences told me that they sat in their own thinking chairs and nothing happened. I explain to them that I don't sit in that thinking chair without an agenda, just hoping that a good idea hits me. What I usually do is think about the things I've jotted down because I couldn't think about them during a busy day. I take the list to my chair, put it in front of me, and give each item as much think-time as it needs. Sometimes I'm evaluating a decision I've already made. Sometimes I'm thinking through a decision I will have to make. Sometimes I'm developing a strategy. Other times I'm trying to be creative in fleshing out an idea.

I want to encourage you to try managing your thinking in this way. If you've never done it before, you will be amazed by the payoff. And know this: 1 minute > 1 hour. A minute of thinking is often more valuable than an hour of talk or unplanned work.

—The 360° Leader

CREATE A TIME AND PLACE IN YOUR LIFE FOR THINKING.

DO FOR OTHERS WHAT THEY
CAN'T DO FOR THEMSELVES

A mbassador and poet Henry Van Dyke observed, "There is a loftier ambition than merely to stand high in the world. It is to stoop down and lift mankind a little higher." What a great perspective! Doing for others what they can't do for themselves is really a matter of attitude. I believe that whatever I've been given is to be shared with others. And because I have an abundance mind-set, I never worry about running out myself. The more I give away, the more I seem to get to give away.

No matter how much or how little you think you have, you have the ability to do for others what they cannot do for themselves. Exactly how you do that will depend on your unique gifts, resources, and history.

Nearly twenty-five years ago, Professor C. Peter Wagner of Fuller Seminary invited me to speak to audiences of pastors around the country about leadership. He put me on a national stage for the first time and gave me credibility that I didn't possess on my own.

Few things are of greater value to a prepared person than an opportunity. Why? Because opportunities increase our potential. Demosthenes, the great orator of ancient Greece, said, "Small opportunities are often the beginning of great enterprises." An opportunity seized is often a source of success. Help people win by giving them opportunities, and you will win with them.

—25 Ways to Win with People

PROVIDE OTHERS WITH SMALL OPPORTUNITIES TO SUCCEED,
AND THEN ACKNOWLEDGE AND REWARD THEIR SUCCESS.

AUGUST 18

SOLUTION ORIENTED

M ost people can see problems. That doesn't require any special ability or talent. Someone who thinks in terms of solutions instead of
just problems can be a difference maker. A team filled with people who
possess that mind-set can really get things done.

Your personality type, upbringing, and personal history may affect
how solution oriented you are naturally. However, anyone can become
solution oriented. Consider these truths that all solution-seeking people
recognize:

Problems are a matter of perspective. Obstacles, setbacks, and failures
are simply parts of life. You can't avoid them. But that doesn't mean you
have to allow them to become problems. The best thing you can do is to
meet them with a solution-oriented mind-set. It's just a matter of attitude.

All problems are solvable. Some of the great problem solvers have
been inventors. Charles Kettering explained, "When I was research head
of General Motors and wanted a problem solved, I'd place a table outside
the meeting room with a sign: 'Leave slide rules here.' If I didn't do that,
I'd find someone reaching for his slide rule. Then he'd be on his feet
saying, 'Boss, you can't do it.'" Kettering believed all problems were
solvable, and he helped to cultivate that attitude in others. If you want to
be solution oriented, then you must be willing to cultivate that attitude
in yourself too.

Problems either stop us or stretch us. Problems either hurt you or help
you. Depending on how you approach them, they'll stop you from suc-
ceeding or stretch you so that you not only overcome them, but also
become a better person in the process. The choice is yours.

—*The 17 Essential Qualities of a Team Player*

Do problems stop or stretch you?

JUST PRACTICING

In *The 17 Indisputable Laws of Teamwork*, I wrote about pioneer aviator Charles Lindbergh, mentioning that even his solo flight across the Atlantic Ocean was really a team effort, since he had the backing of nine businessmen from St. Louis and the help of the Ryan Aeronautical Company, which built his plane. But that doesn't take away from his personal effort. For more than thirty-three hours, he flew alone and covered an incredible 3,600 miles.

That's not the kind of task a person just goes out and does. He has to work up to it. How did Lindbergh do that? A story from his friend Frank Samuels gives insight into the process. In the 1920s, Lindbergh used to fly mail out of St. Louis. Occasionally he would go out to San Diego to check on the progress of his plane, the Spirit of St. Louis, which was being built there. Samuels sometimes went along with him, and the two men would stay overnight in a small hotel there. One night Samuels woke up shortly after midnight and noticed that Lindbergh was sitting by the window looking at the stars. It had been a long day, so Samuels asked, "Why are you sitting there at this hour?"

"Just practicing," answered Lindbergh.

"Practicing what?" asked Samuels.

"Staying awake all night."

When he could have been enjoying a well-deserved rest, Lindbergh was putting forth the effort to improve himself. It's an investment that paid off for him—and it can do the same thing for you.

—The 17 Essential Qualities of a Team Player

WHAT ARE YOU GIVING UP IN ORDER TO IMPROVE YOURSELF?

THE RIGHT PICTURE OF SUCCESS

The picture of success isn't the same for any two people because we're all created differently as unique individuals. But the process is the same for everyone. It's based on principles that do not change. After more than twenty-five years of knowing successful people and studying the subject, I have developed the following definition of success:

Success is . . .
- Knowing your purpose in life,
- Growing to reach your maximum potential, and
- Sowing seeds that benefit others.

You can see by this definition why success is a journey rather than a destination. No matter how long you live or what you decide to do in life, you will never exhaust your capacity to grow toward your potential or run out of opportunities to help others. When you see success as a journey, you'll never have the problem of trying to "arrive" at an elusive final destination. And you'll never find yourself in a position where you have accomplished some final goal, only to discover that you're still unfulfilled and searching for something else to do.

Another benefit of focusing on the journey of success instead of on arriving at a destination or achieving a goal is that you have the potential to become a success *today*. The very moment that you make the shift to finding your purpose, growing to your potential, and helping others, successful is something you *are right now*, not something you vaguely hope one day to be.

–Your Road Map for Success

HAVE YOU BEEN VIEWING SUCCESS AS
A DESTINATION OR A JOURNEY?

PUT OTHERS FIRST IN YOUR THINKING

When you meet people, is your first thought about what they'll think of you or how you can make them feel more comfortable? At work, do you try to make your coworkers or employees look good, or are you more concerned about making sure that you receive your share of the credit? When you interact with family members, whose best interests do you have in mind? Your answers show where your heart is. To add value to others, you need to start putting others ahead of yourself in your mind and heart. If you can do it there, you will be able to put them first in your actions.

But how can anyone add value to others if he doesn't know what they care about? Listen to people. Ask them what matters to them. And observe them. If you can discover how people spend their time and money, you'll know what they value.

Once you know what matters to them, do your best to meet their needs with excellence and generosity. Offer your best with no thought toward what you might receive in return. President Calvin Coolidge believed that "no enterprise can exist for itself alone. It ministers to some great need, it performs some great service, not for itself, but for others; or failing therein it ceases to be profitable and ceases to exist."

—Failing Forward

PUT OTHERS AHEAD OF YOU IN
YOUR MIND AND HEART TODAY.

BREAK LARGE TASKS
DOWN INTO SMALLER ONES

Many times large tasks overwhelm people, and that's a problem because overwhelmed people seldom initiate. Here's how I suggest you proceed in breaking an intimidating goal into more manageable parts:

Divide it by categories. Most large objectives are complex and can be broken into steps for functions. Begin by figuring out what skill sets will be required to accomplish the smaller tasks.

Prioritize it by importance. Don't be driven by urgency. When the urgent starts driving you instead of the important, you lose any kind of initiative edge, and instead of activating your talent, it robs you of the best opportunities to use it.

Order it by sequence. Dividing the task according to its categories helps you to understand *how* you will need to accomplish it. Prioritizing by importance helps you to understand *why* you need to do each part of it. Ordering by sequence helps you to know *when* each part needs to be done. Create a timetable, give yourself deadlines, and stick to them.

Assign it by abilities. Very specifically answer the *who* question. As a leader, I can tell you that the most important step in accomplishing something big is determining who will be on the team. Assign tasks to winners and give them authority and responsibility, and the job will get done.

Accomplish it by teamwork. Even if you break a task down, strategically plan, and recruit great people, you still need one more element to succeed. Everyone has to be able to work together. Teamwork is the glue that can bring it all together.

—*Talent Is Never Enough*

BREAK DOWN AN INTIMIDATING GOAL
TODAY TO MAKE IT MANAGEABLE.

INITIATIVE

A re you an initiator? Are you constantly on the lookout for opportunity, or do you wait for it to come to you? Are you willing to take steps based on your best instincts? Or do you endlessly analyze everything? Former Chrysler chairman Lee Iacocca said, "Even the right decision is the wrong decision if it is made too late."

To improve your initiative, do the following:

Change your mind-set. If you lack initiative, recognize that the problem comes from the inside, not from others. Determine why you hesitate to take action. Does risk scare you? Are you discouraged by past failures? Do you not see the potential that opportunity offers? Find the source of your hesitation, and address it. You won't be able to move forward on the outside until you can move forward on the inside.

Don't wait for opportunity to knock. Opportunity doesn't come to the door knocking. You've got to go out and look for it. Take stock of your assets, talents, and resources. Doing that will give you an idea of your potential. Now, spend every day for a week looking for opportunities. Where do you see needs? Who is looking for expertise you have? What unreached group of people is practically dying for what you have to offer? Opportunity is everywhere.

Take the next step. It's one thing to see opportunity. It's another to do something about it. As someone once quipped, everyone has a great idea in the shower. But only a few people step out, dry off, and do something about it. Pick the best opportunity you see, and take it as far as you can. Don't stop until you've done everything you can to make it happen.

—*The 21 Indispensable Qualities of a Leader*

HELP YOUR TEAM TO SEIZE AN OPPORTUNITY TODAY.

ASK YOURSELF, *AM I REALLY TEACHABLE?*

All the good advice in the world won't help if you don't have a teachable spirit.

To know whether you are *really* open to new ideas and new ways of doing things, answer the following questions:

1. Am I open to other people's ideas?
2. Do I listen more than I talk?
3. Am I open to changing my opinion based on new information?
4. Do I readily admit when I am wrong?
5. Do I observe before acting on a situation?
6. Do I ask questions?
7. Am I willing to ask a question that will expose my ignorance?
8. Am I open to doing things in a way I haven't done before?
9. Am I willing to ask for directions?
10. Do I act defensive when criticized, or do I listen openly for the truth?

If you answered no to one or more of these questions, then you have room to grow in the area of teachability. Remember the words of John Wooden: "Everything we know we learned from someone else!"

—Talent Is Never Enough

SOFTEN YOUR ATTITUDE, LEARN HUMILITY,
AND REMAIN TEACHABLE TODAY.

AUGUST 25

FOCUS ON THE BIG PICTURE

On an October evening in 1968, a group of die-hard spectators remained in Mexico City's Olympic Stadium to see the last finishers of the Olympic marathon. More than an hour before, Mamo Wolde of Ethiopia had won the race to the exuberant cheers of onlookers. But as the crowd watched and waited for the last participants, it was getting cool and dark.

It looked as if the last runners were finished, so the remaining spectators were breaking up and leaving when they heard the sounds of sirens and police whistles coming from the marathon gate into the stadium. And as everyone watched, one last runner made his way onto the track for the last lap of the twenty-six-mile race. It was John Stephen Akhwari from Tanzania. As he ran the 400-meter circuit, people could see that his leg was bandaged and bleeding. He had fallen and injured it during the race, but he hadn't let it stop him. The people in the stadium rose and applauded until he reached the finish line.

As he hobbled away, he was asked why he had not quit, injured as he was and having no chance of winning a medal. "My country did not send me to Mexico City to start the race," he answered. "They sent me to finish the race."

Akhwari looked beyond the pain of the moment and kept his eye on the big picture of why he was there. As you make the success journey, keep in mind that your goal is to finish the race—to do the best you're capable of doing.

—Your Road Map for Success

BE MORE THAN JUST A RACER TODAY. BE A FINISHER.

AUGUST 26

MAKE SOME INTRODUCTIONS

My dad, Melvin Maxwell, has done many incredible things for me during the course of my life. One of the things that impacted me most was his introducing me to great men. As a teenager, I met Norman Vincent Peale, E. Stanley Jones, and other exceptional men of the faith. And because I had declared my intention to go into the ministry, my father asked these preachers to pray for me. I can't express in words what that did for me.

Today, I am often in a position to do for others what my father did for me. I love introducing young people to my heroes. I love helping people make business contacts. There are often times when I meet someone, and as we talk, it just hits me: I need to introduce this person to so-and-so. That can mean walking somebody across the room, making a phone call on his or her behalf, or arranging a meeting. Several years ago, I was talking to Anne Beiler, the founder of Auntie Anne's, the pretzel company, and she mentioned in passing that Chick-fil-A's founder, Truett Cathy, was one of her heroes. Since I knew Truett, I offered to introduce them to each other. I hosted a dinner party for them at my house, and it was a great night.

Please don't get the impression that you have to know someone famous to help others in this area. Sometimes it's as simple as introducing one friend to another or one business associate to another. Just make connections. Be the bridge in people's relationships with others.

—25 Ways to Win with People

CREATE A RELATIONAL BRIDGE FOR SOMEONE TODAY.

AUGUST 27

LEADERS PUSH BOUNDARIES

People are trained to follow rules from the time they are kids: *Stand in line. Do your homework. Put your hand up to ask a question.* Most rules are good because they keep us from living in chaos. And most processes are governed by rules. You drop a brick from a second-story window, and you know it's going to fall to the ground. You forget to place the order for office supplies, and you run out of staples. It's simple cause and effect.

Managers often rely on rules to make sure the processes they oversee stay on track. In fact, self-management is basically having the discipline to follow through with the rules you set for yourself. But to move beyond management, you have to learn to think outside the box.

Leaders push boundaries. They desire to find a better way. They want to make improvements. They like to see progress. All these things mean making changes, retiring old rules, inventing new procedures. Leaders are constantly asking, "Why do we do it this way?" and saying, "Let's try this." Leaders want to take new territory, and that means crossing boundaries.

—*The 360° Leader*

DON'T BE AFRAID TO BREAK WITH TRADITION
IN ORDER TO ACHIEVE PROGRESS.

INTEGRITY

Integrity is not what we do so much as who we are. And who we are, in turn, determines what we do. Our system of values is so much a part of us we cannot separate it from ourselves. It becomes the navigating system that guides us. It establishes priorities in our lives and judges what we will accept or reject.

We are all faced with conflicting desires. No one, no matter how "spiritual," can avoid this battle. Integrity is the factor that determines which desire will prevail. We struggle daily with situations that demand decisions between what we want to do and what we ought to do. Integrity establishes the ground rules for resolving these tensions. It determines who we are and how we will respond before the conflict even appears. Integrity welds what we say, think, and do into a whole person so that permission is never granted for one of those to be out of sync.

Integrity binds our person together and fosters a spirit of contentment within us. It will not allow our lips to violate our hearts. When integrity is the referee, we will be consistent; our beliefs will be mirrored by our conduct. There will be no discrepancy between what we appear to be and what our family knows we are, whether in times of prosperity or adversity.

Integrity is not only the referee between conflicting desires. It is the pivotal point between a happy person and a divided spirit. It frees us to be whole persons no matter what comes our way.

—Developing the Leader Within You

ALLOW YOUR INTEGRITY TO BE THE REFEREE
IN YOUR PERSONAL DECISION-MAKING PROCESS.

AUGUST 29

A WILLINGNESS TO PAY THE PRICE

Time after time, success comes down to sacrifice—willingness to pay the price. The same is true of a winning team. Each member of the team must be willing to sacrifice time and energy to practice and prepare, and to be held accountable. He must be willing to sacrifice his own desires. He must be willing to give up part of himself for the team's success.

It all comes down to the desire and dedication of the individuals on the team. It's as true in business as it is in sports. It's even true in war. In an interview with David Frost, General Norman Schwarzkopf, commander of the Allied forces in the Gulf War, was asked, "What's the greatest lesson you've learned out of all this?" He replied:

> I think that there is one really fundamental military truth. And that's that you can add up the correlation of forces, you can look at the number of tanks, you can look at the number of airplanes, you can look at all these factors of military might and put them together. But unless the soldier on the ground, or the airman in the air, has the will to win, has the strength of character to go into battle, believes that his cause is just, and has the support of his country . . . all the rest of that stuff is irrelevant.

Without each person's conviction that the cause is worth the price, the battle will never be won, and the team will not succeed. There must be commitment.

—Developing the Leaders Around You

ARE YOU COMMITTED ONLY WHEN IT IS
COMFORTABLE, OR ARE YOU WILLING TO PAY
THE PRICE TO HELP YOUR TEAM SUCCEED?

AUGUST 30

DON'T UNDERESTIMATE THE PROCESS

I teach leadership to thousands of people each year at numerous conferences. And one of my deepest concerns is always that some people will go home from the event and nothing will change in their lives. They enjoy the "show" but fail to implement any of the ideas presented to them. I tell people continually: We overestimate the event and underestimate the process. Every fulfilled dream occurred because of dedication to a process. (That's one of the reasons I write books and create programs on CD and DVD—so that people can engage in the ongoing *process* of growth.)

People naturally tend toward inertia. That's why self-improvement is such a struggle. But that's also why adversity lies at the heart of every success. The process of achievement comes through repeated failures and the constant struggle to climb to a higher level.

Most people will grudgingly concede that they must make it through some adversity in order to succeed. They'll acknowledge that they have to experience the occasional setback to make progress. But I believe that success comes only if you take that thought one step farther. To achieve your dreams, you must *embrace* adversity and make failure a regular part of your life. If you're not failing, you're probably not really moving forward.

—Failing Forward

USE ADVERSITY TO IMPROVE YOURSELF AND CLIMB HIGHER.

AUGUST 31

BECOMING MORE SELFLESS

If you want to be a contributing member of a successful team, you have to put others on the team ahead of yourself. How are you when it comes to taking a backseat to others? If someone else gets credit for work well done, does it bother you? If you get bumped from the "starting lineup" of your team, do you shout, pout, or tough it out? All of these things are characteristics of selfless players. To become more selfless . . .

Promote someone other than yourself. If you are in the habit of talking up your achievements and promoting yourself to others, determine to keep silent about yourself and praise others for two weeks. Find positive things to say about people's actions and qualities, especially to their superiors, family, and close friends.

Take a subordinate role. Most people's natural tendency is to take the best place and to let others fend for themselves. All day today, practice the discipline of serving, letting others go first, or taking a subordinate role. Do it for a week and see how it affects your attitude.

Give secretly. Writer John Bunyan maintained, "You have not lived today successfully unless you've done something for someone who can never repay you." If you give to others on your team without their knowing, they cannot repay you. Try it. Get in the habit of doing it and you may not be able to stop.

—*The 17 Essential Qualities of a Team Player*

BEGIN CULTIVATING SELFLESSNESS BY CHOOSING ONE
OF THE THREE ACTIONS FROM THE ABOVE LIST TODAY.

SEPTEMBER

SEPTEMBER 1

IF YOUR FRIENDS AREN'T FRIENDS,
MAKE NEW FRIENDS

If the people close to you are dragging you down, then it may be time to make some changes. Speaker Joe Larson remarked, "My friends didn't believe that I could become a successful speaker. So I did something about it. I went out and found me some new friends!"

When you really think about it, the things that matter most in life are the relationships we develop. Remember:

You may build a beautiful house, but eventually it will crumble.
You may develop a fine career, but one day it will be over.
You may save a great sum of money, but you can't take it with you.
You may be in superb health today, but in time it will decline.
You may take pride in your accomplishments, but someone will
surpass you.
Discouraged? Don't be, for the one thing that really matters, lasts
forever—your friendships.

Life is too long to spend it with people who pull you in the wrong direction. And it's too short not to invest in others. Your relationships will define you. And they will influence your talent—one way or the other. Choose wisely.

—*Talent Is Never Enough*

IF THE PEOPLE CLOSE TO YOU AREN'T ADDING VALUE
TO YOUR LIFE, CONSIDER MAKING SOME NEW FRIENDS.

ALLOWING PROBLEMS

There is a world of difference between a person who has a big problem and a person who makes a problem big. For several years I would do between twenty and thirty hours of counseling each week. I soon discovered that the people who came to see me were not necessarily the ones who had the most problems. They were the ones who were problem conscious and found their difficulties stressful. Naïve at first, I would try to fix their problems, only to discover that they would go out and find others.

A study of three hundred highly successful people, people like Franklin Delano Roosevelt, Helen Keller, Winston Churchill, Albert Schweitzer, Mahatma Gandhi, and Albert Einstein, reveals that one-fourth had handicaps, such as blindness, deafness, or crippled limbs. Three-fourths had either been born in poverty, came from broken homes, or at least came from exceedingly tense or disturbed situations.

Why did the achievers overcome problems, while thousands are overwhelmed by theirs? They refused to hold on to the common excuses for failure. They turned their stumbling blocks into stepping-stones. They realized they could not determine every circumstance in life, but they could determine their choice of attitude toward every circumstance.

The *Los Angeles Times* recently ran this quote: "If you can smile whenever anything goes wrong, you are either a nitwit or a repairman." I would add: or a leader in the making—one who realizes that the only problem you have is the one you allow to be a problem because of your wrong reaction to it. Problems can stop you temporarily. You are the only one who can do it permanently.

—*Developing the Leader Within You*

LEARN TO VIEW YOUR PROBLEMS
AS TEMPORARY STUMBLING BLOCKS.

CELEBRATE SUCCESSES

S ometimes people make great strides and aren't even aware of it. Have you ever started to diet or exercise and after a while felt that you were struggling, only to have a friend tell you how good you look? Or haven't you worked on a project and felt discouraged by your progress, but had a friend marvel at what you had accomplished? It is inspiring and makes you want to work that much harder. If you *haven't* had a friend do that for you, then you may need some new friends—people who practice celebrating.

The closer people are to you and the more important the relationship, the more you ought to celebrate. Celebrate early and often with those closest to you—especially with your spouse and children if you have a family. It's usually easy to celebrate victories on the job or in a hobby or sport. But the greatest victories in life are the ones that occur at home.

My friend Dan Reiland says, "A genuine friend encourages and challenges us to live out our best thoughts, honor our purest motives, and achieve our most significant dreams." That's what we need to do with the important people in our lives.

—*Winning with People*

FIND SOMETHING TO CELEBRATE WITH A FRIEND,
COLLEAGUE, OR FAMILY MEMBER TODAY.

LEADERS PUT THE
EMPHASIS ON INTANGIBLES

The things that people can manage are usually tangible and measurable. They provide concrete evidence. You can logically evaluate them before making decisions.

Leadership is really a game of intangibles. What could be more intangible than influence? Leaders deal with things like morale, motivation, momentum, emotions, attitudes, atmosphere, and timing. How do you measure timing before you do something? How do you put your finger on momentum? It's all very intuitive. To gauge such things, you have to read between the lines. Leaders have to become comfortable—more than that, confident—dealing with such things.

Many times the problems leaders face in organizations are not the real problems. For example, let's say a department is $100,000 over budget at the end of the quarter. Their problem isn't a money problem. The deficit is only evidence of the problem. The real problem may be the morale of the sales force, or the timing of a product launch, or the attitude of the department's leader. A leader needs to learn to focus on such things.

—The 360° Leader

FOCUS ON THE INTANGIBLES TODAY. READ BETWEEN
THE LINES AND LOOK FOR THE UNDERLYING ISSUES.

DECIDE WHAT YOU'RE
NOT WILLING TO CHANGE

I have to admit that I'm a personal growth fanatic. There are few things I enjoy more than learning something new. My father got me started when I was a kid. He actually paid me to read books that would help me learn and grow. Now I'm in my late fifties, and I still love it when I can see myself improving in an area I've targeted for growth. But as much as I am dedicated to progress, there are some things that I'm not willing to change—no matter what—such as my faith and my values. I'd rather die than forfeit my faith in God or my commitment to integrity, family, generosity, and belief in people. Some things are not worth compromising at any price.

I want to encourage you to think about the nonnegotiables in your life. What are you willing to live and die for? Once you identify those things, then *everything* else should be open to change.

— *The Difference Maker*

WHAT ARE THE NONNEGOTIABLES IN YOUR LIFE?

LISTENING

Who would you include in a list of the most influential people in the United States? Certainly the president would make that list. You could argue for Bill Gates to be on it. Stop for a moment and think about the people you would include. Now I want you to add a name that you might not have considered: Oprah Winfrey.

In 1985, Winfrey was practically unknown. What success she had achieved could be attributed to her ability to talk. But Winfrey also did more than her share of listening. She is an inveterate learner, and her listening ability got its start as she absorbed the wisdom of writers. She devoured fiction and biographies, learning about how other people feel and think—and in the process she also learned about herself.

That bent toward listening has served her well in every aspect of her career. Its application is obvious for her television show. She is constantly observing and listening to find issues to address on the air. And when she brings celebrities, authors, or experts on her show, she genuinely listens to what they have to say.

Oprah Winfrey's ability to listen has been rewarded with remarkable success and incredible influence. She is the highest paid entertainer in the world and is worth nearly half a billion dollars. Each week, thirty-three million people in the United States alone watch her show.

When was the last time you really paid close attention to people and what they have to say? Do more than just grab onto facts. Start listening not only for words, but also for feelings, meanings, and undercurrents.

—The 21 Indispensable Qualities of a Leader

LISTEN WITH THE PURPOSE OF UNDERSTANDING PEOPLE
TODAY. SEEK TO GAIN KNOWLEDGE FROM THEIR
EXPERIENCE, THEIR PERSPECTIVE, AND THEIR FEELINGS.

SEPTEMBER 7

SHARE COMMON EXPERIENCES

To really connect with others, you have to do more than find common ground and communicate well. You need to find a way to cement the relationship. Joseph F. Newton said, "People are lonely because they build walls instead of bridges." To build bridges that connect you to people in a lasting way, share common experiences with them.

I have enjoyed sharing experiences with others for years. For example, whenever I hire a new member of my executive staff, I always take that person on the road with me to several of my conferences. I do that not only because I want the new staff member to become familiar with the services the company offers to its customers, but also because we can travel together and get to know each other in a wide variety of settings. Nothing bonds people together like racing through impossible traffic in an unfamiliar city to get to the airport and then running with your bags down the concourse to scramble onto a plane at the last minute!

The common experiences you share with others don't have to be that dramatic (although adversity definitely brings people together). Anything you experience together that creates a common history helps to connect you to others.

— Becoming a Person of Influence

TAKE SOMEONE WITH YOU TODAY.

ONCE CONNECTED, MOVE FORWARD

If you want to influence others, and you desire to get them moving in the right direction, you must connect with them before you try to take them anywhere. Attempting to do it before connecting is a common mistake of inexperienced leaders. Trying to move others before going through the connection process with them can lead to mistrust, resistance, and strained relationships. Always remember that you have to share yourself before you try to share the journey. As someone once observed, "Leadership is cultivating in people today, a future willingness on their part to follow you into something new for the sake of something great." Connection creates that willingness.

—*Becoming a Person of Influence*

IDENTIFY SOMEONE ON YOUR TEAM
WITH WHOM YOU NEED TO CONNECT.

GIVE MORE THAN JUST PRAISE

I always encourage leaders to praise people, but you also have to give them more than just praise.

> If you praise them but don't raise them,
>   it won't pay their bills.
> If you raise them but don't praise them,
>   it won't cure their ills.

Talk is cheap—unless you back it up with money. Good leaders take good care of their people. If you really think about it, the people who cost the organization the most aren't the ones who get paid the most. The ones that cost the most are the people whose work doesn't rise to the level of their pay.

When the pay that people receive doesn't match the results they achieve, then they become highly discouraged. If that happens under your watch as a leader, it will not only take a toll on your people's effort, but it will also take a toll on your leadership.

—*The 360° Leader*

MAKE SURE YOU PEOPLE'S PAY
MATCHES THEIR CONTRIBUTION.

FIND THE KEYS TO THEIR HEARTS

In the 1980s, I had the privilege, along with about thirty other leaders, to spend two days with the father of modern management, Peter Drucker. One of the things he said was, "Leading people is like conducting an orchestra. There are many different players and instruments that the conductor must know thoroughly." Drucker challenged us to really know the key players on our team.

Asking a good question is essential to discovering the keys to a person's heart. Through the years, I have developed a list of questions that have helped me in this endeavor time and time again:

"What do you dream about?" You can learn about people's minds by looking at what they have already achieved, but to understand their hearts, look at what they dream of becoming.

"What do you cry about?" When you understand people's pain, you can't help but understand their hearts.

"What do you sing about?" What brings people joy is often a source of their strength.

"What are your values?" When people give you access to their values, know that you have entered the most sacred chambers of their hearts.

"What are your strengths?" Whatever people perceive as their strengths makes their hearts proud.

"What is your temperament?" Learn that, and you often discover the way to their hearts.

Obviously, you don't want your questions to feel like an interview, and you don't need to find out all of the answers in one sitting. The process can be natural while being intentional.

—*25 Ways to Win with People*

GET TO KNOW ONE OF YOUR KEY PLAYERS BETTER TODAY.

ADVERSITY PROMPTS INNOVATION

Early in the twentieth century, a boy whose family had immigrated from Sweden to Illinois sent twenty-five cents to a publisher for a book on photography. What he received instead was a book on ventriloquism. What did he do? He adapted and learned ventriloquism. The boy was Edgar Bergen, and for more than forty years he entertained audiences with the help of a wooden dummy named Charlie McCarthy.

The ability to innovate is at the heart of creativity—a vital component in success. University of Houston professor Jack Matson recognized that fact and developed a course that his students came to call "Failure 101." In it, Matson assigns students to build mock-ups of products that no one would ever buy. His goal is to get students to equate failure with innovation instead of defeat. That way they will free themselves to try new things. "They learn to reload and get ready to shoot again," says Matson. If you want to succeed, you have to learn to make adjustments to the way you do things and try again.

—*Failing Forward*

WHAT "PROBLEM" OR "DEFEAT" HAVE YOU BEEN
DEALT, AND HOW CAN YOU TURN IT INTO AN ASSET?

CONFRONTATION

Confrontation is very difficult for most people. If you feel uneasy just reading the word *confront*, I'd like to suggest that you substitute the word clarify. *Clarify* the issue instead of confronting the person. Then follow these ten commandments.

1. Do it privately, not publicly.
2. Do it as soon as possible. That is more natural than waiting a long time.
3. Speak to one issue at a time. Don't overload the person with a long list of issues.
4. Once you've made a point, don't keep repeating it.
5. Deal only with actions the person can change. If you ask the person to do something he or she is unable to do, frustration builds in your relationship.
6. Avoid sarcasm. Sarcasm signals that you are angry at people, not at their actions, and may cause them to resent you.
7. Avoid words like *always* and *never*. They usually detract from accuracy and make people defensive.
8. Present criticisms as suggestions or questions if possible.
9. Don't apologize for the confrontational meeting. Doing so detracts from it and may indicate you are not sure you had the right to say what you did.
10. Don't forget the compliments. Use what I call the "sandwich" in these types of meetings: Compliment—Confront—Compliment.

—Developing the Leader Within You

HAVE COURAGE AND CONFRONT THE PERSON
YOU HAVE AVOIDED DEALING WITH.

BECOMING MORE SOLUTION ORIENTED

How do you look at life? Do you see a solution in every challenge or a problem in every circumstance? To make yourself a more solution-oriented team player . . .

Refuse to give up. Think about an impossible situation you and your teammates have all but given up overcoming. Now determine not to give up until you find a solution.

Refocus your thinking. No problem can withstand the assault of sustained thinking. Set aside dedicated time with key teammates to work on the problem. Make sure it's prime think time, not leftover time when you're tired or distracted.

Rethink your strategy. Get out of the box of your typical thinking. Break a few rules. Brainstorm absurd ideas. Redefine the problem. Do whatever it takes to generate fresh ideas and approaches to the problem.

Repeat the process. If at first you don't succeed in solving the problem, keep at it. If you do solve the problem, then repeat the process with another problem. Remember, your goal is to cultivate a solution-oriented attitude that you bring into play all the time.

—*The 17 Essential Qualities of a Team Player*

DO YOU SEE A PROBLEM IN EVERY CIRCUMSTANCE
OR A SOLUTION IN EVERY CHALLENGE?

SUPPORT YOUR LEADER'S VISION

When top leaders hear others articulate the vision they have cast for the organization, their hearts sing. It's very rewarding. It represents a kind of tipping point, to use the words of author Malcolm Gladwell. It indicates a level of ownership by others in the organization that bodes well for the fulfillment of the vision.

Leaders in the middle of the organization who are champions for the vision become elevated in the estimation of a top leader. They get it. They're on board. And they have great value. Each time another person in the organization embraces the vision and passes it on, it's like giving the vision "fresh legs." In other words, when the vision gets handed off, the next person is able to run with it.

If you are unsure about the vision of your leader, then talk to him. Ask questions. Once you think you understand it, quote it back to your leader in situations where it's appropriate to make sure you're in alignment. If you've got it right, you will be able to see it in your leader's face. Then start passing it on to the people in your sphere of influence. It will be good for the organization, your people, your leader, and you. Promote your leader's dreams, and he will promote you.

—The 360° Leader

MAKE SURE YOU HAVE CAPTURED YOUR
LEADER'S VISION SO THAT YOU CAN PASS IT ON.

PROBLEMS CAN ADVANCE YOU

A young woman was complaining to her father about her problems and how difficult her life was.

"Come with me," he said. "I want to show you something." He took her into the kitchen where he put three pots of water on the stove to heat. Meanwhile, he cut up some carrots and put them into the first pot to boil. Into the simmering water in the second pot he put two eggs. In the third pot he poured some ground coffee. After a few minutes, he strained the carrots into one bowl, peeled the eggs and put them into another, and into a cup he poured the strained coffee. Then he placed them before his daughter.

"What's all this supposed to mean?" she asked somewhat impatiently.

"Each of these items can teach us something about the way we handle adversity," he answered. "The carrots started out hard, but the boiling water turned them mushy. The eggs went into the water fragile but came out hard and rubbery. The coffee, on the other hand, changed the water into something better."

"Sweetheart," he said, "you can choose how you will respond to your problems. You can let them make you weak. You can let them make you hard. Or you can use them to create something beneficial. It's all up to you."

—The Difference Maker

WHAT WILL YOU MAKE OUT OF YOUR PROBLEMS TODAY?

SIGNIFICANCE OVER SECURITY

Most people enjoy feeling secure. It's a natural desire, one that psychologist Abraham Maslow recognized as important in the hierarchy of human needs. But to keep moving to a higher level and reach your potential, you also have to be willing to bypass another landmark and trade security for significance.

Bob Buford talks about the landmark ability of shifting your attention to significance in his book *Halftime*. As he sees it, our lives naturally break into two halves, with a midpoint usually falling somewhere between ages thirty and fifty. He says, "The first half of life has to do with getting and gaining, learning and earning . . . The second half is more risky because it has to do with living beyond the immediate." And he adds, "If you do not take responsibility for going into halftime and ordering your life so that your second half is better than the first, you will join the ranks of those who are coasting their way to retirement."[1] According to Buford, the key to making your second half count is to make the shift to significance. The result is that you will experience a life of purpose and see the fulfillment of your life's mission.

No matter when you make the change to significance, whether it's during your "halftime" or at some other time of life, know that it is one of the most significant, life-changing steps—and landmarks—on the success journey. It's a decision that's always worth the price.

—Your Road Map for Success

ARE YOU STRIVING TO MAKE A DIFFERENCE,
OR HAVE YOU BEEN COASTING?

PRACTICING RESPONSIBILITY

Holocaust survivor Elie Wiesel, who won the Nobel Peace Prize in 1986, spent the years after his time in the Nazi concentration camps trying to give back to others. One of the questions he asked young people was, "How will you cope with the privileges and obligations society will feel entitled to place on you?" As he tried to guide them, he shared his sense of responsibility to others:

> What I receive I must pass on to others. The knowledge that I have must not remain imprisoned in my brain. I owe it to many men and women to do something with it. I feel the need to pay back what was given to me. Call it gratitude . . . To learn means to accept the postulate that life did not begin at my birth. Others have been there before me, and I walk in their footsteps.

Practicing responsibility will do great things for you. It will strengthen your talent, advance your skills, and increase your opportunities. It will improve your quality of life during the day and help you to sleep better at night. But it will also improve the lives of the people around you.

If you want your life to be a magnificent story, then realize that you are its author. Every day you have the chance to write a new page in that story. I want to encourage you to fill those pages with responsibility to others and yourself. If you do, in the end you will not be disappointed.

—*Talent Is Never Enough*

How are you filling up the pages of your life?

WHERE PEOPLE NEED PATIENCE WITH YOU

Do you know what your shortcomings are? For example, I know that the people closest to me need patience to put up with my idiosyncrasies. Ironically, the first one is putting up with my impatience! (I'm working on that one.) But there are plenty of others. Just for fun, I asked my assistant, Linda Eggers, to give me a list of the areas where she has been longsuffering. It didn't take her long. Here are the top things she mentioned:

- I am constantly losing my cell phone and glasses.
- Anytime we're discussing planning, I want lots of options.
- I am constantly changing my travel plans and needs.
- I overschedule myself, and as a result, projects take longer than the time allotted.
- I hate to say no.
- I want to be able to call her twenty-four hours a day, seven days a week.

I'm sure there are lots more, but that's enough. If I can keep in mind that others are being patient with me in multiple areas, it helps me to remember to be patient with others. Doing that may have a similar effect on you.

—Winning with People

LOOK AT YOUR OWN QUIRKS, IDIOSYNCRASIES, AND ODDITIES
AS A REMINDER TO BE MORE PATIENT WITH OTHERS.

BRING SOMETHING TO THE TABLE

For years I have used the expression "bring something to the table" to describe a person's ability to contribute to a conversation or to add value to others at a meeting. Not everyone does that. In life, some people always want to be the "guest." Wherever they go, they are there to be served, to have their needs met, to be the recipient. Because they possess that attitude, they never bring anything to the table for anyone else. After a while, that can really wear out the person who is always playing host.

As the leader of an organization, I am always looking for people who bring something to the table in the area of ideas. If they can be creative and generate ideas, that's great. But I also highly value people who are constructive, who take an idea that someone puts on the table and make it better. Often the difference between a good idea and a great idea is the value added to it during the collaborative thinking process.

If you always try to bring something of value to the table when you meet with your boss, you may be able to avoid a similar fate at work. If you don't, at the end of the day you just may get a note from the boss. Only yours will be a pink slip.

—The 360° Leader

THE NEXT TIME YOU MEET WITH SOMEONE,
BE SURE TO BRING SOMETHING TO THE TABLE.

DO THINGS TOGETHER AS A TEAM

I once read the statement, "Even when you've played the game of your life, it's the feeling of teamwork that you'll remember. You'll forget the plays, the shots, and the scores, but you'll never forget your teammates." That is describing the community that develops among teammates who spend time doing things together.

The only way to develop community and cohesiveness among your teammates is to get them together, not just in a professional setting but in personal ones as well. There are lots of ways to get yourself connected with your teammates, and to connect them with one another. Many families who want to bond find that camping does the trick. Business colleagues can socialize outside work (in an appropriate way). The where and when are not as important as the fact that team members share common experiences.

— *The 17 Indisputable Laws of Teamwork*

ENCOURAGE YOUR TEAM TO SPEND TIME TOGETHER
TO SHARE AN ENJOYABLE COMMON EXPERIENCE.

DEALING WITH THE BAD APPLE

If you think you have a bad apple on your team, you need to take the person aside and discuss the situation with him. Doing it the right way is important. Take the high road: As you approach him, share what you have observed, but give him the benefit of the doubt. Assume that your perception might be wrong and you want clarification. (If you have several people with bad attitudes, start with the ringleader.) If it truly is your perception and the team is not being hurt, then you haven't done any damage, and you have smoothed the relationship between you and the other person.

However, if it turns out that your perception was correct and the person's attitude is the problem, give him clear expectations and an opportunity to change. Then hold him accountable. If he changes, it's a win for the team. If he doesn't, remove him from the team. You cannot allow him to remain because you can be sure his rotten attitude will ruin the team.

—*The 17 Indisputable Laws of Teamwork*

DEAL WITH ANY BAD APPLES ON YOUR TEAM.

WHEN YOU PARTNER WITH OTHERS

Thomas Jefferson observed, "A candle loses nothing when it lights another candle." That is the real nature of partnership. I find that many people don't think that way. They believe that sharing means losing something. But I don't think that's true.

Every person possesses one of two mind-sets: scarcity or abundance. People with a scarcity mind-set believe that there's only so much to go around, so you have to scrap for everything you can and protect whatever you have at all costs. People with an abundance mind-set believe there's always enough to go around. If you have an idea, share it; you can always come up with another one. If you have money, give some of it away; you can always make more. If you have only one piece of pie, let someone else eat it; you can bake another one.

I believe that in this area, you get from life what you expect. You can hoard what little you have and receive no more. Or you can give what you have, and you will be rewarded with abundance. Your attitude makes the difference. So if you partner with another person and give generously, one way or another you're going to get back more than you gave.

—*Winning with People*

CONSIDER HOW YOUR MIND-SET—OF EITHER SCARCITY
OR ABUNDANCE—IS IMPACTING YOUR LEADERSHIP.

LISTEN WITH YOUR HEART

Herb Cohen, often called the world's best negotiator, says, "Effective listening requires more than hearing the words transmitted. It demands that you find meaning and understanding in what is being said. After all, meanings are not in words, but in people." Many people put their focus on the ideas being communicated, and they almost seem to forget about the person. You can't do that and listen with the heart.

There's a difference between listening passively and listening aggressively. To listen with your heart, your listening has to be active. In his book *It's Your Ship*, Captain Michael Abrashoff explains that people are more likely to speak aggressively than to listen aggressively. When he decided to become an intentional listener, it made a huge difference in him and his team.

—25 Ways to Win with People

CHOOSE TO BE AN AGGRESSIVE LISTENER TODAY.

ADVERSITY MOTIVATES

Nothing can motivate a person like adversity. Olympic diver Pat McCormick discusses this point: "I think failure is one of the great motivators. After my narrow loss in the 1948 trials, I knew how really good I could be. It was the defeat that focused all my concentration on my training and goals." McCormick went on to win two gold medals in the Olympics in Helsinki in 1952 and another two in Melbourne four years later.

If you can step back from the negative circumstances facing you, you will be able to discover their positive benefits. That is almost always true; you simply have to be willing to look for them—and not take the adversity you are experiencing too personally.

If you lose your job, think about the resilience you're developing. If you try something daring and survive, evaluate what you learned about yourself—and how it will help you take on new challenges. If a bookstore gets your order wrong, figure out whether it's an opportunity to learn a new skill. And if you experience a train wreck in your career, think of the maturity it's developing in you. Besides, Bill Vaughan maintains that "in the game of life it's a good idea to have a few early losses, which relieves you of the pressure of trying to maintain an undefeated season." Always measure an obstacle next to the size of the dream you're pursuing. It's all in how you look at it.

—*Failing Forward*

EMBRACE THE ADVERSITIES YOU MAY BE FACING IN YOUR LIFE, AND RETRAIN YOURSELF TO VIEW THEM AS BENEFICIAL.

GROWTH OF PEOPLE =
GROWTH OF COMPANY

People are the principal asset of any company, whether it makes things to sell, sells things made by other people, or supplies intangible services. Nothing moves until your people can make it move. In actual studies of leadership in American business, the average executive spends three-fourths of his working time dealing with people. The largest single cost in most business is people. The largest, most valuable asset any company has is its people. All executive plans are carried out, or fail to be carried out, by people.

According to William J. H. Boetcker, people divide themselves into four classes:

1. Those who always do less than they are told
2. Those who will do what they are told, but no more
3. Those who will do things without being told
4. Those who will inspire others to do things

It's up to you.

As Ralph Waldo Emerson said, "Trust men and they will be true to you: treat them greatly and they will show themselves great."

—Developing the Leader Within You

CULTIVATE AN ENVIRONMENT THAT
INSPIRES YOUR PEOPLE TO DO GREAT THINGS.

IMPROVING YOUR TENACITY

You beat 50 percent of the people in America by working hard," says A. L. Williams. "You beat another 40 percent by being a person of honesty and integrity and standing for something. The last 10 percent is a dogfight in the free enterprise system."

To improve your tenacity:

Work harder and/or smarter. If you tend to be a clock-watcher who never works beyond quitting time no matter what, then you need to change your habits. Put in an additional sixty to ninety minutes of work every day by arriving at work thirty to forty-five minutes early and staying an equal amount of time after your normal hours. If you are someone who already puts in an inordinate number of hours, then spend more time planning to make your working hours more efficient.

Stand for something. To succeed, you must act with absolute integrity. However, if you can add to that the power of purpose, you will possess an additional edge. Write on an index card how your day-to-day work relates to your overall purpose. Then review that card daily to keep your emotional fires burning.

Make your work a game. Nothing feeds tenacity like our natural competitive nature. Try to harness that by making your work a game. Find others in your organization who have similar goals and create a friendly competition with them to motivate you and them.

—*The 17 Essential Qualities of a Team Player*

APPROACH YOUR DAY WITH TENACITY.

SEPTEMBER 27

DEFINING PROBLEMS

Philosopher Abraham Kaplan makes a distinction between problems and predicaments. A problem is something you can do something about. If you can't do something about it, then it's not a problem. It's a predicament. That means it's something that must be coped with, endured.

When people treat a predicament as a problem, they can become frustrated, angry, or depressed. They waste energy. They make bad decisions. And when people treat problems as predicaments, they often settle, give up, or see themselves as victims.

More than twenty-five years ago when I was dealing with some difficult issues, I wrote something to help me see problems in the right light. It became my new "definition" of problems. Maybe it will help you too:

P – predictors: helping to mold our future
R – reminders: showing us that we cannot succeed alone
O – opportunities: pulling us out of ruts, prompting creative thinking
B – blessings: opening doors we would otherwise not go through
L – lessons: providing instruction with each new challenge
E – everywhere: telling us that no one is excluded from difficulties
M – messages: warning us about potential disaster
S – solvable: reminding us that every problem has a solution

If you can separate the predicaments from the problems, then you put yourself in a much better position to deal with the predicaments and to solve the problems.

—The Difference Maker

SEPARATE YOUR PREDICAMENTS FROM YOUR PROBLEMS
TODAY, AND DEAL WITH THEM ACCORDINGLY.

GET TO THE BOTTOM LINE

Playwright Victor Hugo said, "Short as life is, we make it still shorter by the careless waste of time." I haven't met a good leader yet who didn't want to get quickly to the bottom line. Why? Because they want results. Their motto is, "Never mind about the delivery; just show me the baby."

When you first begin working with a leader, you may need to spend some time giving insight into the process by which you came to a decision. Early on in the relationship, you have to earn your credibility. But as time goes by and the relationship builds, just get to the point. Just because you possess all the data needed to explain what you're doing doesn't mean you need to share it. If your leader wants more detail or wants to know about the process you used, she can ask you for it.

—The 360° Leader

PRACTICE GETTING TO THE BOTTOM LINE TODAY

SHARE IDEAS

What is an idea worth? Every product begins with an idea. Every service begins with an idea. Every business, every book, every new invention begins with an idea. Ideas are what make the world move forward. So when you give people an idea, you give them a great gift.

One of the things I love about writing books is the process that it takes me through. It usually starts with a concept that I'm anxious to teach. I get a few ideas down on paper, and then I call together a group of good creative thinkers to help me test the concept, brainstorm ideas, and flesh out the outline. Every time we've done this, people have given me great ideas that I never would have come up with on my own. I have to say I'm very grateful.

One of the things I enjoy most about creative people is that they love ideas, and they always seem to have more coming. The more they give away, the more new ideas they seem to have. Creativity and generosity feed each other. That's one of the reasons I'm never reluctant to share ideas with others. I'm convinced that I will run out of time long before I run out of ideas. It's better to give some away and contribute to another person's success than to have them lying dormant in me.

—25 Ways to Win with People

SURROUND YOURSELF WITH CREATIVE PEOPLE,
AND LET THEIR IDEAS INSPIRE YOUR OWN CREATIVITY.

HOW TO RAISE UP LEADERS
WHO REPRODUCE LEADERS

In an article published by the *Harvard Business Review*, author Joseph Bailey examined what it took to be a successful executive. In conducting his research, he interviewed more than thirty top executives and found that every one of them learned firsthand from a mentor. If you want to raise up leaders who reproduce other leaders, you need to mentor them.

We've been told that in hospital emergency rooms, nurses have a saying: "Watch one, do one, teach one." It refers to the need to learn a technique quickly, jump right in and do it with a patient, and then turn around and pass it on to another nurse. The mentoring process for developing leaders works in a similar way. It happens when you take potential leaders under your wing, develop them, empower them, share with them how to become persons of influence, and then release them to go out and raise up other leaders. Every time you do that, you plant seeds for greater success. And as novelist Robert Louis Stevenson advised, "Don't judge each day by the harvest you reap but by the seeds you plant."

— *Becoming a Person of Influence*

IF YOU ARE NOT ALREADY MENTORING
OTHERS, GET STARTED TODAY.

OCTOBER

TAKE A RISK

In life, there are no safe places or risk-free activities. Helen Keller, author, speaker, and advocate for disabled persons, asserted, "Security is mostly a superstition. It does not exist in nature, nor do the children of men as a whole experience it. Avoiding danger is no safer in the long run than outright exposure. Life is either a daring adventure or nothing."

Everything in life brings risk. It's true that you risk failure if you try something bold because you might miss it. But you also risk failure if you stand still and don't try anything new. G. K. Chesterton wrote, "I do not believe in a fate that falls on men however they act; but I do believe in a fate that falls on them unless they act." The less you venture out, the greater your risk of failure. Ironically, the more you risk failure—and actually fail—the greater your chances of success.

—*Failing Forward*

ARE YOU WILLING TO TAKE A RISK—EVEN FAIL—
TO HAVE A DARING ADVENTURE?

OCTOBER 2

IT'S A MIND-SET

Teachability is an attitude, a mind-set that says, "No matter how much I know (or think I know), I can learn from this situation." That kind of thinking can help you turn adversity into advantage. It can make you a winner even during the most difficult circumstances. Sydney Harris sums up the elements of a teachable mind-set: "A winner knows how much he still has to learn, even when he is considered an expert by others. A loser wants to be considered an expert by others before he has learned enough to know how little he knows."

Business author Jim Zabloski writes,

> Contrary to popular belief, I consider failure a necessity in business. If you're not failing at least five times a day, you're probably not doing enough. The more you do, the more you fail. The more you fail, the more you learn. The more you learn, the better you get. The operative word here is *learn*. If you repeat the same mistake two or three times, you are not learning from it. You must learn from your own mistakes and from the mistakes of others before you.

The ability to learn from mistakes has value not just in business but in all aspects of life. If you live to learn, then you will really learn to live.

— *Failing Forward*

DO YOU THINK YOU HAVE "ARRIVED," OR
DO YOU MAINTAIN AN ATTITUDE OF TEACHABILITY?

PLANNED NEGLECT

William James said that the art of being wise is the "art of knowing what to overlook." The petty and the mundane steal much of our time. Too many of us are living for the wrong things.

Dr. Anthony Campolo tells about a sociological study in which fifty people over the age of ninety-five were asked one question: "If you could live your life over again, what would you do differently?" It was an open-ended question, and a multiplicity of answers constantly reemerged and dominated the results of the study. These were three answers:

- If I had it to do over again, I would reflect more.
- If I had it to do over again, I would risk more.
- If I had it to do over again, I would do more things that would live on after I am dead.

A young concert violinist was asked the secret of her success. She replied, "Planned neglect." Then she explained, "When I was in school, there were many things that demanded my time. When I went to my room after breakfast, I made my bed, straightened the room, dusted the floor, and did whatever else came to my attention. Then I hurried to my violin practice. I found I wasn't progressing as I thought I should, so I reversed things. Until my practice period was completed, I deliberately neglected everything else. That program of planned neglect, I believe, accounts for my success."

—*Developing the Leader Within You*

PUT FIRST THINGS FIRST TODAY AND
NEGLECT THINGS THAT DON'T REALLY MATTER.

OCTOBER 4

ASSISTING OTHERS

Alex Haley, the author of *Roots*, used to keep a picture in his office of a turtle sitting atop a fence. He kept it there to remind him of a lesson he had learned years before: "If you see a turtle on a fence post, you know he had some help." Haley remarked, "Anytime I start thinking, 'Wow, isn't this marvelous what I've done!' I look at that picture and remember how this turtle—me—got up on that post."

Both developed leaders and the people who developed them are like that turtle. They've gotten a lot of help. Their view from the fence post is made possible by others. Through the development process, the new leaders and the developers have value added to their lives.

Adding value to a person is much more than personal promotion or organizational improvement. It is true that people who have been developed get promoted. And it is equally true that organizations improve and expand when they have leaders devoted to the development of others. But adding value is much more than that. It is the enrichment of people's quality of life. It is the expansion of their life purpose and capabilities. People development is life-changing for everyone involved. In *Bringing Out the Best in People*, Alan McGinnis said, "There is no more noble occupation in the world than to assist another human being."

—Developing the Leaders Around You

WHO HAS HELPED YOU UP ONTO THE
"FENCE POST," AND WHO ARE YOU HELPING?

REFOCUS ON THE MISSION

R alph Waldo Emerson observed, "Concentration is the secret of strength in politics, in war, in trade, in short, in all management of human affairs." Where should you focus that concentration? On the mission. And when you make a mistake, don't chase after it. Don't try to defend it. Don't throw good money after it. Just refocus your attention on the mission and then move on. You must always keep your eye on what it is you desire to do. I have yet to meet a person focused on yesterday who had a better tomorrow.

John Foster Dulles, secretary of state in the Eisenhower administration, observed, "The measure of success is not whether you have a tough problem to deal with, but whether it is the same problem you had last year." A problem solved is a springboard to future success, to bigger and better things. The key is to focus on what you are learning, not on what you are losing. If you do that, then you will open the door to future possibilities.

A positive attitude can help you do that. It can help you learn from the present and look to the future. Norman Vincent Peale said, "Positive thinking is how you think about a problem. Enthusiasm is how you feel about a problem. The two together determine what you do about a problem." And that's what really matters in the end.

—*The Difference Maker*

IF YOU HAVE A TOUGH PROBLEM THAT WON'T GO AWAY, CHECK TO MAKE SURE YOUR ATTITUDE ISN'T AT FAULT.

YOUR ATTITUDE INFLUENCES OTHERS

Leadership is influence. People catch our attitudes just like they catch our colds—by getting close to us. One of the most gripping thoughts to ever enter my mind centers on my influence as a leader. It is important that I possess a great attitude, not only for my own success, but also for the benefit of others.

Dr. Frank Crane reminds us that a ball rebounds from the wall with precisely the force with which it was thrown against the wall. There is a law in physics to the effect that action is equal to reaction. The law is also true in the realm of influence. In fact, its effects multiply with a leader's influence. The action of a leader multiplies in reaction because there are several followers. To a smile given, many smiles return. Anger unleashed toward others results in much anger returned from many.

I believe that a leader's attitude is caught by his followers more quickly than his actions. An attitude is reflected by others even when they don't follow the action. An attitude can be expressed without a word being spoken.

The effect of a leader's attitude on others is the main reason for the importance of considering a candidate's attitude when hiring executives. Practicing psychologists list areas needing significant appraisal when employees are being considered for executive promotion: ambition; attitudes toward policy; attitudes toward colleagues; supervisory skills; and attitudes toward excessive demands on time and energy. A candidate who is out of balance in one or more of these areas would be likely to project a negative attitude and, therefore, prove to be a poor leader.

—*Developing the Leader Within You*

MARE SURE YOUR ATTITUDE IS A
POSITIVE INFLUENCE ON YOUR TEAM.

ACCEPT THE FACT THAT
PEOPLE ARE DIFFERENT

I've written in previous books about how, when I was young, I used to believe that everyone ought to be like me in order to be successful. I've matured quite a bit since then. Some of my growth has come as a result of traveling and meeting many kinds of people. Books such as Florence Littauer's *Personality Plus* have also helped me. I've come to realize with time that I've got major gaps in my skills and abilities, as everyone does, and if people with different talents and temperaments work together, we all win and get a lot more done. We also enjoy the journey of life much more.

If you have a healthy self-image, you may fall into the same trap I did. However, you cannot win with people if you secretly harbor the belief that everyone ought to be more like you. Accept that people are different, and celebrate that God made us that way.

—25 Ways to Win with People

APPRECIATE THE DIFFERENCES YOU FIND IN YOUR
COLLEAGUES, FAMILY MEMBERS, AND FRIENDS.

OCTOBER 8

PRACTICE YOUR CRAFT TODAY

William Osler, the physician who wrote *The Principles and Practice of Medicine* in 1892, once told a group of medical students:

> Banish the future. Live only for the hour and its allotted work. Think not of the amount to be accomplished, the difficulties to be overcome, or the end to be attained, but set earnestly at the little task at your elbow, letting that be sufficient for the day; for surely our plain duty is, as Carlyle says, "Not to see what lies dimly at a distance, but to do what lies clearly at hand."

The only way to improve is to practice your craft until you know it inside and out. At first, you do what you know to do. The more you practice your craft, the more you know. But as you do more, you will also discover more about what you ought to do differently. At that point you have a decision to make: Will you do what you have always done, or will you try to do more of what you think you should do? The only way you improve is to get out of your comfort zone and try new things.

People often ask me, "How can I grow my business?" or, "How can I make my department better?" The answer is for you personally to grow. The only way to grow your organization is to grow the leaders who run it. By making yourself better, you make others better. Retired General Electric CEO Jack Welch said, "Before you are a leader, success is all about growing yourself. When you become a leader, success is all about growing others." And the time to start is today.

—*The 360° Leader*

WHAT NEW THING OUTSIDE OF YOUR
COMFORT ZONE WILL YOU ATTEMPT TODAY?

OCTOBER 9

HAVE I ALREADY MADE MY POINT?

Investment expert Warren Buffet said, "Sometimes it's not how hard you row the boat. It's how fast the stream is going." Whenever you're dealing with your leader, you need to pay attention to the flow of the stream.

It is very important to learn to communicate your point of view clearly to your leader. It is your responsibility to communicate what you know and give your perspective on an issue. But it's one thing to communicate and another to coerce your leader. The choice your leader makes is not your responsibility. Besides, if you have made your point clearly, you are unlikely to help your cause by continuing to hammer away at it with your leader. President Dwight D. Eisenhower said, "You do not lead by hitting people over the head—that's assault, not leadership." If you keep repeating yourself after your point's been made, you're just trying to get your own way.

—The 360° Leader

TAKE RESPONSIBILITY FOR YOUR PART TODAY
AND ALLOW OTHERS TO TAKE THEIRS.

A NAVIGATOR STAYS WITH THE PEOPLE

A good navigator takes the trip with the people he is guiding. He doesn't give directions and then walk away. He travels alongside his people as a friend. Author and conference speaker Richard Exley explained his idea of friendship this way: "A true friend is one who hears and understands when you share your deepest feelings. He supports you when you are struggling; he corrects you, gently and with love, when you err; and he forgives you when you fail. A true friend prods you to personal growth, stretches you to your full potential. And most amazing of all, he celebrates your successes as if they were his own."

As you come alongside some of the people within your influence and mentor them, you and they may experience difficult times together. You won't be perfect and neither will they, but just keep in mind Henry Ford's words: "Your best friend is he who brings out the best that is within you." Do your best to follow that objective, and you will help a lot of people.

—Becoming a Person of Influence

NAVIGATE FOR YOUR PEOPLE TODAY
AND BRING OUT THE BEST IN THEM.

DON'T MISS OUT

P eople miss many opportunities for connection and the chance to build deeper relationships because they do not make themselves approachable. And notice that I am purposely using the phrase "make themselves." Approachability has little to do with other people's boldness or timidity. It has everything to do with how you conduct yourself and what messages you send to others.

Years ago I saw a piece called "The Art of Getting Along," which stated,

> Sooner or later, a man, if he is wise, discovers that life is a mixture of good days and bad, victory and defeat, give and take. He learns that it doesn't pay to be a too-sensitive soul, that he should let some things go over his head like water off a duck's back. He learns that he who loses his temper usually loses out, that all men have burnt toast for breakfast now and then, and that he shouldn't take the other fellow's grouch too seriously . . . He learns that most others are as ambitious as he is, that they have brains as good or better, that hard work, not cleverness, is the secret of success. He learns that no man ever gets to first base alone, and that it is only through cooperative effort that we move on to better things. He realizes (in short) that the "art of getting along" depends about 98 percent on his own behavior toward others.

If you want to make yourself agreeable and approachable to others, then you need to put them at ease.

—Winning with People

ARE YOU MAKING YOURSELF APPROACHABLE?

FEAR IS A PART OF PROGRESS

One of the secrets of success is not letting what you cannot do interfere with what you can do. Today I am known most for my public speaking. But when I first started speaking, I wasn't effective. I remember being really fearful. Then when I got the chance to speak at an event as a senior in college, I was terrible. People who knew me then described my speaking style as "stiff." But I kept at it. I began to study effective communicators and spoke to small audiences at every opportunity. It took me seven years to become comfortable while speaking. Only then could I develop and hone my communication style.

In time I got chances to speak to larger audiences. The first time I spoke to over a thousand people was at Veterans Memorial Auditorium in Columbus, Ohio, in the 1970s. In the 1980s, I spoke to an audience of more than 10,000 for the first time during a youth rally at the University of Illinois. In the 1990s, I spoke to 68,000 people at the RCA Dome in Indianapolis. And in the 2000s, I've spoken live in events that were simulcast to even larger audiences.

I don't tell you this to brag. I say it because when I was afraid during that first speaking engagement, I had no idea where it would lead me. But I didn't let my fear rule me. Instead, I accepted it as the price I would have to pay for personal progress.

Shakespeare said, "He is not worthy of the honeycomb that shuns the hive because the bees have stings." Don't let your fear keep you from taking small steps in your development. You never know where they might lead.

—*The Difference Maker*

PUT FEAR ASIDE AND TAKE A SMALL STEP
TO FURTHER DEVELOP YOURSELF.

FROM HERE EVERYTHING
LOOKS DIFFERENT

W hen it comes to winning with people, everything begins with the ability to think about people other than ourselves. People who remain self-centered and self-serving will always have a hard time getting along with others. To help them break that pattern of living, they need the big picture. If you would like to improve your ability to see the big picture and put others first, then do the following:

Get out of your "own little world." To change focus, people need to get out of their own little world. If you have a narrow view of people, go places you have never gone, meet the kinds of people you do not know, and do things you have not done before. It will change your perspective, as it has done mine.

Check your ego at the door. An egotist can be described *not* as a person who thinks too much of himself, but as someone who thinks too little of other people. That's a good description. We often mistakenly believe that the opposite of love is hate. But I believe that's incorrect. The opposite of loving others is being self-centered. If your focus is always on yourself, you'll never be able to build positive relationships.

Understand what brings fulfillment. Ultimately the things that bring fulfillment involve others. A person who is entirely self-focused will always feel restless and hungry.

If you want to live a fulfilling life, you need healthy relationships. And to build those kinds of relationships, you need to get over yourself.

—*Winning with People*

REMIND YOURSELF THAT THE ENTIRE
POPULATION OF THE WORLD—WITH ONE MINOR
EXCEPTION—IS COMPOSED OF OTHERS.

LEARN YOUR CRAFT TODAY

O n a wall in the office of a huge tree farm hangs a sign. It says, "The best time to plant a tree is twenty-five years ago. The second best time is today." There is no time like the present to become an expert at your craft. Maybe you wish you had started earlier. Or maybe you wish you had found a better teacher or mentor years ago. None of that matters. Looking back and lamenting will not help you move forward.

A friend of the poet Longfellow asked the secret of his continued interest in life. Pointing to a nearby apple tree, Longfellow said, "The purpose of that apple tree is to grow a little new wood each year. That is what I plan to do." The friend would have found a similar sentiment in one of Longfellow's poems:

> Not enjoyment and not sorrow
> Is our destined end or way;
> But to act that each tomorrow
> Find us further than today.

You may not be where you're supposed to be. You may not be what you want to be. You don't have to be what you used to be. And you don't have to ever arrive. You just need to learn to be the best you can be right now. As Napoleon Hill said, "You can't change where you started, but you can change the direction you are going. It's not what you are going to do, but it's what you are doing now that counts."

—*The 360° Leader*

FOR THE SAKE OF TOMORROW, DO TODAY
WHAT YOU HAVE BEEN PUTTING OFF.

IF AT FIRST YOU DO SUCCEED, TRY SOMETHING HARDER

The willingness to take greater risks is a major key to achieving success, and you may be surprised that it can solve two very different kinds of problems.

First, if you've been hitting all the goals you set for yourself, then you need to increase your willingness to take chances. The road to the next level is always uphill, so you can't coast there.

Conversely, if you find yourself in a place where it seems that you don't achieve many of your goals, you may be playing it too safe. Once again, the answer is a willingness to take greater risks. (It's ironic that opposite ends of the spectrum come together in the area of risk.)

Think about the next big goal ahead of you. Write down your plan for reaching it. Then go over that plan to see whether you have included enough risks. If not, find parts of that process where you can push the envelope, take more chances, and increase your opportunity for success.

—Failing Forward

INCREASE YOUR RISK THRESHOLD TODAY.

CHOICES

Poet, critic, and dictionary writer Samuel Johnson observed, "He who has so little knowledge of human nature as to seek happiness by changing anything but his own disposition will waste his life in fruitless efforts and multiply the grief which he purposes to remove." Most people want to change the world to improve their lives, but the world they need to change first is the one inside themselves. That is a choice—one that some are not willing to make.

The longer you live, the more your life is shaped by your choices. You decide what you will eat. (This is one of the most common ways small children begin to assert their independence.) You decide what toys to play with. You decide whether you will do your homework or watch TV. You choose which friends to spend time with. You choose whether to finish high school, whether you will go to college, who you will marry, what you will do for a living. The longer you live, the more choices you make—and the more responsible you are for how your life is turning out.

I don't know what kind of circumstances you've had to face in your life. You may have had a really tough time. You may have faced extreme hardship or suffered terrible tragedies. However, your attitude is still your choice.

—*The 17 Essential Qualities of a Team Player*

WHAT KIND OF ATTITUDE HAVE YOU *CHOSEN*?

OCTOBER 17

INFLUENCE OTHERS

If your dream is big and will require the teamwork of a group of people, then any potential leaders you select to go with you on the journey will need to be people of influence. After all, that's what leadership is—influence. And when you think about it, all leaders have two things in common: they're going somewhere, and they're able to persuade others to go with them.

As you look at the people around you, consider the following:

- *Who influences them?* You can tell a lot about *who* they will influence and *how* they will go about doing it by knowing who their heroes and mentors are.
- *Who do they influence?* You'll be able to judge their current level of leadership effectiveness by who they influence.
- *Is their influence increasing or decreasing?* You can tell whether a person is a *past* leader or a *potential* leader by examining which direction the level of influence is going.

To be a good judge of potential leaders, don't just see the person— see all the people that person influences. The greater the influence, the greater the leadership potential and the ability to get others to work with you to accomplish your dream.

—Your Road Map for Success

INVEST YOURSELF IN THE PEOPLE WITH
THE GREATEST LEVEL OF INFLUENCE.

THE NATURE OF NURTURE

In some regards, people respond similarly to the way some animals do. And like animals, people need to be cared for, not just physically, but emotionally. If you look around, you'll discover that there are people in your life who want to be fed—with encouragement, recognition, security, and hope. That process is called nurturing, and it's a need of every human being.

If you desire to become an influencer in others' lives, start by nurturing them. Many people mistakenly believe that the way to become an influencer is to become an authority figure—correct others' errors, reveal the weak areas they can't easily see in themselves, and give so-called constructive criticism. But what clergyman John Knox said more than four hundred years ago is still true: "You cannot antagonize and influence at the same time."

At the heart of the nurturing process is genuine concern for others. As you try to help and influence the people around you, you must have positive feelings and concern for them. If you want to make a positive impact on them, you cannot dislike, despise, or disparage them. You must give them love and respect.

—*Becoming a Person of Influence*

FEED THE PEOPLE AROUND YOU TODAY WITH
ENCOURAGEMENT, RECOGNITION, SECURITY, AND HOPE.

THE LAW OF EXPLOSIVE GROWTH

You can grow by leading followers. But if you want to maximize your leadership and help your organization reach its potential, you need to develop leaders. There is no other way to experience explosive growth. Here's how to move forward with leader's math:

* If you develop yourself, you can experience personal success.
* If you develop a team, your organization can experience growth.
* If you develop leaders, your organization can achieve explosive growth.

You will be able to reach your potential and help your organization reach its loftiest goals only if you begin developing leaders instead of merely attracting followers. Leaders who develop leaders experience an incredible multiplication effect in their organizations that can be achieved in no other way.

—The 21 Irrefutable Laws of Leadership

FOCUS YOUR ENERGY ON DEVELOPING LEADERS,
NOT JUST LEADING FOLLOWERS.

THE LAW OF SOLID GROUND

How important is trust for a leader? It is the most important thing. Trust is the foundation of leadership. How does a leader build trust? By consistently exemplifying character. A person's character quickly communicates many things to others. Here are the most important ones:

1. *Character communicates consistency.* Leaders without inner strength can't be counted on day after day because their ability to perform changes constantly.
2. *Character communicates potential.* Poor character is like a time bomb ticking away. It's only a matter of time before it blows up a person's ability to perform and the capacity to lead.
3. *Character communicates respect.* How do leaders earn respect? By making sound decisions, by admitting their mistakes, and by putting what's best for their followers and the organization ahead of their personal agendas.

—The 21 Irrefutable Laws of Leadership

WHAT IS YOUR CHARACTER COMMUNICATING?

TALK YOUR CRAFT TODAY

Once you reach a degree of proficiency in your craft, then one of the best things you can do for yourself is talk your craft with others on the same and higher levels than you. Many people do this naturally. Guitarists talk about guitars. Parents talk about raising children. Golfers talk about golf. They do so because it's enjoyable, it fuels their passion, it teaches them new skills and insights, and it prepares them to take action.

I enjoy talking about leadership with good leaders all the time. In fact, I make it a point to schedule a learning lunch with someone I admire at least six times a year. Before I go, I study up on them by reading their books, studying their lessons, listening to their speeches, or whatever else I need to do. My goal is to learn enough about them and their "sweet spot" to ask the right questions. If I do that, then I can learn from their strengths. But that's not my ultimate goal. My goal is to learn what I can transfer from their strength zones to mine. That's where my growth will come from—not from what they're doing. I have to apply what I learn to my situation.

The secret to a great interview is listening. It is the bridge between learning about them and learning about you. And that's your objective.

—The 360° Leader

MAKE AN APPOINTMENT TO INTERVIEW SOMEONE FROM
WHOM YOU CAN LEARN LESSONS ABOUT YOUR CRAFT.

GIVE TODAY YOUR ATTENTION

I love what former First Lady Barbara Bush said about the future, comparing it to a train ride:

> We get on board that train at birth, and we want to cross the continent because we have in mind that somewhere out there is a station. We pass by sleepy little towns looking out the window of life's train, grain fields and silos, level grade crossings, buses full of people on the roads beside us. We pass by cities and factories, but we don't look at any of it because we want to get to the station . . . This station changes for us during life. To begin with, for most of us, it's turning 18, getting out of high school. Then the station is that first promotion and then the station becomes getting the kids out of college, and then the station becomes retirement and then . . . all too late we recognize the truth—that this side of that city whose builder is God, there really isn't a station. The joy is in the journey and the journey is the joy.
>
> Sooner or later, you realize there is no station and the truth of life is the trip. Read a book, eat more ice cream, go barefoot more often, hug a child, go fishing, laugh more. The station will come soon enough. And as you go, find a way to make this world more beautiful.

Focusing on the destination is not a good idea. Tomorrow may come; it may not. The only place we really have any power is in the present.

—*The Difference Maker*

DO WHAT YOU CAN IN THE HERE AND NOW,
MAKING THE MOST OF THE JOURNEY.

OCTOBER 23

BEING APPROACHABLE

We've all met people who seemed cold and forbidding. And we've all met people who treat us like old friends from day one. This isn't an issue with just high-profile people. How approachable are the most important people in your life? When you need to ask your boss a question, is it easy or difficult? When you need to talk to your spouse about a difficult subject, do you expect a dialogue or a fight?

For that matter, what about you? Can the people closest to you talk to you about nearly anything? When was the last time someone brought you bad news? Or strongly disagreed with your point of view on an issue? Or confronted you concerning something you did wrong? If it has been a while, you may not be a very approachable person.

Some people treat the idea of becoming approachable as frivolous; it's a nice thing if one can be bothered to cultivate it. But truly it's much more than that. It is a powerful asset to have in one's relational toolbox.

—*Winning with People*

DO A 360-DEGREE SURVEY OF YOUR APPROACHABILITY.
FIND OUT IF YOUR BOSSES, EMPLOYEES, COLLEAGUES,
AND FAMILY MEMBERS FIND YOU EASY TO TALK TO.

TAKE THE HIGH ROAD

The high road truly is the path less traveled. I say that because taking the high road requires thinking and acting in ways that are not natural or common. However, those who practice the High Road Principle become instruments of grace to others and recipients of grace.

People who embrace the high road make excellence their goal. That's something that can be accomplished if we:

- Care more than others think is wise
- Risk more than others think is safe
- Dream more than others think is practical
- Expect more than others think is possible
- Work more than others think is necessary

When we conduct ourselves according to our highest standards, we are less likely to be defensive and take the low road when attacked by others. I say that because when you know you've done all you can do, you can let criticism roll off your back like rain.

—*Winning with People*

CHOOSE TO TAKE THE HIGH ROAD TODAY,
REGARDLESS OF WHAT OTHERS MAY DO OR SAY.

ADD VALUE TO PEOPLE

It all starts with your attitude toward people. Human relations expert Les Giblin remarked, "You can't make the other fellow feel important in your presence if you secretly feel that he is a nobody." Isn't that true? Don't you find it difficult to do something kind for people when you dislike them?

The way we see people is often the difference between manipulating and motivating them. If we don't want to help people, yet we want them to help us, then we get in trouble. We manipulate people when we move them for our *personal* advantage. However, we motivate people when we move them for *mutual* advantage. Adding value to others is often a win-win proposition.

How do you see people? Are they potential recipients of value you can give, or do they tend to be nuisances along your path to success? Author Sydney J. Harris said, "People want to be appreciated, not impressed. They want to be regarded as human beings, not as sounding boards for other people's egos. They want to be treated as an end in themselves, not as a means towards the gratification of another's vanity." If you want to add value to people, you have to value them first.

—25 Ways to Win with People

ARE YOU MANIPULATING OR MOTIVATING PEOPLE?

IS TIME RUNNING OUT?

There's an old saying, "Better one word in time than two afterward." If that was true in ages past, it is even more applicable today in our fast-paced society where information and markets move so quickly.

Constantine Nicandros, former president of Conoco, said, "The competitive marketplace is strewn with good ideas whose time came and went because inadequate attention was given to moving rapidly and hitting an open window of opportunity. The same marketplace is strewn with broken glass of windows of opportunities hit after they were slammed shut."

If waiting will make it impossible for your organization to seize an opportunity, take a risk and push forward. Your leader can always choose not to take your advice, but no leader wants to hear, "You know, I thought that might happen" after it's too late. Give your leader the chance to decide.

—*The 360° Leader*

PRESENT THE OPPORTUNITIES YOU SEE
TO YOUR LEADER BEFORE TIME RUNS OUT.

PROBLEMS GIVE MEANING TO LIFE

A wise philosopher once commented that an eagle's only obstacle to overcome for flying with greater speed and ease is the air. Yet, if the air were withdrawn and the proud bird were to fly in a vacuum, it would fall instantly to the ground, unable to fly at all. The very element that offers resistance to flying is at the same time the condition for flight.

The main obstacle that a powerboat has to overcome is the water against the propeller, yet, if it were not for this same resistance, the boat would not move at all.

The same law, that obstacles are conditions of success, holds true in human life. A life free of all obstacles and difficulties would reduce all possibilities and powers to zero. Eliminate problems, and life loses its creative tension. The problem of mass ignorance gives meaning to education. The problem of ill health gives meaning to medicine. The problem of social disorder gives meaning to government.

We all have a tendency all of our lives to want to get rid of problems and responsibilities. When that temptation arises, remember the youth who was questioning a lonely old man. "What is life's heaviest burden?" he asked. The old fellow answered sadly, "Having nothing to carry."

—Developing the Leader Within You

ALLOW YOUR PROBLEMS TO MOTIVATE YOU
TOWARD GREATER CREATIVITY AND STRENGTH.

EXPRESS BELIEF IN PEOPLE'S POTENTIAL

Philosopher-poet Johann Wolfgang von Goethe said, "Treat a man as he appears to be and you make him worse. But treat a man as if he already were what he potentially could be, and you make him what he should be."

Think about the people who have made a difference in your life: the teacher who made you believe you could achieve; the boss who gave you a chance to show that you could do it; the counselor who let you know you had what it takes to change and have a better life; the man or woman who loved you enough to say, "I do." Not only were they *there* at pivotal times, in many cases they probably *created* those pivotal times in your life.

In almost every instance where the impact was positive, the person believed in you. He or she probably saw something in you that perhaps you didn't even see in yourself. Wouldn't you like to be that person to others? If the answer is yes, then try to love others and see them as 10s. If you have a family, start with your spouse and your kids. And then broaden the circle from there. Believe the best in others, and you will bring out their best.

—*Winning with People*

TODAY CREATE A PIVOTAL MOMENT FOR SOMEONE
BY EXPRESSING YOUR BELIEF IN HIM OR HER.

EMBRACE HEALTHY COMPETITION

What is the quickest way for you to measure your effectiveness in your profession? Maybe you have long-term measurements in place, such as monthly or yearly goals. But what if you want to know how you're doing today? How would you go about measuring it? You could look at your to-do list. But what if you set the bar too low for yourself? You could ask your boss. But maybe the best way would be to see what others in your line of work are doing. If you are significantly behind or ahead of them, wouldn't that tell you something? And if you were behind, wouldn't you try to figure out what you're doing wrong? It may not be the only way to assess yourself, but it certainly can provide a good reality check.

—*The 360° Leader*

SPEND SOME TIME TODAY EXAMINING PEOPLE IN YOUR PROFESSION TO SEE HOW YOU MEASURE UP AGAINST THEM.

PERSONAL DEVELOPMENT

I have made it a practice to set aside time to develop those around me. One leader said, "You have purposefully mentored and coached me now for more than a decade." I give my leaders time for counsel and advice. I help them wrestle with difficult situations. I also schedule time for equipping them on a regular basis. Several leaders have cited the monthly leadership instruction that I give as being valuable. Another reminded me of the experiences I've shared. She said, "He always wants the people around him to be able to experience with him the privileges and opportunities he has been given."

I try to give my people what I can. Sometimes it is time with them. At other times I am able to give guidance. If I can share a valuable experience, I do. As an example, that same staff member mentioned how with my help she was able to have breakfast in Korea with Dr. Cho, pastor of the largest church in the world. Another one of my staff members had always dreamed of meeting Billy Graham in person. When I had an opportunity to meet with the great evangelist, I shared that experience with that staff member by taking him with me. These two incidents were exciting to my staff members, but they were no more valuable then the more common growing experiences that I try to share with them day to day. I look for opportunities to share myself with my people, and you should too.

—*Developing the Leaders Around You*

WHAT CAN YOU DO FOR SOMEONE TODAY
TO HELP DEVELOP THEM?

WHAT CAN I LEARN FROM WHAT HAPPENED?

I enjoy reading the comic strip *Peanuts* by Charles Schulz. In one of my favorites, Charlie Brown is at the beach building a beautiful sand castle. As he stands back to admire his work, it is suddenly consumed by a huge wave. Looking at the smooth sand mound that had been his creation a moment before, he says, "There must be a lesson here, but I don't know what it is."

That's the way many people approach adversity. They are so consumed by the events that they become bewildered and miss the whole learning experience. But there is always a way to learn from failures and mistakes. Poet Lord Byron was right when he stated, "Adversity is the first path to truth."

It's difficult to give general guidelines about how to learn from mistakes because every situation is different. But if you maintain a teachable attitude as you approach the process and try to learn *anything* you can about what you could do differently, you will improve yourself. When a person has the right mind-set, every obstacle introduces him to himself.

—*Failing Forward*

CARVE OUT SOME TIME TODAY TO REFLECT
ON RECENT MISTAKES YOU'VE MADE.

NOVEMBER

ADAPTABILITY

Teamwork and personal rigidity just don't mix. If you want to work well with others and be a good team player, you have to be willing to adapt yourself to your team. Team players who exhibit adaptability have certain characteristics. Adaptable people are . . .

Teachable: Diana Nyad said, "I am willing to put myself through anything; temporary pain or discomfort means nothing to me as long as I can see that the experience will take me to a new level. I am interested in the unknown, and the only path to the unknown is through breaking barriers." Adaptable people always place a high priority on breaking new ground. They are highly teachable.

Emotionally Secure: People who are not emotionally secure see almost everything as a challenge or a threat. They meet with rigidity or suspicion the addition of another talented person to the team, an alteration in their position or title, or a change in the way things are done. But secure people aren't made nervous by change itself. They evaluate a new situation or a change in their responsibilities based on its merit.

Creative: When difficult times come, creative people find a way. Creativity fosters adaptability.

Service Minded: People who are focused on themselves are less likely to make changes for the team than people focused on serving others. If your goal is to serve the team, adapting to accomplish that goal isn't difficult.

The first key to being a team player is being willing to adapt yourself to the team—not an expectation that the team will adapt to you!

—*The 17 Essential Qualities of a Team Player*

ARE YOU WILLING TO ADAPT TO
YOUR TEAM IN ORDER TO SUCCEED?

THE 20/80 PRINCIPLE

M any years ago, while working toward a business degree, I learned about the Pareto Principle. It is commonly called the 20/80 principle. Although I received little information about this principle at the time, I began applying it to my life. Twenty years later I find it a most useful tool for determining priorities for any person's life or for any organization.

Every leader needs to understand the Pareto Principle in the area of people oversight and leadership. For example, 20 percent of the people in an organization will be responsible for 80 percent of the company's success.

The following strategy will enable a leader to increase the productivity of an organization:

1. Determine which people are the top 20 percent producers.
2. Spend 80 percent of your "people time" with the top 20 percent.
3. Spend 80 percent of your personal developmental dollars on the top 20 percent.
4. Determine what 20 percent of the work gives 80 percent of the return and train an assistant to do the 80 percent less effective work. This "frees up" the producer to do what he/she does best.
5. Ask the top 20 percent to do on-the-job training for the next 20 percent.

Remember, we teach what we know; we reproduce what we are. Like begets like.

—Developing the Leader Within You

BRING A 20/80 FOCUS TO EVERYTHING YOU DO TODAY.

MAKE YOURSELF MORE VALUABLE

We've talked about the phrase "you cannot give what you do not have." There are people who possess good hearts and the desire to give, yet they have very little to offer. Why? Because they have not first added value to themselves. Making yourself more valuable is not an entirely selfish act. When you acquire knowledge, learn a new skill, or gain experience, you not only improve yourself, but you also increase your ability to help others.

In 1974 I committed myself to the pursuit of personal growth. I knew that it would help me to be a better minister, so I began to continually read books, listen to tapes, attend conferences, and learn from better leaders. At the time, I had no idea that this commitment would be the most important thing I would ever do to help others. But that has turned out to be the case. As I improve myself, I am better able to help others improve. The more I grow, the more I can help others grow. The same will be true for you.

—25 Ways to Win with People

To MAKE YOURSELF MORE VALUABLE, TAKE
STEPS TO EXPAND YOUR KNOWLEDGE, YOUR
EXPERIENCE, OR YOUR SKILLS TODAY.

TEACH PEOPLE TO BE SELF-ENLARGERS

It has been said that the goal of all teachers should be to equip students to get along without them. The same can be said of leaders who seek to enlarge others. As you work with others and help them to enlarge themselves, give them what they need so that they learn to take care of themselves. Teach them to find resources. Encourage them to get out of their comfort zone on their own. And point them toward additional people who can help them learn and grow. If you can help them to become lifelong learners, you will have given them an incredible gift.

We've heard it said, "No one becomes rich unless he enriches another." When you enrich others by helping them grow and enlarge themselves, you not only bring joy to them and yourself, but you also increase your influence and their ability to touch others' lives.

—*Becoming a Person of Influence*

COACH YOUR PEOPLE TO CREATE PERSONAL GROWTH
PLANS FOR THEMSELVES FOR THE COMING YEAR.

CASTING VISION

I f you are the leader of your team, then you carry the responsibility for communicating the team's vision and keeping it before the people continually. That's not necessarily easy. Whenever I endeavor to cast vision with the members of my team, I use the following checklist. I try to make sure that every vision message possesses the following:

- Clarity: brings understanding to the vision (answers what the people must know and what I want them to do)
- Connectedness: brings the past, present, and future together
- Purpose: brings direction to the vision
- Goals: bring targets to the vision
- Honesty: brings integrity to the vision and credibility to the vision caster
- Stories: bring relationships to the vision
- Challenge: brings stretching to the vision
- Passion: brings fuel to the vision
- Modeling: brings accountability to the vision
- Strategy: brings process to the vision

I believe your team members will find the vision more accessible and will more readily buy into it if you follow this checklist. And if they do, you will see that they have greater direction and confidence.

—The 17 Indisputable Laws of Teamwork

RECOMMUNICATE THE VISION TO YOUR PEOPLE TODAY.

MAKE FAILURE YOUR BEST FRIEND

When you are able to learn from any bad experience and thereby turn it into a good experience, you make a major transition in life. For years I've taught something that I think gives useful insight on the subject of change:

People change when they . . .
Hurt enough that they have to,
Learn enough that they want to, and
Receive enough that they are able to.

I learned the truth of that statement on a whole new level on December 18, 1998. While at my company's Christmas party, I felt an excruciating pain in my chest, and I went down for the count. I suffered a serious heart attack. My heart attack was a painful and surprising experience, but I feel that God was very good to me in that process. Several excellent physicians rallied around me and made it possible for me not only to survive but also to avoid any permanent heart damage.

My cardiologist, Dr. Marshall, told me that men who survive an early heart attack and learn from it live longer and healthier lives than those who never suffer a heart attack. I am determined to learn from the experience. I changed my diet. I exercise and try to live a more balanced life. I have to admit that it's sometimes a struggle, but I'm persevering. I've taken to heart Jim Rohn's comment: "Don't let your learning lead to knowledge; let your learning lead to action."

—*Failing Forward*

USE PAINFUL EXPERIENCES AS A CATALYST TO NOT ONLY
LEARN BUT TO LEAD YOU TO GREATER ACTION.

LEARN YOUR MAILMAN'S NAME

In 1937 the granddaddy of all people-skills books was published. It was an overnight hit, eventually selling more than fifteen million copies. That book was *How to Win Friends and Influence People*, by Dale Carnegie. What made that book so valuable was Carnegie's understanding of human nature. I love his simple words of wisdom. Something that I learned early from Carnegie was this: remember and use a person's name. "We should be aware of the *magic* contained in a name . . . The name sets the individual apart; it makes him or her unique among all others. The information we are imparting or the request we are making takes on a special importance when we approach the situation with the name of the individual. From the waitress to the senior executive, the name will work magic as we deal with others."

What was true in 1937 is even more applicable in our fast-paced world. These days an account number or a title too often replaces a person's name. Remembering names can help enhance your personal image, improve your style, and, most importantly, increase your impact on others.

—*25 Ways to Win with People*

MAKE IT A POINT TO LEARN THE NAMES
OF PEOPLE YOU MEET TODAY.

BE WILLING TO CHANGE

One of the greatest generals in military history was Napoleon Bonaparte. Made a full general at age twenty-six, he utilized shrewd strategy, bold cunning, and lightning speed to his advantage to win many victories. The Duke of Wellington, one of the general's most formidable enemies, said, "I consider Napoleon's presence in the field to equal forty thousand men in the balance."

"I will tell you the mistake you are always making," Napoleon said, addressing an opponent he had defeated. "You draw up your plans the day before battle, when you do not yet know your adversary's movements." Napoleon recognized in his losing opponent a weakness that he himself did not have: lack of adaptability. If you are willing to change and adapt for the sake of your team, you always have a chance to win.

—The 17 Essential Qualities of a Team Player

ARE YOU WILLING TO IMPROVISE AND ADAPT
AS CONDITIONS CHANGE IN ORDER TO SUCCEED?

THE BENEFIT OF INTEGRITY: TRUST

The bottom line when it comes to integrity is that it allows others to trust you. And without trust, you have nothing. Trust is the single most important factor in personal and professional relationships. It is the glue that holds people together. And it is the key to becoming a person of influence.

At one time you could assume that others would trust you until you gave them a reason not to. But today with most people, you must prove your trustworthiness first. That's what makes integrity so important if you want to become a person of influence. Trust comes from others only when you exemplify solid character.

It has been said that you don't really know people until you have observed them when they interact with a child, when the car has a flat tire, when the boss is away, and when they think no one will ever know. But people with integrity never have to worry about that. No matter where they are, who they are with, or what kind of situation they find themselves in, they are consistent and live by their principles.

—Becoming a Person of Influence

DO YOU BEHAVE IN A MANNER CONSISTENT
WITH PRINCIPLES OF INTEGRITY NO MATTER
WHERE OR WITH WHOM YOU FIND YOURSELF?

FEED THE RIGHT EMOTION

In life, both faith and fear will arise within you, and you choose which one will prevail. Someone once wrote,

> Two natures beat within my breast,
> The one is foul, the other blessed.
> The one I love, the other I hate;
> The one I feed will dominate.

The thing is, both of those emotions will *always* be present in you. The emotion you continually feed is the one that will dominate your life. You can't expect fear simply to disappear. If you continually focus on your fears, entertain them, and give in to them, they will increase. The way to ultimately overcome them is to starve them. Don't give your fears any of your time or energy. Don't feed them with gossip or negative news shows or frightening movies. Focus on your faith and feed it. The more energy and time you give it, the stronger it becomes. And anytime you feel afraid of doing something but go ahead and do it anyway, you will be reprogramming your attitude. When you feel fear, it will mean "go" instead of "stop," and "fight harder" instead of "give up."

—*The Difference Maker*

WHAT EMOTION ARE YOU FEEDING?
CHOOSE TO FEED YOUR FAITH AND COURAGE.

LEADERSHIP DEVELOPS DAILY, NOT IN A DAY

Becoming a leader is a lot like investing successfully in the stock market. If your hope is to make a fortune in a day, you're not going to be successful. What matters most is what you do day by day over the long haul. If you continually invest in your leadership development, letting your "assets" compound, the inevitable result is growth over time.

- *Phase 1:* I Don't Know What I Don't Know. As long as a person doesn't know what he doesn't know, he isn't going to grow.
- *Phase 2:* I Know That I Need to Know. Many people find themselves placed in a leadership position only to look around and discover that no one is following them. When that happens, we realize that we need to learn how to lead.
- *Phase 3:* I Know What I Don't Know. To grow as a leader, I have to realize I don't have all the answers or the skills as a leader. I need others on my journey of growth.
- *Phase 4:* I Know and Grow, and It Starts to Show. When you recognize your lack of skill and begin the daily discipline of personal growth, exciting things start to happen.
- *Phase 5:* I Simply Go Because of What I Know. Your ability to lead becomes almost automatic. You develop great instincts. And that's when the payoff is incredible.

—*The 21 Irrefutable Laws of Leadership*

DO YOU KNOW WHERE YOU ARE
IN THE LEADERSHIP PROCESS?

MAKE OTHERS FEEL IMPORTANT

A lan Zimmerman tells the story of Cavett Roberts, a successful lawyer, salesman, and founder of the National Speakers Association:

> Roberts looked out his window one morning and saw a skinny twelve-year-old boy going door to door selling books. The boy was headed for his house. Roberts turned to his wife and said, "Just watch me teach this kid a lesson about selling" . . . Mrs. Roberts watched as the twelve-year-old boy knocked on the door. Mr. Roberts opened the door and quickly explained that he was a very busy man. He had no interest in buying any books. But he said, "I'll give you one minute, but I have to leave then—have a plane to catch."
>
> The young salesman was not daunted by Roberts's brush-off. He simply stared at the tall, gray-haired, distinguished-looking man, a man that he knew was fairly well known and quite wealthy. The boy said, "Sir, could you be the famous Cavett Roberts?" To which Mr. Roberts replied, "Come on in, son."
>
> Mr. Roberts bought several books from the youngster—books that he might never read. The boy had mastered the principle of making the other person feel important, and it worked.

When talking about charisma, it all boils down to this: The person *without* charisma walks into a group and says, "Here I am." The person *with* charisma walks into a group and says, "There you are."

—*Winning with People*

WHEN YOU WALK INTO A ROOM, DO YOU
FOCUS ON OTHERS AND SAY, "THERE YOU ARE"?

IT'S A FAMILY TRIP

Fairly early in our marriage, Margaret and I realized that in my career, I would often have the opportunity to travel. And we decided that any time I got the chance to go someplace interesting or to attend an event that we knew would be exciting, she would come along with me, even when it was difficult financially.

I love taking my family with me—including on business trips—because I get to share the opportunities and rewards of the journey. Those trips have been fun. But our travels around the globe don't in any way compare to another trip I've taken them on: the success journey.

But many people are now realizing that the hope of happiness at the expense of breaking up a family is an illusion. You can't give up your marriage or neglect your children and gain true success. Building and maintaining strong families benefit us in every way, including in helping us make the success journey.

I believe my greatest accomplishment in life was getting Margaret to marry me. We're partners in everything, and I know that I wouldn't have experienced any measure of success in life without her. Several years ago I realized that all the success in the world means nothing if you aren't loved and respected the most by those closest to you. When I reach the end of my days, I don't want Margaret, Elizabeth, or Joel Porter to say that I was a good author, speaker, pastor, or leader. My desire is that the kids think I'm a good father and that Margaret thinks I'm a good husband. That's what matters most. It's the measure of true success.

—Your Road Map for Success

DO THOSE CLOSEST TO YOU LOVE
AND RESPECT YOU THE MOST?

SAY WHAT YOU MEAN,
AND MEAN WHAT YOU SAY

B ecoming a leader is about building trust with people. When asked what he considered the most essential qualification for a politician, Winston Churchill said, "It's the ability to foretell what will happen tomorrow, next month, and next year—and to explain afterward why it did not happen." Churchill understood the dynamics of politics as well as anyone in the twentieth century. Political leaders find themselves under tremendous pressure. Maybe that's why some of them crack under it and tell people what they want to hear rather than what the politicians really believe. And those who do crack create a negative reputation that all politicians have to labor under.

If you want to develop trust with others, you must be more than competent. You must also be credible and consistent. The way to achieve those qualities is to make sure that what you *say*, what you *do*, and what you *say you do* all match. If you do that, the people who work with you will know they can depend on you.

—The 360° Leader

Ask those who know you best if your words
and actions consistently match.

NOVEMBER 15

REMEMBER A PERSON'S STORY

There are so many good reasons to learn a person's story. Here are just a few that keep motivating me to continue this practice with others:

- *Requesting* a person's story says, "You could be special."
- *Remembering* a person's story says, "You are special."
- *Reminding* a person of his or her story says, "You are special to me."
- *Repeating* a person's story to others says, "You should be special to them."

The result? You become special to the person who shared a story with you.

When you meet someone new, after the introductions and initial pleasantries, don't hesitate. Dive in and ask to hear the person's story. You can do it any number of ways: you can flat-out ask, "What's your story?" You can request that he tell you about himself. You can ask where he is from or how he got into the field he's in. Use your own style.

—25 Ways to Win with People

USE SOMEONE'S STORY AS A CONNECTING POINT TODAY.

REFUSING TO TAKE A RISK

L ife means risk. People who sabotage themselves shouldn't worry about failure as much as they should be concerned about the chances they miss when they don't even try. Speech writer Charles Parnell observed, "Too many people are having what might be called 'near-life experiences.' They go through life bunting, so afraid of failure that they never try to win the big prizes, never knowing the thrill of hitting a home run or even taking a swing at one."

French writer, poet, and art critic Guillaume Apollinaire wrote,

> Come to the edge.
> No, we will fall.
> Come to the edge.
> No, we will fall.
> They came to the edge.
> He pushed them and they flew.

Those who fly always first get out on the edge. If you want to seize an opportunity, you must take a risk. If you want to grow, you must make mistakes. If you want to reach your potential, you will have to take chances. If you don't, you will be resigned to a life of mediocrity. The people who don't make mistakes end up working for those who do. And in the end, they often end up regretting the safe life they lived.

—*The Difference Maker*

IN SOME WAY, GET OUT ON THE EDGE THIS WEEK.

THE POWER OF COLLABORATION

A re you a collaborative person? You may not be working against the
team, but that doesn't necessarily mean you're working for it. Do you
bring cooperation and added value to your teammates—even to the
people you don't enjoy being with?

To become a collaborative team player . . .

Think win-win-win. Usually when you collaborate with others, you win,
they win, and the team wins. Find someone on the team with a similar role
whom you have previously seen as a competitor. Figure out ways you can
share information and work together to benefit both you and the team.

Complement others. Another way to collaborate is to get together with
someone who has strengths in your area of weakness and vice versa. Seek
out others on the team with complementary gifts and work together.

Take yourself out of the picture. Get in the habit of asking what's best
for the team. For example, the next time you are at a problem-solving
meeting and everyone is contributing ideas, instead of promoting yourself, ask yourself how the team would do if you were not involved in the
solution. If it would do better, then propose ideas that promote and
involve people other than yourself.

—*The 17 Essential Qualities of a Team Player*

BE MINDFUL TO BRING A SPIRIT OF COLLABORATION
AND COOPERATION INTO EVERYTHING YOU DO TODAY.

DON'T CUT CORNERS

A common obstacle to success is the desire to cut corners and take the short road to success. But shortcuts never pay off in the long run. As Napoleon said, victory belongs to the most persevering.

Most people tend to underestimate the time it takes to achieve something of value, but to be successful, you have to be willing to pay your dues. James Watt spent twenty years laboring to perfect his steam engine. William Harvey labored night and day for eight years to prove how blood circulated in the human body. And it took another twenty-five years for the medical profession to acknowledge he was right.

Cutting corners is a sign of impatience and poor self-discipline. But if you are willing to follow through, you can achieve a breakthrough. That's why Albert Gray says, "The common denominator of success lies in forming the habit of doing things that failures don't like to do."

If you continually give in to your moods or impulses, then you need to change your approach to doing things. The best method is to set standards for yourself that *require* accountability. Suffering a consequence for not following through helps you stay on track. Once you have your new standards in place, work according to them, not your moods. That will get you going in the right direction.

Self-discipline is a quality that is won through practice. Psychologist Joseph Mancusi noted, "Truly successful people have learned to do what does not come naturally. Real success lies in experiencing fear or aversion and acting in spite of it."

—*Failing Forward*

REMEMBER THAT SHORTCUTS NEVER
PAY OFF IN THE LONG RUN.

ACHIEVEMENT OVER AFFIRMATION

Affirmation from others is fickle and fleeting. If you want to make an impact during your lifetime, you have to trade the praise you could receive from others for the things of value that you can accomplish. You can't be "one of the boys" and follow your destiny at the same time.

A friend once explained something to me that illustrates this concept very well. He grew up near the Atlantic Ocean, where people catch blue crabs for dinner. He told me that as they catch the crabs, they'll toss them into a bucket or basket. He said that if you have only one crab in the basket, you need a lid to keep it from crawling out, but if you've got two or more, you don't. That didn't make any sense to me until he explained further. He said that when there are several crabs, they will drag each another down so that none of them can get away.

I've found that some unsuccessful people act the same way. They do all kinds of things to keep others from getting ahead, trying to prevent them from improving themselves or their situation. They use all kinds of devices to keep others in the basket with them: playing politics, promoting mediocrity, role-playing, and so on. But the good news is that if people try to do that, you don't have to buy into their belief system. You can stay out of the basket by refusing to be a crab. You may have to face opposition and live through times of insecurity, but you'll also experience freedom, increased potential, and satisfaction. Raise yourself up, and raise others with you.

—Your Road Map for Success

TAKE THE HIGH ROAD AND SPEAK WELL OF OTHERS,
NO MATTER WHAT THEY SAY ABOUT YOU.

EXPAND BEYOND YOUR STRENGTHS

E ven outside of work, I think we all tend to respect and gravitate to people whose strengths are like our own. Sports stars hang out together. Actors marry other actors. Entrepreneurs enjoy trading stories with other entrepreneurs. The problem is that if you spend time only with people like yourself, your world can become terribly small and your thinking limited.

If you are a creative type, go out of your way to meet people who are analytical. If you have a type-A personality, then learn to appreciate the strengths of people who are more laid back. If your thing is business, spend time with people who work in nonprofit environments. If you are white-collar, learn to connect with blue-collar people. Anytime you get a chance to meet people with strengths very different from your own, learn to celebrate their abilities and get to know them better. It will broaden your experience and increase your appreciation for people.

—The 360° Leader

GO OUT OF YOUR WAY TO SPEND TIME WITH SOMEONE
WHO DOESN'T THINK OR ACT THE WAY YOU DO.

NOVEMBER 21

AVOID GOSSIP

It's been said that great people talk about ideas, average people talk about themselves, and small people talk about others. That's what gossip does. It makes people small. There really is no upside to gossip. It diminishes the person being talked about. It diminishes the person who is saying unkind things about others, and it even diminishes the listener. That's why you should avoid not only spreading gossip but also being a recipient of it. If you stop people from unloading gossip on you, it will make you feel better about the person who's being talked about, as well as about yourself. Besides, whoever gossips to you will gossip about you.

British prime minister Winston Churchill said, "When the eagles are silent, the parrots begin to jabber." Good leaders are like eagles: they soar; they inspire; they fly high. And they don't talk just to hear themselves. They don't vent about someone to others to make themselves feel better. If they have a problem with a person, they go to that individual and address the issue directly—never through a third party. They praise publicly and criticize privately. And they never say anything about others that they wouldn't want them to hear—because they probably will.

—The 360° Leader

DO NOT ENGAGE IN GOSSIP OR ALLOW
ANYONE TO DRAW YOU INTO IT.

NOTES OF ENCOURAGEMENT
ARE REMEMBERED

For years I have made it a practice to write personal notes to others. I often forget what I have written, but occasionally someone who has received a note from me will tell me what an encouragement it was. It is in those moments that I am reminded of the sustained and repeated encouragement people receive from the written word.

You never can tell when something you write to others will light them up in down times or sustain them when life gets difficult. In the first *Chicken Soup for the Soul* book, teacher Sister Helen Mrosla recounted how a spur-of-the-moment assignment in class became a source of encouragement for her students. On a day when her junior high math students were especially ornery, she asked them to write down what they liked about each of their fellow students. She then compiled the results over the weekend and handed out the lists on the following Monday.

Years later when one of those students, Mark, was killed in Vietnam, she and some of those former students got together for the funeral. Afterward, Mark's father told the group, "They found this on Mark when he was killed," and he showed them a folded, refolded, and taped paper— the one he had received years before from his teacher. Right after that, Charlie, one of Mark's classmates, said, "I keep my list in my desk drawer." Chuck's wife said, "Chuck put his in our wedding album." "I have mine, too," Marilyn said, "in my diary."

Each person cherished the kind words of encouragement they had received. That's the power of a few kind words.

—*25 Ways to Win with People*

WRITE A NOTE OF ENCOURAGEMENT TO SOMEONE TODAY.

LEARN TO BE FLEXIBLE

Perhaps the most relentless enemy of achievement, personal growth, and success is inflexibility. A friend sent me "The Top Ten Strategies for Dealing with a Dead Horse," which I think is hilarious:

1. Buy a stronger whip.
2. Change riders.
3. Appoint a committee to study the horse.
4. Appoint a team to revive the horse.
5. Send out a memo declaring the horse isn't really dead.
6. Hire an expensive consultant to find "the real problem."
7. Harness several dead horses together for increased speed and efficiency.
8. Rewrite the standard definition of *live horse*.
9. Declare the horse to be better, faster, and cheaper when dead.
10. Promote the dead horse to a supervisory position.

I bet you've seen just about every one of these "solutions" enacted in your place of work. But there's really only one effective way to deal with that problem: when your horse is dead, for goodness' sake, dismount. You don't have to love change to be successful, but you need to be willing to accept it.

— *Failing Forward*

LOOK FOR A "DEAD HORSE" PROBLEM IN YOUR
ORGANIZATION AND DEAL WITH IT APPROPRIATELY.

COMMITMENT

How important is commitment to you? Are you someone who values loyalty and follow-through? When things get tough, are you in the habit of standing firm? Or do you have a tendency to compromise or even quit? More specifically, how committed are you to your team? Is your support solid? Is your dedication undeniable? To improve your level of commitment . . .

Tie your commitments to your values. Because your values and your ability to fulfill your commitments are closely related, take some time to reflect on them. First, make a list of your personal and professional commitments. Then try to articulate your core values. Once you have both lists, compare them. You will probably find that you have commitments unrelated to your values. Reevaluate them. You will also find that you have values that you are not living out. Commit yourself to them.

Take a risk. Being committed involves risk. You may fail. Your teammates may let you down. You may discover that fulfilling your goals doesn't give you the results you desire. But take the risk of committing anyway. George Halas, former owner of the NFL Chicago Bears, asserted, "Nobody who ever gave his best regretted it."

Evaluate your teammates' commitment. If you find it difficult to commit in particular relationships and you cannot find a reason for it in yourself, consider this: you cannot make a commitment to uncommitted people and expect to receive a commitment from them. Examine the relationship to see whether you are reluctant because the potential recipient is untrustworthy.

—*The 17 Essential Qualities of a Team Player*

INCREASE YOUR LEVEL OF COMMITMENT AND
STAND FIRM ON MATTERS RELATED TO YOUR VALUES.

LET FAILURE POINT YOU TO SUCCESS

O liver Goldsmith was born the son of a poor preacher in Ireland in the 1700s. Growing up, he wasn't a great student. In fact, his school-master labeled him a "stupid blockhead." He did manage to earn a college degree, but he finished at the bottom of his class. He was unsure of what he wanted to do. At first he tried to become a preacher, but it didn't suit him, and he was never ordained. Next he tried law but failed at it. He then settled on medicine, but he was an indifferent doctor and was not passionate about his profession. He was able to hold several posts only temporarily. Goldsmith lived in poverty, was often ill, and once even had to pawn his clothes to buy food.

It looked like he would never find his way. But then he discovered an interest and aptitude for writing and translating. At first, he worked as a Fleet Street reviewer and writer. But then he began to write works that came out of his own interests. He secured his reputation as a novelist with *The Vicar of Wakefield*, a poet with "The Deserted Village," and a play-wright with *She Stoops to Conquer*.

My friend, Tim Masters, says that failure is the productive part of success. It provides the road you don't have to travel again, the moun-tain you don't have to climb again, and the valley you don't have to cross again. At the time you're making mistakes, they may not feel like "the kiss of Jesus," which was Mother Teresa's term for failures that drive us to God. But if we have the right attitude, they can lead us to what we ought to be doing.

—The Difference Maker

EMBRACE YOUR FAILURES AS BLESSINGS IN DISGUISE.

THE POWER OF PEOPLE SKILLS

By far the greatest single obstacle to success that I see in others is a poor understanding of people. A while back the *Wall Street Journal* printed an article on the reasons that executives fail. At the top of the list was a person's inability to effectively relate to others.

I was talking to some people a couple of days ago, and they were complaining about not winning a business contract that they had bid on. "It wasn't fair," one person told me. "All the people involved knew each other, and we didn't have a chance. It's all politics." But what he went on to describe wasn't politics. It was relationships.

Authors Carole Hyatt and Linda Gottlieb indicate that people who fail on the job commonly cite "office politics" as the reason for their failures, but the reality is that what they call politics is often nothing more than regular interaction with other people.

If you haven't learned how to get along with people, you will always be fighting a battle to succeed. However, making people skills a strength will take you farther than any other skill you develop. People like to do business with people they like. Or to put it the way President Theodore Roosevelt did: "The most important single ingredient in the formula of success is knowing how to get along with people."

—Failing Forward

ARE YOUR PEOPLE SKILLS AS GOOD
AS THEY POSSIBLY CAN BE?

BURN THE SHIPS

How do you define true commitment? Let me tell you how Hernán Cortés defined it. In 1519, under the sponsorship of Cuba's Governor Velásquez, Cortés sailed from Cuba to the Mexican mainland with the goal of gaining riches for Spain and fame for himself. Though only thirty-four years old, the young Spanish captain had prepared his whole life for such a chance.

But the soldiers under his command were not as dedicated as he. After he landed, there was talk that the men might mutiny and return to Cuba with his ships. What was his solution? He burned the ships. How dedicated are you to your team? Are you totally committed, or do you have an "out," just in case things don't work out? Remember, there is no such thing as a halfhearted champion.

—The 17 Essential Qualities of a Team Player

ARE YOU COMMITTED ENOUGH TO BURN THE SHIPS
IF NECESSARY TO INSURE THE SUCCESS OF YOUR TEAM?

GIVE CREDIT TO THE TEAM

In his book *Good to Great*, Jim Collins points out that the leaders of the best organizations, what he calls "level-5 leaders," are characterized by humility and a tendency to avoid the spotlight. Does that mean those leaders aren't talented? Of course not. Does it mean they have no egos? No. It means they recognize that everyone on the team is important, and they understand that people do better work and do it with greater effort when they are recognized for their contribution.

If you want to help your team go farther and help team members to sharpen their talent and maximize their potential, when things don't go well, take more than your fair share of the blame, and when things go well, give all of the credit away.

—*Talent Is Never Enough*

PRAISE OTHERS FOR THEIR CONTRIBUTION TODAY, AND
TAKE THE BLAME FOR ANYTHING THAT DOESN'T GO WELL.

RECOGNIZE THE VALUE OF A NAME

How do you feel when someone calls you by the wrong name? How about when you kindly correct the person and spend time with him, and he still gets your name wrong? How about when people haven't seen you for a long time, and they still remember your name? Doesn't it make you feel good? (And doesn't it also impress you?) When people care enough to know your name, they make you feel valued.

My friend Jerry Lucas is known as "Dr. Memory." He has spent the years following his hugely successful run in the NBA helping schoolchildren and adults improve their memories through a variety of innovative techniques. One of the things he teaches is called the SAVE Method. Here's how it works:

S — Say the name three times in conversation.
A — Ask a question about the name or about the person.
V — Visualize the person's prominent physical or personality feature.
E — End the conversation with the name.

Years ago Jerry showed how useful his method could be by remembering the names of every guest in the audience at the *Tonight Show*. I believe it can also help you remember the first and last names of the people you meet.

If you work at it, you *will* become better at remembering people's names.

—*25 Ways to Win with People*

USE WHATEVER METHOD YOU MUST
TO REMEMBER PEOPLE'S NAMES.

NOVEMBER 30

MEASURING INTEGRITY

If a good reputation is like gold, then having integrity is like owning the mine. The following questions may help you nail down areas that need attention.

1. How well do I treat people from whom I can gain nothing?
2. Am I transparent with others?
3. Do I role-play based on the person(s) I'm with?
4. Am I the same person when I'm in the spotlight as I am when I'm alone?
5. Do I quickly admit wrongdoing without being pressed to do so?
6. Do I put other people ahead of my personal agenda?
7. Do I have an unchanging standard for moral decisions, or do circumstances determine my choices?
8. Do I make difficult decisions, even when they have a personal cost attached to them?
9. When I have something to say about people, do I talk to them or about them?
10. Am I accountable to at least one other person for what I think, say, and do?

Take some time to reflect on each question, honestly considering it before answering. Then work on the areas where you're having the most trouble.

—*Becoming a Person of Influence*

WORRY LESS ABOUT WHAT OTHERS THINK, AND GIVE
YOUR ATTENTION TO YOUR INNER CHARACTER TODAY.

DECEMBER

DECEMBER 1

LEARN TO LISTEN

The first step in teachability is learning to listen. American writer and philosopher Henry David Thoreau wrote, "It takes two to speak the truth—one to speak and one to hear." Being a good listener helps us to know people better, to learn what they have learned, and to show them that we value them as individuals.

Abraham Lincoln was one of the most teachable presidents. When he began his career, he was not a great leader. But he grew into his presidency. He was always an avid listener, and as president, he opened the doors of the White House to anyone who wanted to express an opinion to him. He called these frequent sessions his "public opinion baths." He also asked nearly everyone he met to send him ideas and opinions. As a result, he received hundreds of letters every month—many more than other presidents had received in the past. From this practice, he learned much. And even if he didn't embrace the arguments, he learned more about how the letter writers thought, and he used that knowledge to help him craft his policies and persuade others to adopt them.

As you go through each day, remember that you can't learn if you're always talking. As the old saying goes, "There's a reason you have one mouth but two ears." Listen to others, remain humble, and you will begin to learn things every day that can help you to expand your talent.

—*Talent Is Never Enough*

PRACTICE USING FEWER WORDS TODAY.
AND GENUINELY LISTENING TO OTHERS.

ADVANCE BASED ON YOUR CHARACTER

Every time you face mistakes and attempt to move forward in spite of them is a test of character. There always comes a time when giving up is easier than standing up, when giving in looks more attractive than digging in. And in those moments, character may be the only thing you have to draw on to keep you going.

Championship-winning NBA coach Pat Riley said, "There comes a moment that defines winning from losing. The true warrior understands and seizes the moment by giving an effort so intensive and so intuitive that it could be called one from the heart." After you've been knocked down, and you've had the will to get back up, the intelligence to plan your comeback, and the courage to take action, know this: You will experience one of those defining moments. And it will define you—as an achiever or a quitter.

—Failing Forward

WORK FROM THE HEART TODAY.

DECEMBER 3

PROBLEM MANAGEMENT

Under excellent leadership a problem seldom reaches gigantic proportions, because it is recognized and fixed in its early stages. Great leaders usually recognize a problem in the following sequence:

1. They sense it before they see it (intuition).
2. They begin looking for it and ask questions (curiosity).
3. They gather data (processing).
4. They share their feelings and findings to a few trusted colleagues (communicating).
5. They define the problem (writing).
6. They check their resources (evaluating).
7. They make a decision (leading).

Great leaders are seldom blindsided. They realize that the punch that knocks them out is seldom the hard one—it's the one they didn't see coming. Therefore, they are always looking for signs and indicators that will give them insight into the problem ahead and their odds of fixing it. They treat problems like the potential trespasser of an Indiana farm who read this sign on a fence post, "If you cross this field, you better do it in 9.8 seconds. The bull can do it in 10 seconds."

—*Developing the Leader Within You*

PAY ATTENTION TO YOUR INTUITION, AND
FOLLOW UP WHEN SOMETHING STRIKES YOU.

ANYTHING WE DO
CAN BE MADE IMPORTANT

Most moments in life become special only if we treat them that way. The average day is average only because we don't make it something more. The most excellent way to elevate an experience is to give it our best. That makes it special. An average conversation becomes something better when you listen with great interest. A common relationship transforms when you give it uncommon effort. An unremarkable event becomes something special when you spice it up with creativity. You can make anything more important by giving your best to it.

—*25 Ways to Win with People*

COMMIT TO GIVE THIS DAY YOUR VERY BEST.

DECEMBER 5

KNOWING WHO TO DEVELOP

Often I am asked in leadership conferences, "How do you know which staff person to hire?" I always laugh and say, "You never know for sure," and my track record underscores that comment! However, here are some guidelines I have tried to follow when looking for staff:

- Know what you need before you start looking for someone.
- Take time to search the field.
- Call many references.
- Have several interviews.
- Include your associates in some interviews and ask for their input.
- Interview the candidates' spouses.
- Check out the candidates' track records.
- If possible, have a trial run to see if job and potential staff match.
- Ask hard questions, such as, "Why did you leave?"; "What can you contribute?"; "Are you willing to pay the price?"
- Trust your instincts.

If someone you're considering looks good on paper but makes you feel bad inside, go slowly. In fact, back off and let an associate take over the interviewing process; then compare conclusions. I only hire a person if it looks good *and* feels good.

—Developing the Leader Within You

REMEMBER THAT YOU CAN LOSE WITH GOOD PLAYERS
ON YOUR TEAM, BUT YOU CANNOT WIN WITHOUT THEM.

COMMUNICATIVE

How are you doing when it comes to communication? Are you well connected to all of your teammates? Have you neglected some people or excluded them from your circle of communication? Or have you isolated yourself from others for the sake of being more productive? Anytime you're on a team but not communicating with team members, the team suffers.

To improve your communication . . .

Be candid. Open communication fosters trust. Having hidden agendas, communicating to people via a third party, and sugarcoating bad news hurt team relationships. Think about a poor relationship you have with someone on your team. If you haven't been candid with that person, then determine to change your ways. Your goal should be to speak truthfully but kindly to your teammates.

Be quick. If you tend to sit on things instead of saying them, force yourself to follow the twenty-four-hour rule. When you discover an issue with teammates, find the first reasonable opportunity to address it with them. And invite others to do the same with you.

Be inclusive. Some people hoard information unless forced to divulge it. Don't take that approach. Include others if you can. Certainly you need to be discreet with sensitive information, but remember this: people are up on things they're in on. Open communication increases trust, trust increases ownership, and ownership increases participation.

—The 17 Essential Qualities of a Team Player

ENGAGE YOUR TEAM WITH
EFFECTIVE COMMUNICATION TODAY.

DECEMBER 7

BOUNCING BACK

About twenty years ago, *Time* magazine described a study by a psychologist of people who had lost their jobs three times due to plant closings. The writers were amazed by what they discovered. They expected the people being laid off to be beaten down and discouraged. Instead they found them to be incredibly resilient. Why was that? They concluded that people who had weathered repeated adversity had learned to bounce back. People who had lost a job and found a new one twice before were much better prepared to deal with adversity than someone who had always worked at the same place and had never faced adversity.

It may sound ironic, but if you have experienced a lot of failure, you are actually in a better position to achieve success than people who haven't. When you fail, and fail, and fail again—and keep getting back up on your feet and keep learning from your failures—you are building strength, tenacity, experience, and wisdom. And people who develop such qualities are capable of sustaining their success, unlike many for whom good things come early and easily. As long as you don't give up, you're in a really good place.

—*The Difference Maker*

IT MAY SOUND IRONIC, BUT IF
YOU'VE FAILED A LOT, CELEBRATE.

WATCH ANOTHER PERSON BLOOM

Scott Adams, creator of the popular *Dilbert* cartoon, tells this story about his beginnings as a cartoonist:

> You don't have to be a "person of influence" to be influential. In fact, the most influential people in my life probably are not even aware of the things they've taught me. When I was trying to become a syndicated cartoonist, I sent my portfolio to one cartoon editor after another—and received one rejection after another. One editor even called and suggested that I take art classes. Then Sarah Gillespie, an editor at United Media and one of the real experts in the field, called to offer me a contract. At first, I didn't believe her. I asked if I'd have to change my style, get a partner— or learn how to draw. But she believed I was already good enough to be a nationally syndicated cartoonist. Her confidence in me completely changed my frame of reference and altered how I thought about my own abilities. This may sound bizarre, but from the minute I got off the phone with her, I could draw better.

There is no telling what might happen if you were to begin encouraging the dreams of the people around you.

—25 Ways to Win with People

ENCOURAGE SOMEONE TODAY AND YOU MIGHT
GET TO WATCH THEM BLOOM TOMORROW.

MANAGE YOUR PERSONAL LIFE

You can do everything right at work and manage yourself well there, but if your personal life is a mess, it will eventually turn everything else sour. What would it profit a leader to climb to the top of the organizational chart but to lose a marriage or alienate the children? As someone who spent many years counseling people, I can tell you, no career success is worth it.

For years one of my definitions of *success* has been this: having those closest to me love and respect me the most. That is what is most important. I want the love and respect of my wife, my children, and my grandchildren before I want the respect of anyone I work with. Don't get me wrong, I want the people who work with me to respect me too, but not at the expense of my family. If I blow managing myself at home, then the negative impact will spill over into every area of my life, including work.

If you want to lead up, you must always lead yourself first. If you can't, you have no credibility. I've found the following to be true:

+ If I can't lead myself, others won't follow me.
+ If I can't lead myself, others won't respect me.
+ If I can't lead myself, others won't partner with me.

That applies whether the influence you desire to exert is on the people above you, beside you, or below you. The better you are at making sure you're doing what you should be doing, the better chance you have for making an impact on others.

—*The 360° Leader*

How well are you leading yourself at home?

DECEMBER 10

CULTIVATE DETERMINATION

A uthor Napoleon Hill noted, "Effort only fully releases its reward after a person refuses to quit." To develop persistence over the long haul, you have to cultivate inward determination on a continual basis. And if you do, someday your story may be similar to one of these:

- Admiral Peary attempted to reach the North Pole seven times before he made it on try number eight.
- Oscar Hammerstein had five flop shows that lasted less than a combined total of six weeks before *Oklahoma*, which ran for 269 weeks and grossed $7 million.
- John Creasey received 743 rejection slips from publishers before one word was ever published—he eventually published 560 books, which have sold more than 60 million copies.
- Eddy Arcaro lost 250 consecutive races before he won his first.
- Albert Einstein, Edgar Allan Poe, and John Shelley were all expelled from school for being mentally slow.

Learn to become a determined individual. And remember, the only difference between a little shot and a big shot is that the big shot kept shooting.

—*Failing Forward*

HOW DETERMINED ARE YOU TO ACHIEVE
YOUR GOALS AND LEAD YOUR TEAM TO SUCCESS?

DECEMBER 11

PASS THE CREDIT ON TO OTHERS

Passing the credit on to others is one of the easiest ways to win with people. I love what H. Ross Perot once said about passing on credit: "Reward employees while the sweat's still on their brow." Isn't it true that one of the very best times to give credit to others is when the amount of work and sacrifice something took is still fresh in their minds? Why wait? You may have heard management expert Ken Blanchard's teaching that you should catch people while they're doing something good. What a great idea! The sooner you give credit to someone else, the bigger the payoff.

In 2003, when I interviewed UCLA basketball coach John Wooden, he told me how he would often teach his players who scored to give a smile, wink, or nod to the player who gave them a good pass. "What if he's not looking?" asked a team member. Wooden replied, "I guarantee he'll look." Everyone enjoys having his contribution acknowledged.

—25 Ways to Win with People

CATCH SOMEONE DOING SOMETHING RIGHT
TODAY AND PRAISE THEM PUBLICLY.

DECEMBER 12

LOOK FOR COURAGE INSIDE,
NOT OUTSIDE, YOURSELF

During the Great Depression, Thomas Edison delivered his last public message. In it he said, "My message to you is: Be courageous! I have lived a long time. I have seen history repeat itself again and again. I have seen many depressions in business. Always America has come out stronger and more prosperous. Be as brave as your fathers before you. Have faith! Go forward!" Edison knew that when we experience fear, we must be willing to move forward. That is an individual decision. Courage starts internally before it is displayed externally.

I love the story about the shortest letter to the editor written to England's newspaper the *Daily Mail*. When the editor invited readers to send in their answers to the question, "What's wrong with the world?" writer G. K. Chesterton is reputed to have sent the following:

> Dear Sir,
> I am.
> Yours sincerely,
> G. K. Chesterton

Courage, like all other character qualities, comes from within. It begins as a decision we make and grows as we make the choice to follow through.

—*Talent Is Never Enough*

HAVE THE COURAGE TO FIRST FIGHT
THE BATTLES THAT COME FROM WITHIN.

THE LAW OF THE INNER CIRCLE

When we see any incredibly gifted person, it's always tempting to believe that talent alone made him successful. To think that is to buy in to a lie. Nobody does anything great alone. Leaders do not succeed alone. A leader's potential is determined by those closest to him. What makes the difference is the leader's inner circle.

To practice the Law of the Inner Circle, you must be intentional in your relationship building. As you consider whether individuals should be in your inner circle, ask yourself the following questions.

1. Do they have high influence with others?
2. Do they possess strengths in my areas of weakness?
3. Do they add value to me and my organization?
4. Do they positively impact other inner circle members?

—The 21 Irrefutable Laws of Leadership

BE HIGHLY INTENTIONAL AND STRATEGIC
IN BUILDING YOUR INNER CIRCLE.

DECEMBER 14

COMPETENCY

The word *competent* sometimes is used to mean "barely adequate." When I talk about the quality of competence that is desirable in teammates, I mean it in the sense of its most basic definition, which means "to be well qualified, fit." Highly competent people have some things in common:

They are committed to excellence. John Johnson in *Christian Excellence* writes, "Success bases our worth on a comparison with others. Excellence gauges our value by measuring us against our own potential. Success grants its rewards to the few but is the dream of the multitudes. Excellence is available to all living beings but is accepted by the . . . few."

They never settle for average. The word mediocre literally means "halfway up a stony mountain." To be mediocre is to do a job halfway, to leave yourself far short of the summit. Competent people never settle for average.

They pay attention to detail. Dale Carnegie said, "Don't be afraid to give your best to what seemingly are small jobs. Every time you conquer one it makes you that much stronger. If you do little jobs well, the big ones tend to take care of themselves."

They perform with consistency. Highly competent people perform with great consistency. They give their best all the time, and that's important. If 99.9 percent were good enough, then 22,000 checks would be deducted from the wrong bank accounts in the next 60 minutes, and 12 babies would be given to the wrong parents today alone.

—*The 17 Essential Qualities of a Team Player*

PERFORM WITH THE HIGHEST LEVEL OF COMPETENCE
AND DEMAND THE SAME OF ALL YOUR TEAM MEMBERS.

FIND A PURPOSE

More than anything else, having a sense of purpose keeps a person going in the midst of adversity. Business consultant Paul Stoltz did an extensive study on what it takes for individuals to persist through setbacks.

According to Stoltz, the most important ingredient of persistence is, "Identifying your mountain, your purpose in life, so that the work you do is meaningful. I run into people every day who are basically climbing the wrong mountain. People who have spent 20 years or more of their lives doing something that has no deep purpose for them. Suddenly they look back and go, 'What have I been doing?'"

If you are a purpose-driven person naturally, then you probably already possess an innate sense of direction that helps you overcome adversity. But if you're not, then you may need some help. Use the following steps to help you *develop a desire*.

- Get next to people who possess great desire.
- Develop discontent with the status quo.
- Search for a goal that excites you.
- Put your most vital possessions into that goal.
- Visualize yourself enjoying the rewards of that goal.

If you follow this strategy, you may not immediately find your ultimate purpose, but you will at least start moving in that direction. As Abraham Lincoln said, "Always bear in mind that your resolution to succeed is more important than any other thing."

—Failing Forward

How sure are you that you are
climbing the right mountain?

DECEMBER 16

THE INFLUENCE MYTH

I once read that President Woodrow Wilson had a housekeeper who constantly lamented that she and her husband didn't possess more prestigious positions in life. One day the lady approached the president after she heard that the secretary of labor had resigned.

"President Wilson," she said, "my husband is perfect for his vacant position. He is a laboring man, knows what labor is, and understands laboring people. Please consider him when you appoint the new secretary of labor."

"I appreciate your recommendation," answered Wilson, "but you must remember, the secretary of labor is an important position. It requires an influential person."

"But," the housekeeper said, "if you made my husband the secretary of labor, he would be an influential person!"

People who have no leadership experience have a tendency to overestimate the importance of a leadership title. You may be able to grant someone a position, but you cannot grant him real leadership. Influence must be earned.

A position gives you a chance. It gives you the opportunity to try out your leadership. It asks people to give you the benefit of the doubt for a while. But given some time, you will earn your level of influence—for better or worse. Good leaders will gain in influence beyond their stated position. Bad leaders will shrink their influence down so that it is actually less than what originally came with the position. Remember, a position doesn't make a leader, but a leader can make the position.

—The 360° Leader

ARE YOU COUNTING ON YOUR POSITION TO LEAD
OTHERS, OR ARE YOU STRIVING TO EARN INFLUENCE?

DECEMBER 17

LOOK BEYOND YOUR PERSONAL PREJUDICES

French novelist André Gide said that "an unprejudiced mind is probably the rarest thing in the world." Unfortunately, that is probably true. I think all human beings have prejudices of some sort. We prejudge people we haven't met because of their race, ethnicity, gender, occupation, nationality, religion, or associations. And it really does limit us.

If we desire to grow beyond not only our circle of acquaintances but also some of the limitations created by our own thoughts, then we need to break down the walls of prejudice that exist in our minds and hearts. Novelist Gwen Bristow said, "We can get the new world we want, if we want it enough to abandon our prejudices, every day, everywhere. We can build this world if we practice now what we said we were fighting for."

—*The 360° Leader*

RECOGNIZE YOUR PREJUDICES AND WORK TO BREAK DOWN THE INTERNAL WALLS YOU HAVE CREATED BECAUSE OF THEM.

LEARN A NEW DEFINITION OF FAILURE

Thomas Edison believed, "Many of life's failures are people who did not realize how close they were to success when they gave up." If you can change the way you see failure, you gain the strength to keep running the race. Get a new definition of *failure*. Regard it as the price you pay for progress. If you can do that, you will put yourself in a much better position to fail forward.

How can you help yourself learn a new definition of *failure* and develop a different perspective concerning failure and success? By making mistakes. Chuck Braun of Idea Connection Systems encourages trainees to think differently through the use of a mistake quota. He gives each student a quota of thirty mistakes to make for each training session. And if a student uses up all thirty? He receives another thirty. As a result, the students relax, think of mistakes in a whole new light, and begin learning.

Remember, mistakes don't define *failure*. They are merely the price of achievement on the success journey.

—*Failing Forward*

HOW CLOSE TO SUCCESS MIGHT YOUR TEAM BE? ARE YOU WILLING TO KEEP FIGHTING TO MAKE A BREAKTHROUGH?

DECEMBER 19

INTEGRITY

It's crucial to maintain integrity by taking care of the little things. Many people misunderstand that. They think they can do whatever they want when it comes to the small things because they believe that as long as they don't have any major lapses, they're doing well. But that's not the way it works. *Webster's New Universal Unabridged Dictionary* describes *integrity* as "adherence to moral and ethical principles; soundness of moral character; honesty." Ethical principles are not flexible. A little white lie is still a lie. Theft is theft—whether it's $1, $1,000, or $1 million. Integrity commits itself to character over personal gain, to people over things, to service over power, to principle over convenience, to the long view over the immediate.

Nineteenth-century clergyman Phillips Brooks maintained, "Character is made in the small moments of our lives." Anytime you break a moral principle, you create a small crack in the foundation of your integrity. And when times get tough, it becomes harder to act with integrity, not easier. Character isn't created in a crisis; it only comes to light. Everything you have done in the past—and the things you have neglected to do—come to a head when you're under pressure.

Developing and maintaining integrity require constant attention. Josh Weston, chairman and CEO of Automatic Data Processing, Inc., says, "I've always tried to live with the following simple rule: 'Don't do what you wouldn't feel comfortable reading about in the newspapers the next day.'" That's a good standard all of us should keep.

—*Becoming a Person of Influence*

WHAT ARE YOU DOING IN THE
SMALL MOMENTS OF YOUR LIFE?

THE LAW OF THE PICTURE

When times are tough, uncertainty is high, and chaos threatens to overwhelm everyone, followers need a clear picture from their leaders the most. The living picture they see in their leader produces energy, passion, and motivation to keep going. As you strive to improve as an example to your followers, remember these things:

1. *Followers are always watching what you do.* Just as children watch their parents and emulate their behavior, so do employees watching their bosses. People do what people see.

2. *It's easier to teach what's right than to do what's right.* Author Norman Vincent Peale stated, "Nothing is more confusing than people who give good advice but set a bad example." I would say a related thought is also true: "Nothing is more *convincing* than people who give good advice and set a good example."

3. *We should work on changing ourselves before trying to improve others.* A great danger to good leadership is the temptation to try to change others without first making changes to yourself.

4. *The most valuable gift a leader can give is being a good example.* Leadership is more caught than taught. How does one "catch' leadership? By watching good leaders in action!

—*The 21 Irrefutable Laws of Leadership*

WHAT LIVING PICTURE ARE YOU GIVING YOUR FOLLOWERS?

THE VOICES OF VISION

Where does vision come from? To find the vision that is indispensable to leadership, you have to become a good listener. You must listen to several voices.

The Inner Voice: Vision starts within. Do you know your life's mission? What stirs your heart? What do you dream about? If what you're pursuing in life doesn't come from a desire within—from the very depths of who you are and what you believe—you will not be able to accomplish it.

The Unhappy Voice: Where does inspiration for great ideas come from? From noticing what doesn't work. Discontent with the status quo is a great catalyst for vision. Are you on complacent cruise control? Or do you find yourself itching to change your world? No great leader in history has fought to prevent change.

The Successful Voice: Nobody can accomplish great things alone. To fulfill a big vision, you need a good team. But you also need good advice from someone who is ahead of you in the leadership journey. If you want to lead others to greatness, find a mentor. Do you have an adviser who can help you sharpen your vision?

The Higher Voice: Although it's true that your vision must come from within, you shouldn't let it be confined by your limited capabilities. A truly valuable vision must have God in it. Only He knows your full capabilities. Have you looked beyond yourself, even beyond your own lifetime, as you've sought your vision? If not, you may be missing your true potential and life's best for you.

—The 21 Indispensable Qualities of a Leader

MAKE SURE YOUR VISION CONTAINS ALL THAT
IT MUST FOR YOU TO REACH YOUR POTENTIAL.

DEVELOP NEW STRATEGIES TO SUCCEED

Lester Thurlow points out that "a competitive world has two possibilities for you. You can lose, or, if you want to win, you can change." Once you develop a plan and put it into action, you're not finished. In fact, if you want to succeed, you're never finished. Success is in the journey, the continual process. And no matter how hard you work, you will not create the perfect plan or execute it without error. You will never get to the point that you no longer make mistakes, that you no longer fail. But that's okay.

Failures are milestones on the success journey. Each time you plan, risk, fail, reevaluate, and adjust, you have another opportunity to begin again, only better than the last time. As sixty-seven-year-old Thomas Edison said as his laboratory burned to the ground, "Thank goodness all our mistakes were burned up. Now we can start again fresh."

—Failing Forward

GIVE UP ON THE NOTION OF EVER ARRIVING AT PERFECTION.

DECEMBER 23

TAKING THE FAMILY ALONG

NBA coach Pat Riley said, "Sustain a family life for a long period of time and you can sustain success for a long period of time. First things first. If your life is in order you can do whatever you want." There is definitely a correlation between family success and personal success. Not only does building a strong family lay the groundwork for future success, but it also gives life deeper meaning.

I believe that few people have ever been truly successful without a positive, supportive family. No matter how great people's accomplishments are, I think they're still missing something when they're working without the benefit of those close relationships. True, some people are called to be single, but they are rare. For most people, a good family helps you know your purpose and develop your potential, and it helps you enjoy the journey along the way with an intensity that isn't possible otherwise. And when it comes to sowing seeds that benefit others, who could possibly derive greater benefit from you than your own family members?

—*Your Road Map for Success*

IF YOU HAVE A FAMILY, BE SURE YOU AREN'T
NEGLECTING THEM AS YOU PURSUE CAREER SUCCESS.

A LITTLE EXTRA CHANGE

M ost people are resistant to change. They desire improvement, but they resist changing their everyday routine. That's a problem because, as leadership expert Max DePree says, "We cannot become what we need to be by remaining what we are." To sharpen your talent through practice, you need to do more than just be *open* to change. You need to *pursue* change—and you need to do it a little bit more than other achievers. Here's what to look for and how to focus your energy to get the kinds of changes that will change you for the better:

- Don't change just enough to get away from your problems— change enough to solve them.
- Don't change your circumstances to improve your life—change yourself to improve your circumstances.
- Don't do the same old things expecting to get difference results— get different results by doing something new.
- Don't wait to see the light to change—start changing as soon as you feel the heat.
- Don't see change as something hurtful that must be done—see it as something helpful that can be done.
- Don't avoid paying the immediate price of change—if you do, you will pay the ultimate price of never improving.

Poet and philosopher Johann von Schiller wrote, "He who has done his best for his own time has lived for all times." You can do your best only if you are continually seeking to embrace positive change.

—Talent Is Never Enough

FIND SOMETHING TODAY THAT YOU NEED
TO CHANGE ABOUT YOURSELF AND GET STARTED.

GIVE WITH NO STRINGS ATTACHED

Jesuit theologian Pierre Teilhard de Chardin said, "The most satisfying thing in life is to have been able to give a large part of one's self to others." Anyone who has unselfishly helped another person knows this to be true. Yet not everyone is able to adopt an ongoing mind-set of giving toward others. Why is that? I believe it has nothing to do with circumstances. I've met generous people with almost nothing who were willing to share what little they possessed. And I've met well-off people who were stingy with their time, money, and talents. The issue is really attitude.

People who give with no strings attached almost always have an abundance mentality. They are generous because they believe that if they give, they will not run out of resources. Pastor and former college professor Henri Nouwen states, "When we refrain from giving, with a scarcity mentality, the little we have will become less. When we give generously, with an abundance mentality, what we give away will multiply."

I have found this to be true. Someone once asked me why he should adopt an abundance mentality, and he was surprised by my answer. I told him that if you believe in abundance, that's what life gives you. If you believe in scarcity, then that's what you get. I don't know why that is, but after fifty years of paying attention to people's attitudes and watching how life unfolded for them, I know it to be true. So if you desire to be more generous, change your thinking and your attitude when it comes to abundance. Not only will it allow you to be more generous, but also it will change your life.

—*25 Ways to Win with People*

GIVE FIRST, NO MATTER WHAT
YOUR CIRCUMSTANCES MAY BE.

BECOMING AN EMPOWERER

The ability to empower others is one of the keys to personal and professional success. John Craig remarked, "No matter how much work you can do, no matter how engaging your personality may be, you will not advance far in business if you cannot work through others." And business executive J. Paul Getty asserted, "It doesn't make much difference how much other knowledge or experience an executive possesses; if he is unable to achieve results through people, he is worthless as an executive."

When you become an empowerer, you work with and through people, but you do much more. You enable others to reach the highest levels in their personal and professional development. Simply defined, empowering is giving your influence to others for the purpose of personal and organizational growth. It's sharing yourself—your influence, position, power, and opportunities—with others with the purpose of investing in their lives so that they can function at their best. It's seeing people's potential, sharing your resources with them, and showing them that you believe in them completely.

The act of empowering others changes lives, and it's a win-win situation for you and the people you empower. Giving others your authority isn't like giving away an object, such as your car, for example. If you give away your car, you're stuck. You no longer have transportation. But empowering others by giving them your authority has the same effect as sharing information: You haven't lost anything. You have increased the ability of others without decreasing yourself.

—*Becoming a Person of Influence*

WHEREVER POSSIBLE, GIVE OTHERS YOUR
POWER SO THAT THEY CAN ACHIEVE MORE.

THE LAW OF DIVIDENDS

A t this stage of my life, everything I do is a team effort. When I first started teaching seminars, I did everything. Certainly there were other people pitching in, but I was just as likely to pack and ship a box as I was to speak. Now, I show up and teach. My wonderful team takes care of everything else. Even the book you're reading was a team effort. My team is my joy. I would do anything for the people on my team because they do everything for me:

- My team makes me better than I am.
- My team multiplies my value to others.
- My team enables me to do what I do best.
- My team gives me more time.
- My team represents me where I cannot go.
- My team provides community for our enjoyment.
- My team fulfills the desires of my heart.

Building a team for the future is just like developing a financial nest egg. It may start slowly, but what you put in brings a high return—similar to the way that compound interest works with finances. Try it and you will find that the Law of Dividends really works. *Investing in the team compounds over time.*

—*The 17 Indisputable Laws of Teamwork*

INVESTING IN YOUR TEAM PAYS DIVIDENDS NOT ONLY
FOR THEM AND THE ORGANIZATION, BUT ALSO FOR YOU.

YOUR ATTITUDE IS YOUR MOST IMPORTANT ASSET

Our attitude may not be the asset that makes us great leaders, but without good ones we will never reach our full potential. Robert Half International, a San Francisco consulting firm, recently asked vice presidents and personnel directors at one hundred of America's largest companies to name the single greatest reason for firing an employee. The responses are very interesting and underscore the importance of attitude in the business world:

* Incompetence: 30 percent
* Inability to get along with other workers: 17 percent
* Dishonesty or lying: 12 percent
* Negative attitude: 10 percent
* Lack of motivation: 7 percent
* Failure or refusal to follow instructions: 7 percent
* All other reasons: 8 percent

Notice that although incompetence ranked first on the list, the next five were all attitude problems. The Carnegie Institute not long ago analyzed the records of ten thousand persons and concluded that 15 percent of success is due to technical training. The other 85 percent is due to personality, and the primary personality trait identified by the research is attitude. Our attitudes determine what we see and how we handle our feelings. These two factors greatly determine our success.

—*Developing the Leader Within You*

MAKE SURE YOUR ATTITUDE IS YOUR GREATEST ASSET— AND NOT YOUR GREATEST LIABILITY.

DECEMBER 29

MAKE YOURSELF AN ENLARGER

Albert Schweitzer maintained that "the great secret of success is to go through life as a man who never gets used up." When you make it a goal to continually learn and enlarge yourself, you become the kind of person who can never be "used up." You're always recharging your batteries and finding better ways to get things done. To determine whether you are still growing, ask yourself what you're still looking forward to. If you can't think of anything or you're looking back instead of ahead, your growth may be at a standstill.

It has been said, "The greatest obstacle to discovery is not ignorance. It is the illusion of knowledge." Many people lose sight of the importance of personal growth once they finish their formal education. But don't let that happen to you. Any day that passes without personal growth is an opportunity lost to improve yourself and to enlarge others.

—Becoming a Person of Influence

MAKE IT A POINT TO LEARN SOMETHING NEW TODAY.

GET UP, GET OVER IT, GET GOING

Undoubtedly some great task lies ahead of you. Maybe you suspect that accomplishing it is the key to your purpose, but you've been afraid to tackle it. Perhaps you're worried that you will not be able to overcome the failure that could result from attempting it.

Plan to do it. Don't jump into it frivolously. (If you've tried and failed at it once already, then you probably wouldn't be frivolous.) Get back up on your feet, and use this strategy to move forward:

F – finalize your goal.
O – order your plans.
R – risk failing by taking action.
W – welcome mistakes.
A – advance based on your character.
R – reevaluate your progress continually.
D – develop new strategies to succeed.

If you're willing to stay determined, work according to a plan, and keep getting up when you get knocked down, you will be able to achieve your goals—and someday your dreams.

—Failing Forward

WHATEVER TASK LIES AHEAD OF YOU
TODAY, PLAN TO MOVE FORWARD.

THE LAW OF LEGACY

I believe that every person leaves some kind of legacy. For some it's positive. For others it's negative. But here's what I know: we have a choice about what legacy we will leave, and we must work and be intentional to leave the legacy we want.

Know the legacy you want to leave. Most people simply accept their lives—they don't lead them. I believe that people need to be proactive about how they live, and I believe that is especially true for leaders. Someday people will summarize your life in a single sentence. My advice: pick it now!

Live the legacy you want to leave. I believe that to have any credibility as a leader, you must live what you say you believe. If you want to create a legacy, you need to live it first. You must become what you desire to see in others.

Choose who will carry on your legacy. I don't know what you want to accomplish in life, but I can tell you this: a legacy lives on in people, not things. Too often leaders put their energy into organizations, buildings, systems, or other lifeless objects. But only people live on after we are gone. Everything else is temporary.

Make sure you pass the baton. Just about anybody can make an organization look good for a moment, but the best leaders lead today with tomorrow in mind. They make sure they invest in leaders who will carry their legacy forward. Why? Because a leader's lasting value is measured by succession.

—*The 21 Irrefutable Laws of Leadership*

SPEND TIME REFLECTING ON THE LASTING
INVESTMENTS YOU WOULD LIKE TO MAKE
AND CREATING A PLAN TO ACHIEVE THEM.

ABOUT THE AUTHOR

JOHN C. MAXWELL is an internationally recognized leadership expert, speaker, and author who has sold over 16 million books. His organizations have trained more than 2 million leaders worldwide. Dr. Maxwell is the founder of EQUIP and INJOY Stewardship Services. Every year he speaks to Fortune 500 companies, international government leaders, and audiences as diverse as the United States Military Academy at West Point, the National Football League, and ambassadors at the United Nations. A *New York Times*, *Wall Street Journal*, and *Business Week* best-selling author, Maxwell was named the World's Top Leadership Guru by Leadershipgurus.net. He was also one of only 25 authors and artists named to Amazon.com's 10th Anniversary Hall of Fame. Three of his books, *The 21 Irrefutable Laws of Leadership*, *Developing the Leader Within You*, and *The 21 Indispensable Qualities of a Leader* have each sold over a million copies.

ANNOTATED BIBLIOGRAPHY

The following are brief descriptions of the books from John C. Maxwell that were used to create this collection, all published in Nashville, Tennessee, by Thomas Nelson, Inc.

DEVELOPING THE LEADER WITHIN YOU

To a culture confused over the difference between management and leadership, *New York Times* best-selling author John C. Maxwell demonstrates what sets "leader-managers" apart from "run-of-the-mill managers." Whether you find yourself leading two people or two hundred, you feel the responsibility of training them to achieve all that they are capable of becoming. In this endearing volume, Maxwell shares his heart for developing exceptional leaders. Timeless principles applied in your life—and the life of your organization—will bring about positive change through personal integrity and self-discipline. This resource is a must have for anyone in, or desiring to be in, leadership! (First published in 1993.)

DEVELOPING THE LEADERS AROUND YOU
How to Help Others Reach Their Full Potential

John C. Maxwell is committed to more than just being a leader—he's also committed to nurturing and mentoring thousands of potential leaders around him. This passion is what caused him to found INJOY and EQUIP, and it is the driving force in everything he does. Both practical and inspirational, *Developing the Leaders Around You* is crammed with strategies that help you effectively transform your goals into reality by building leadership in the people around you. Emphasizing that an organization can't grow until its members grow, Maxwell encourages readers to foster a productive team spirit, make difficult decisions, handle confrontation, and to nurture, encourage, and equip people to be leaders. (First published in 1995.)

Becoming a Person of Influence
How to Positively Impact the Lives of Others

No matter who you are or what you do, *Becoming a Person of Influence* is within your grasp. John C. Maxwell and Jim Dornan share time-proven tools to help you reach and break new goals. With humor, heart, and unique insight, they share what they've gleaned from decades of experience in both business and nonprofit arenas. Best of all, their insights are practical and easy to apply to everyday life. Whether your desire is to build a business, strengthen your children, or reach the world, you can achieve it by raising your level of influence in the lives of others. Through this book you will learn simple, insightful ways to interact more positively with others, and watch your personal and organizational success go off the charts. (First published in 1997.)

Your Road Map for Success
You Can Get There from Here

Defining success is a difficult task. Most people equate it with wealth, power, and happiness. However, true success is not a thing you acquire or achieve. Rather, it is a journey you take your whole life long. In a refreshingly straightforward style, John C. Maxwell shows you the keys to knowing your purpose in life, growing to your maximum potential, and sowing seeds that benefit others along the way. He will show you that success is found on the well-traveled journey, not at a destination. *Your Road Map for Success* features new and expanded material, making this a needed book for all leadership libraries. (First published in 1997 as *The Success Journey*.)

The 21 Irrefutable Laws of Leadership
Follow Them and People Will Follow You

Completely revised and updated for its tenth anniversary, this book has helped over a million people hone their leadership skills. In *The 21 Irrefutable Laws of Leadership*, John C. Maxwell combines insights learned from his forty-plus years of leadership successes and mistakes with observations from the worlds of business, politics, sports, religion, and the military. Every chapter has been revised. Two *entirely* new chapters have been written: The Law of Addition (replacing The Law of E. F. Hutton) and The Law of the Picture (replacing The Law of Reproduction). Application pieces follow every chapter. A leadership evaluation is included. PLUS seventeen new stories from John. "A book is a conversation between the author and reader," says Maxwell. "It's been ten years since I wrote this book. I've grown a lot since then. I've taught these laws in dozens of countries around the world. This new edition gives me the opportunity to share what I've learned." If you've never read *The 21 Irrefutable Laws of Leadership,* you've been missing out on one of the best-selling leadership book of all time. If you have read the original version, you'll love this new expanded and updated one. (First published in 1998.)

The 21 Indispensable Qualities of a Leader
Becoming the Person Others Will Want to Follow

What do you dream of? In your wildest imagination, what do you see yourself doing? Now, what is standing between you and that dream? The answer is leadership. The key to transforming yourself from someone who understands leadership to a person who successfully leads in the real world is character. Your character qualities activate and empower your leadership ability—or stand in the way of your success! Dr. Maxwell says, "Part of any leader's development comes from learning the laws of leadership, for those are the tools that teach how leadership works. But leaders are effective because of who they are on the inside. To go to the highest level of leadership, you must develop these character qualities from the inside out." If you look at all great leaders, you'll find that they possess the twenty-one qualities contained in this book, which is a complementary companion to the *New York Times* bestseller *The 21 Irrefutable Laws of Leadership.* If you can become the leader you ought to be on the inside, you will be able to become the leader you want to be on the outside. "If you are able to do that," says Maxwell, "you'll find there's nothing in this world you cannot do." (First published in 1999.)

FAILING FORWARD
Turning Mistakes into Stepping Stones for Success

It seems that some people are born to achieve anything they want. Some would say they are lucky, are blessed, or have the Midas touch. But what truly is the reason for their success? Family background, wealth, greater opportunities, high morals, an easy childhood? In *Failing Forward*, John C. Maxwell reveals the answer: "The difference between average people and achieving people is their perception of, and response to, failure." The not-talked-about, terrible truth is that all roads to achievement lead through the land of failure. Every person you admire has walked this road: the Wright brothers, Arnold Palmer, Mary Kay Ash, Truett Cathey, Erma Bombeck, Tony Gwynn, Amelia Earhart, Sergio Zyman, Hank Aaron, George Bernard Shaw, and Mother Teresa all experienced failure and learned how to turn it into a stepping-stone for success. Leadership expert Peter Drucker says, "The better a man is, the more mistakes he will make, for the more new things he will try." Mistakes really do pave the road to achievement. Let John C. Maxwell teach you the fifteen steps to turning mistakes into stepping-stones for success! (First published in 2000.)

THE 17 INDISPUTABLE LAWS OF TEAMWORK
Embrace Them and Empower Your Team

In this popular book, John C. Maxwell tackles the laws of teamwork. Written in the style of the bestseller *The 21 Irrefutable Laws of Leadership*, this book is sure to impact leaders all over the world. In business, ministry, sports, and families, teamwork is essential. The old autocratic approach simply doesn't work. And after thirty-plus years of leadership experience and building successful organizations, Maxwell knows that the only way to win—and win big—is by developing great teams. Drawing from history, headlines, and his own life, each law has been proven and each law when followed will lead you closer to your goals. Teamwork is necessary, and knowing how to build effective teams will benefit every area of your life. (First published in 2001.)

THE 17 ESSENTIAL QUALITIES OF A TEAM PLAYER
Becoming the Kind of Person Every Team Wants

If you want to have a better team, you have to develop better players. Great team players, like great teams, are formed from the inside out. Where can a person go to learn how to become a better team player? Your choices are definitely limited. In this companion to *The 17 Indisputable Laws of Teamwork*, John C. Maxwell takes the pain out of knowing what makes a team tick. The qualities that John teaches quickly take you to the heart of teamwork. Anybody can understand them and apply them—whether at home, on the job, or on the ball field. If you learn the seventeen essential qualities of a team player, you can become the kind of person every team wants. If everyone on your team does it, there will be no holding you back. (First published in 2002.)

WINNING WITH PEOPLE
Discover the People Principles That Work for You Every Time

Ask successful CEOs, entrepreneurs, top salespeople, and pastors what characteristic is most needed for success in leadership positions, and they'll tell you that it's the ability to work with people. How many times have you heard someone referred to as a either being or not being a "people person"? This term is used all the time to describe people we work with, but how do you become a people person? Can you learn to be a more people-oriented leader? How do you learn to deal with people who might be lacking in those relational skills? In *Winning with People*, John C. Maxwell has translated decades of experience into twenty-five People Principles that anyone can learn. The People Principles are divided according to the questions we must ask ourselves if we want to win with people: Readiness—Are we prepared for relationships? Connection—Are we willing to focus on others? Trust—Can we build mutual trust? Investment—Are we willing to invest in others? Synergy—Can we create a win-win relationship? Every section contains valuable principles that, when put into practice, will help you develop essential relationship skills. (First published in 2004.)

25 Ways to Win with People
How to Make Others Feel Like a Million Bucks

Dr. John C. Maxwell and Les Parrott, Ph.D., have joined together to author *25 Ways to Win with People*. Each brings his own unique perspective to winning with people—one as a seasoned communicator and leadership authority, the other as relationship expert and professor of psychology. Dr. Maxwell shares practical examples of how he wins with people in everyday life. Dr. Parrott backs up those insights with evidence from recent psychological research. Together, they show how anyone can win with people by making others feel like a million bucks. (First published in 2005.)

The 360° Leader
Developing Your Influence from Anywhere in the Organization

In his forty-plus years of teaching leadership, John C. Maxwell has encountered this question again and again: How do I apply leadership principles if I'm not the boss? It's a valid question that Maxwell answers in *The 360° Leader*. You don't have to be the main leader, asserts Maxwell, to make a significant impact in your organization. Good leaders are not only capable of leading their followers but are also adept at leading their superiors and their peers. Debunking myths and shedding light on the challenges, Maxwell offers specific principles for Leading Down, Leading Up, and Leading Across. 360-Degree Leaders can lead effectively, regardless of their position in an organization. By applying Maxwell's principles, you will expand your influence and ultimately be a more valuable team member. (First published in 2005.)

The Difference Maker
Making Your Attitude Your Greatest Asset

How can two people with the same skills and abilities, in the same situation, end up with two totally different outcomes? Leadership expert John C. Maxwell says the difference maker is attitude. For those who have ever wondered what may be separating them from achieving the kind of personal and professional success they've always dreamt of, Maxwell has some words of insight: "Your attitude colors every aspect of your life. It is like the mind's paintbrush." In *The Difference Maker*, Maxwell shatters common myths about attitude—what it can do for you and what it can't—and shows you how to overcome the five biggest attitude obstacles. Most importantly, you'll learn not only how to develop an attitude that will have a tremendous impact on career, family, and daily living, but also how to maintain that attitude for the rest of your life. Maxwell believes attitude is the one thing that can make all the difference in your life—and now shows you how you can make it your best asset. (First published in 2006.)

TALENT IS NEVER ENOUGH
Discover the Choices That Will Take You Beyond Your Talent

As long as there are people in the world, there will be plenty of talent. If that were enough, though, everyone would reach their potential. What's missing are things people need in addition to their talent. Many business leaders today place too much emphasis on talent alone. Renowned leadership expert John C. Maxwell contends that this is the wrong way to approach success. "If talent alone is enough, then why do you and I know highly talented people who are not highly successful?" Society's landscape is strewn with people who could have been great—those who show amazing promise but never reach their full potential. And then there are the others, such as Thomas Jefferson, Joe Namath, Winston Churchill, Bono, Oprah, and Charles Dickens, who went to the next level by multiplying and maximizing their talent and improved the world around them in the process. Maxwell believes first that you have talent, and second, that you can improve it. In this book he shares the secret of thirteen key choices you can make to become a talent-*plus* person. (First published in 2007.)

SOURCES BY BOOK

THE 17 ESSENTIAL QUALITIES OF A TEAM PLAYER
January 18; January 22; April 9; April 14; April 24; May 7; May 18;
May 28; May 29; June 5; June 22; July 1; July 7; July 14; July 18;
August 5; August 18; August 19; August 31; September 13;
September 26; October 16; November 1; November 8; November 17;
November 24; November 27; December 6; December 14

THE 17 INDISPUTABLE LAWS OF TEAMWORK
January 2; February 6; February 11; February 18; March 30;
April 4; April 7; May 11; May 13; June 15; June 25; July 19; July 30;
August 4; September 20; September 21; November 5; December 27

THE 21 INDISPENSABLE QUALITIES OF A LEADER
January 3; January 6; January 9; January 24; January 25;
January 27; February 3; February 21; March 2; March 12;
March 18; March 21; April 1; April 10; April 19; April 29; May 5;
May 16; June 11; August 23; September 6; December 21

THE 21 IRREFUTABLE LAWS OF LEADERSHIP
January 7; January 10; January 11; January 17; January 23; February 8;
February 19; February 24; July 3; July 28; October 19; October 20;
November 11; December 13; December 20; December 31

25 WAYS TO WIN WITH PEOPLE
January 8; January 12; January 19; January 29; February 1; February 4;
February 7; February 12; February 20; March 1; March 5; March 15;
March 26; April 23; April 25; May 12; May 21; June 2; June 13;
June 24; June 26; July 21; July 24; August 9; August 17; August 26;

September 10; September 23; September 29; October 7; October 25;
November 3; November 7; November 15; November 22; November 29;
December 4; December 8; December 11; December 25; February 29

THE 360° LEADER

January 1; January 5; January 14; January 15; January 21; February 2;
February 9; February 10; March 9; March 10; March 13; March 14;
March 17; March 20; March 24; March 31; April 8; April 30;
May 3; May 4; May 9; May 14; June 4; June 21; June 29; June 30;
July 8; July 20; July 27; July 31; August 2; August 15; August 16;
August 27; September 4; September 9; September 14; September 19;
September 28; October 8; October 9; October 14; October 21;
October 26; October 29; November 14; November 20;
November 21; December 9; December 16; December 17

BECOMING A PERSON OF INFLUENCE

February 16; February 28; March 7; March 25; April 2; May 31;
June 12; August 7; September 7; September 8; September 30;
October 10; October 18; November 4; November 9;
November 30; December 19; December 26; December 29

DEVELOPING THE LEADER WITHIN YOU

January 26; February 15; February 22; February 26; March 6;
March 22; April 16; April 17; April 20; May 10; May 22; June 10;
June 28; July 13; August 1; August 8; August 28; September 2;
September 12; September 25; October 3; October 6; October 27;
November 2; December 3; December 5; December 28

DEVELOPING THE LEADERS AROUND YOU

March 16; March 19; March 28; April 5; April 12; April 22;
April 27; May 2; May 8; May 17; May 25; June 1; June 14; June 19;
June 23; July 2; July 25; July 29; August 29; October 4; October 30

The Difference Maker

January 16; February 14; April 28; May 19; May 26; June 8;
June 17; July 4; July 10; July 22; August 6; August 11; September 5;
September 15; September 27; October 5; October 12; October 22;
November 10; November 16; November 25; December 7

Failing Forward

February 25; February 27; March 3; March 11; March 23; April 3;
April 18; May 6; May 15; May 24; May 30; June 6; June 16; June 27;
July 6; July 15; July 26; August 10; August 21; August 30; September 11;
September 24; October 1; October 2; October 15; October 31;
November 6; November 18; November 23; November 26; December 2;
December 10; December 15; December 18; December 22; December 30

Talent Is Never Enough

April 13; April 26; May 27; June 7; June 18; June 20; July 5;
July 11; July 12; July 17; July 23; August 3; August 13; August 14;
August 22; August 24; September 1; September 17; November 28;
December 1; December 12; December 24; August 12

Winning with People

January 4; February 5; March 4; April 6; April 11; April 15; May 20;
June 9; September 3; September 18; September 22; October 11;
October 13; October 23; October 24; October 28; November 12

Your Road Map for Success

January 13; January 20; January 28; January 30; January 31; February 13;
February 17; February 23; March 8; March 27; March 29; April 21;
May 1; May 23; June 3; July 9; July 16; August 20; August 25;
September 16; October 17; November 13; November 19; December 23

SOURCES BY DAY
AND PARALLEL PASSAGES

BOOKS BY DR. JOHN C. MAXWELL
CAN TEACH YOU HOW TO BE A REAL SUCCESS

RELATIONSHIPS

Encouragement Changes Everything
25 Ways to Win With People
Winning With People
Relationships 101
The Treasure of a Friend
The Power of Partnership in the Church
Becoming a Person of Influence
Be A People Person
The Power of Influence
Ethics 101

ATTITUDE

Success 101
The Difference Maker
The Journey From Success to Significance
Attitude 101
Failing Forward
Your Bridge to a Better Future
Living at the Next Level
The Winning Attitude
Be All You Can Be
The Power of Thinking Big
Think on These Things
The Power of Attitude
Thinking for a Change

EQUIPPING

The Choice Is Yours
Mentoring 101
Talent is Never Enough
Equipping 101
Developing the Leaders Around You
The 17 Essential Qualities of a Team Player
Success One Day at a Time
The 17 Indisputable Laws of Teamwork
Your Road Map for Success
Today Matters
Partners in Prayer

LEADERSHIP

Maxwell Daily Reader
Leadership Promises For Your Work Week
Leadership Gold
Go for Gold
The 21 Most Powerful Minutes
in a Leader's Day
Revised & Updated 10th Anniversary
Edition of The 21 Irrefutable
Laws of Leadership
The 360 Degree Leader
Leadership Promises for Every Day
Leadership 101
The Right to Lead
The 21 Indispensable Qualities of a Leader
Developing the Leader Within You
The Power of Leadership

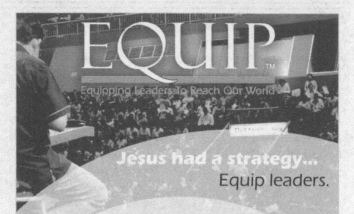

EQUIP™
Equipping Leaders To Reach Our World

Jesus had a strategy...
Equip leaders.

Founded by leadership expert and author John C. Maxwell, EQUIP's passion is the Great Commission plain and simple.

EQUIP's strategy is developing Christian leaders worldwide with the skills needed to provide leadership to their communities, workplaces, and churches, to ultimately fulfill the Great Commission.

"My vision for EQUIP is that it be continually committed to developing leaders whose potential is great but opportunities for learning leadership have been limited."

John C. Maxwell, Founder of EQUIP

If you share our passion for fulfilling the Great Commission by empowering great leaders

visit www.iEQUIP.org.

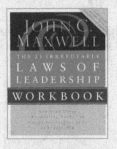

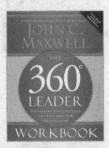

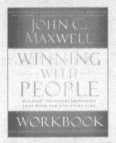

C ONTINUE DEVELOPING your own essential leadership skills with one of these great workbooks from one of the world's most recognized leadership experts— John Maxwell.

THOMAS NELSON
Since 1798

John Maxwell's REAL Leadership Series

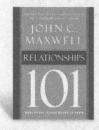

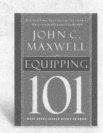

RELATIONSHIPS 101
ISBN 0-7852-6351-9

EQUIPPING 101
ISBN 0-7852-6352-7

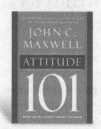

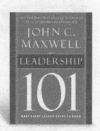

ATTITUDE 101
ISBN 0-7852-6350-0

LEADERSHIP 101
ISBN 0-7852-6419-1

THOMAS NELSON
Since 1798

thomasnelson.com

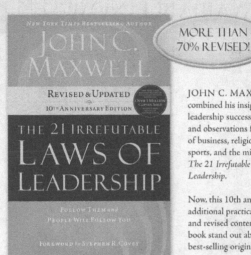

MORE THAN 70% REVISED!

JOHN C. MAXWELL has combined his insights from leadership successes, mistakes and observations from the worlds of business, religion, politics, sports, and the military in *The 21 Irrefutable Laws of Leadership*.

Now, this 10th anniversary edition's additional practical applications and revised content make this book stand out above the best-selling original.

21 Irrefutable Laws of Leadership (0-7852-0837-6)

The Leadership expert, John C. Maxwell, brings an in-depth look at God's laws for leaders and leadership.

Includes:
• New articles and notes
• Revised indexes
• New interior page design

Available in hardcover and black bonded leather.

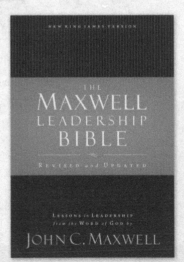

Maxwell Leadership Bible, 2nd Edition (0-7180-2015-4)

AVAILABLE NOW

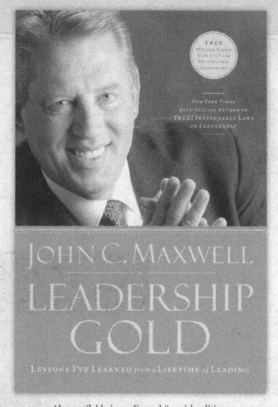

Also available in audio and Spanish editions

Leadership Gold delivers leadership guru John C. Maxwell's most valuable lessons from forty years of leading.

THOMAS NELSON
Since 1798

CPSIA information can be obtained
at www.ICGtesting.com
Printed in the USA
LVHW032134171120
671861LV00002B/1